The British Party System

For Margaret

The British Party System

Stephen Ingle

Basil Blackwell

First published 1987

Basil Blackwell Ltd
108 Cowley Road, Oxford, OX4 1JF, UK

Basil Blackwell Inc.
432 Park Avenue South, Suite 1503
New York, NY 10016, USA

British Library Cataloguing in Publication Data

Ingle, Stephen
  The British party system.
  1. Political parties—Great Britain
  I. Title
  324.241   JN1117
  ISBN 0-631-14485-4
  ISBN 0-631-14486-2 Pbk

Library of Congress Cataloging in Publication Data

Ingle, Stephen
  The British party system
  Includes index.
  1. Political parties—Great Britain—History
  I. Title
  JN11177.I54   1987   324.241′009   87–841
  ISBN 0-631-14485-4
  ISBN 0-631-14486-2 (pbk.)

Typeset in 10½ on 12 pt Baskerville
by Columns of Reading
Printed in Great Britain by Billing and Sons Ltd., Worcester

Contents

Preface

We live in an overtly political age. Remorseless media coverage of political events is reinforced by drama and fiction with political themes or messages, and even popular comedy and satire frequently feed upon politics. The game of party politics has a bigger, if less well informed, audience than the game of soccer. At an altogether deeper level, too, party politics has a pervasive influence. A substantial if diminishing number of citizens are confident that if only party A would replace party B in government, Britain would become happier, or fairer, or freer, or more prosperous, or more equal, or more industrious, or indeed any combination of these. Even the realist, who probably does not believe any of this, may still think that on balance party A would make a better fist of government than party B.

Few people bother to concern themselves with the nature of parties. They are, so to speak, part of the furniture; in fact apparently the most important part. We could hardly imagine a room without them. But chairs, tables, and so on have a utility value which is directly related to their design. They were made for the job. Parties, on the other hand, were not. They have grown up, changed, adapted to different circumstances. Their utility value has only a marginal relation to their 'design' and a much greater relation to the way that they have adapted to social changes.

People ought not to take parties for granted because they take them seriously. I know of a married couple, now elderly, who voted conscientiously in both general and local elections until the 1960s, with the husband voting Labour and the wife Conservative. Then on one particularly wet and windy evening in early May, when it was colder than it had any right to be, they made a pact; since the vote of each cancelled the other's they should, henceforth, both refrain from voting at all. Over twenty years later the wife confided that, pact notwithstanding, she had voted in every election since. The irony was, though, that the Conservative candidate in her constituency could entertain no greater hope than to save his/her deposit. The moral of this story is that voters take parties and party allegiances seriously.

What I hope to do in this book is not to provide a detailed account of how the major parties operate but to give an account of what parties are like within the context of the functions they are generally supposed to fulfil. These functions will not be taken for granted but stated. The intention, then, is not simply to describe parties but to say if, as presently constructed, they are up to the job.

There are a few points to be made, though, before we begin. First, I have chosen not to include minor parties. There are several reasons for this. I wished to concentrate on the two-party system, which is generally believed to have dominated British politics, and on the impact upon that system of a third major force, the Alliance. Also, I felt that within the compass of one book I could hardly do more than offer a polite nod in the direction of the minor parties, which would have been particularly unfair to the rich traditions embodied in the nationalist parties.

Second, the structure of the book is not intended to be rigid. The themes in the various chapters are interrelated because, in the real world, the history, ideology, organization and membership of parties are interdependent. In a sense it is the focus of the camera that is being changed, not the subject of the photograph. William Morris tells us that in his nineteenth-century work on European natural history Horrebow includes a chapter entitled 'Snakes in Ireland' which comprises the single sentence: 'There are no snakes in Ireland.' I decided at the beginning that to impose a rigid structure upon the chapters themselves would have been inappropriate. In other words, though similar in structure, comparable chapters follow the contours of the subjects rather than impose a shape upon them.

In addition I shall have nothing to say about local politics, except in passing, since generalizations on that uniquely differentiated system are very difficult to make and can be misleading. Finally, a word on terminology. I shall not shrink from using words in common currency, such as 'left', 'right', 'soft left', 'centre-right', 'wet' and 'dry', where I consider them useful. They are not without ambiguity but then, the phenomena they seek to describe are no more less ambiguous. All the same, where appropriate I shall try to give a connotation to them. Neither shall I shrink from using the words 'socialist' and 'socialism' to refer, in shorthand, to aspects of the Labour party, because, again, this is commonly done and convenient. At the appropriate time, though, I shall be examining the relationship between Labour's dominant ideology and socialism in some detail.

What I propose, then, is to look at the historical development of the British party system, so as to provide a background for what follows but also to make some comments upon the kinds of functions that the system has been expected to fulfil in different periods. I shall then be looking at Britan's oldest political party, the Conservative party, in three chapters dealing with the development of the ideology of conservatism, the leadership and organization of the party, and its membership. There follows a similar exercise in respect of the Labour party. I shall then try to deal with these themes in respect of the Alliance parties, though within the scope of a single chapter. I then consider the relationship between the party system and the making and scrutinizing of government policy since, after all, this is the principal arena within which political parties operate, and finally, in a concluding chapter, I shall be making some general comments on the party system and its likely future development. This study was approximately two years in preparation and due to be published in June 1987. The prime minister's decision to hold an election in that month made it sensible, though, to postpone publication and to take account of the results of that election. Although the main themes of the book remain unaltered, fresh material has been added as a consequence.

Acknowledgements

I should like first to extend my thanks to several members of the Politics Department at Hull who, through their writings and conversation, have helped me to formulate my own views, for which they are not otherwise to blame. I refer to Jack Hayward, Robert Berki (now Head of European Studies), Noël O'Sullivan and Andrew Cox. I owe a particular debt to Philip Norton, with whom I discussed the themes of the book at some length on a number of occasions and whose book collection in this area proved more comprehensive than mine or the University's, and whose charge on overdue books was more reasonable. I shall also like to thank my secretary, Mrs Melanie Bucknell, who struggled with some of the typescript and organized a series of interviews for me, and Sean Magee of Basil Blackwell, who always seemed to manage the right blend of forbearance and encouragement. I owe a debt, too, to the dozen and a half MPs to whom I spoke, some at very considerable length, and whose information was of great value.

Finally, I have to thank my family, especially my wife, for allowing me to cocoon myself in my study or beat the occasional retreat to the Yorkshire Dales during the last twenty months. They have no direct responsibility for what follows, but without their support it would not have been possible.

Stephen Ingle

1 What Are Political Parties?

'We MUST have a bit of a fight, but I don't much care about going on long', said Tweedledum.

'What's the time now?' Tweedledee looked at his watch and said 'Half-past four'. 'Let's fight till six, and then have some dinner', said Tweedledum.

Lewis Carroll (*Alice Through The Looking Glass*)

Difficult though it is to define political parties or indeed to ascertain where or when they originated in Britain, it is sensible to seek to understand what they are by studying their history, which is what is proposed in this chapter. The party system as it has come to be understood in Britain assumes that groups or parties competing for power do so according to a set of rules which, though they may change substantially over time, normally command the support of the competing groups: a defining characteristic of British parties, that is to say, is the fact that they have always tended to stop fighting 'at dinner time' whoever is winning. If we are to understand properly the nature of British political parties then we should seek their origins in the time when political disputes began to be settled not by recourse to open violence among groups but by more constitutional means.

To define political parties scrupulously is not necessarily advantageous, as Epstein's definition indicates: 'Almost everything that is called a party in any Western democratic nation can be so regarded . . .'.[1] Ball's definition is tighter. He insists on the following characteristics: a degree of permanence; a commitment to fighting elections and gaining influence on the legislature; a commitment to gaining executive power, or to influencing those who have done so through strength in the legislature; a distinct identity.[2] It might be felt that this definition locates rather than describes the activities of parties but at least it makes more explicit the commitment to mutually acceptable rules which has been hinted at above.

It is a standard if totally unwarranted assumption that the two-party system in modern Britain represents somehow the end product of a mysterious teleological process. But this assumption confuses the essential with the accidental, for to take the present system as given, natural and immutable, affects our views not only of the possible future but also of the past. For example, it causes a number of writers to declare that no party system existed before the early part of the nineteenth century, with 1832 and the Great Reform Act being the starting-point, simply because it was from this time that the party system began clearly to resemble today's. But in fact there is no set shape to political parties, no preordained set of characteristics to a party system. Parties are principally organizations of people seeking to wield political power in the name of some interest which binds them together and which distinguishes them from other groups, and that interest may be, for example, religious, geographical, ideological or economic, or a combination of these and others. To speak of a party system in Britain is to go back to Tweedledum and Tweedledee and to the idea of a common commitment that conflict between groups should be adjudicated according to mutually accepted rules. Clearly a precondition of mutual acceptability is the possibility of victory for all competing groups either individually or in combination, and on a regular basis; an expectation represented in modern times by the well-known 'swing of the pendulum' theory of the psephologists. The credentials of a party system tend to be judged largely by the absence of overt violence and intimidation; it is taken for granted that a party system can only properly operate in a constitutional framework, best of all in a constitutional democracy. The essential function of political parties is not to avoid conflict but to canalize it into constitutional waters; their structure will change to meet changing circumstances – in nineteenth-century Britain, for example, the advent of mass democracy – but their functions will remain basically unchanged.

When does the story of British political parties begin? Most writers on parties like to begin with the Whigs and the Tories but unfortunately there is considerable doubt when even they originated. According to Samuel Johnson, the first Whig was the Devil himself.

But if going back to the Fall of the Angels is considered excessive, indications of nascent political parties might be discerned as early as the fourteenth century, in the struggle between the king and his supporters, the 'court party', on the one hand, and the baronial opposition on the other. More specifically, when they were out of power, the Lancastrians sought consistently to limit monarchical power during the period, and even when the Lancastrian Henry IV gained the throne he felt obliged to institutionalize the influence of the Council.[3] Certainly by the seventeenth century historians refer regularly to the existence of parties. In the great debate in the House of Commons on 8 February 1641, for example, on the continuance of the episcopacy, Gardiner speaks of two parties standing opposed to each other 'not merely on some incidental question, but on a great principle of action which constituted a permanent bond between those who took one side or the other'.[4] Similarly in 1680 there was a division between parties over the extent of the legitimate powers of the crown, and the bloodless Revolution of 1688 resulted in a permanent decline in the powers of the crown and its supporters and in the triumph of those who sought to restrict royal power, who became known as the Whigs. From now on parties would contest power within parliament, but already 'the seventeenth century had given them a myth and a martyrology and the name of two gangs of ruffians, Whig and Tory'.[5] All the same the emergence of something recognisably like parties at Westminster should not obscure the fact that no such divisions were considered important by the population at large; even at Westminster 'party' was not always a decisive consideration thereafter. Yet the positions adopted in the Glorious Revolution demarcated the two sides. As David Hume wrote: 'Factions were indeed extremely animated against each other. The very names, by which each party denominated its antagonist, discover the virulence and rancour which prevailed . . . The court party reproached their antagonists with their affinity to the fanatical conventiclers of Scotland who were known by the name of Whigs; the country party found a resemblance between the courtiers and the popish banditti in Ireland, to whom the appellation Tory was affixed'.[6]

It would be fair to conclude that by the end of the seventeenth century, in the terms of our definition, two parties existed. They did not operate in a clearly structured party system, however, and there was no general recognition of benefits to be gained by two parties competing for power: the Tories desired only to dominate the Whigs and the Whigs the Tories.

It was probably the decisiveness of the Whigs' victory after 1688 which prevented a party system from developing directly thereafter: to be branded an unrepentant supporter of the Stuarts and a malcontent (i.e. a Tory) was clearly to deny oneself any opportunity of exercising political influence. Thus in the eighteenth-century parliaments the great protagonists tended to be the powerful aristocratic (nominally Whig) families and their political dependants. They possessed neither programmes nor organization, simply the hierarchical ties of patron and client. All the same, there were distinctions between these families and they tended to grow during the reign of George III, though the king was personally opposed to divisive alliances between aristocratic families and in favour of all-party ministries. The Whigs under Rockingham formed themselves into an opposition against the King and his essentially Tory supporters, and actually held office on two occasions. Yet at the end of the eighteenth century less than half the members of either House would have wanted to be categorized as either Whigs or Tories. Certainly these groups might federate to form governments but they lacked both the sanctions and the rewards to encourage any permanent loyalty in the Commons; these prerogatives belonged either to the king or to the great magnates like the Duke of Newcastle. Nothing more formal than an elementary whipping-in of known supporters on particular issues took place, together with the informal gatherings at the great houses or clubs and some cursory canvassing. Whig and Tory could usually be identified in George III's Houses of Parliament but what made a man what he was, in Plucknett's words, was 'not what he proposed to do in the future, but what he thought about the past'.[7]

Towards the end of the eighteenth century three major issues had a profound effect upon British politics. The parties, characterized by the historian Feiling as possessing 'a continuous tradition and some elementary framework of party, and a descent of political ideas',[8] were given greater definition and impetus by those issues. They were: parliamentary reform, the American War and above all the French Revolution. 'The Whig rhetoric', according to one commentator, 'spoke of reform, parliament and the people', though within their own ranks they were divided as to the definitions and implications of these terms, from the radical Wilkes to the Whig Grey. The Tories were for 'King, Church and Constitution, but the varieties of interpretations they gave these causes was illustrated by their divisions over Catholic emancipation and the reform of parliament'.[9] Within this new framework the idea of governments resigning when they had lost the confidence of the House began to take shape, thus encouraging a greater degree of permanence and sense of cohesion among the groupings. A more formal party system was beginning to emerge.

It has to be remembered, though, that politics at this time did not concern the vast bulk of the population, with the electorate prior to the Great Reform Act comprising only approximately 435,000. Moreover, those who contended for power came exclusively from the same class. In Ostrogorski's words, 'England on the eve of its transformation [i.e. by the Great Reform Act] can be summed up in a single sentence. It was the absolute domination of the aristocratic class.'[10] Ostrogorski went on to make the point that the power and social homogeneousness of the ruling class were buttressed by the notion of gentlemanly behaviour which was an 'unwritten charter' like the constitution of the realm. According to a table prepared about 1815, the House of Commons contained no fewer than 471 members who owed their seats to the goodwill of peers and landed gentlemen and it was certainly considered ungentlemanly not to support one's patron. In Disraeli's *Coningsby* Lord Monmouth says to his grandson: 'You go along with your family, sir, like a gentleman; you are not to consider your opinions like a philosopher or political adventurer.' It is an interesting but not often remarked feature of the pre-reformed House of Commons that although Burke wrote to his Bristol constituents explaining that he owed them not his vote but his judgement, at the same time members thought it only gentlemanly to follow the instructions of an individual patron. As Charles James Fox remarked in 1797: 'When gentlemen represent populous towns and cities, then it is a disputed point whether they ought to obey their voice, or follow the dictates of their conscience, but if they represent a noble lord or a duke, then it becomes no longer a question of doubt; and he is not considered a man of honour who does not implicitly obey the orders of a single constituent.' The division of the unreformed House of Commons into parties, then, in no way impaired the homogeneousness of the single unified ruling class; it only served to preserve cohension within the ranks.[11]

This is not to say that the concept of party as it had developed by the end of the eighteenth century was an unreal one. According to Barker the basis of party is not so much ideology or organization as the emergence of a leadership which could retain allegiance.[12] This allegiance would in turn promote continuity, though as Gilmour points out: 'The continuity was of power and opposition, not of names and parties'.[13] Barker argues that party signifies something much more basic than modern definitions suggest; he believes it to represent a response to deep human instincts – the stimulus of leadership and the warmth of personal contact. Most men have a natural desire for some system of sides or teams to which they can pledge their loyalty. It was natural enough, given the traditional division of 'ins' and 'outs', power and opposition, for some kind of two-party system to emerge: not an ideological division, though, but one based on 'bodies of common sentiment' for a 'side and its colour'. This partisanship was a feature not only of the late eighteenth but also of the nineteenth and even twentieth centuries, and there are countless examples in literature of the emotions evoked, especially at the hustings, by this 'common sentiment', as Dickens's description of Eatanswill in *The Pickwick Papers* shows:

It appears then that the Eatanswill people, like the people of many other small towns, consider themselves of the utmost and most mighty importance, and that every man in Eatanswill, conscious of the weight that attached to his example, felt himself bound to unite heart and soul, with one of the two great parties that divided the town – the Blues and the Buffs. Now the Blues lost no opportunity in opposing the Buffs, and the Buffs lost no opportunity in opposing the Blues; and the consequence was, that whenever the Blues and Buffs met together at public meeting, town hall, fair or market place, disputes and high words arose between them. With these dissensions it is almost superfluous to say that everything in Eatanswill was made a party question. If the Buffs proposed to new skylight the market place, the Blues got up public meetings, and denounced the proceeding; if the Blues proposed the erection of an additional pump in the High Street, the Buffs rose as one man and stood aghast at the enormity. There were Blue shops and Buff shops, Blue inns and Buff inns – there was a Blue aisle and a Buff aisle in the very church itself.

Descriptions of actual elections are to be found in a number of novels, for example in George Elliot's *Felix Holt*. This description was based upon Miss Elliot's personal experiences at the Nuneaton hustings in 1832 when the Riot Act was read out and a detachment of Scots Greys ordered in. Later in the century Disraeli and George Meredith were also to give descriptions of 'vigorous' election campaigns based upon personal experience. Anthony Trollope, later still, described his fornight's canvassing in the East Yorkshire borough of Beverley as 'the most wretched fortnight of my manhood'. Fictionalized, these experiences were offered to posterity in the novel *Ralph the Heir*. Around the turn of the century H. G. Wells, and in the twentieth century John Galsworthy, were to show how little things had changed. It is important to remember, though, that most of the participants in the earlier electoral excitement would not even have had the vote and virtually none would have felt that either party represented their interests. The loyalty and commitment were obviously self-generating, suggesting that Barker's 'deep human instinct' theory has substance. Certainly the popular feelings evoked had little to do with the structure of power at Westminster.

What was to transform the nineteenth-century constitution, however, was the advent of a new social class with wealth and influence and a fairly distinctive political philosophy. During the early part of the nineteenth-century a new bustling capitalist class of manufacturers came into its own, with new tastes, new desires and new ambitions. The thrust of these new men was to prove impossible to resist, and their energy and ambition is perhaps best epitomised by one Sir Thomas Throgmorton of whom the *Quarterly Review* of 1825 reported that he would appear at dinner wearing a suit of cloth which had been on the backs of sheep that very morning. But what was the radicalism that so many of these men supported? According to John Stuart Mill it represented a frontal attack on 'the wretched supposition that the English institutions were models of excellence'. Certainly radicalism, with its belief that democratic suffrage constituted, in Mill's words, 'the most essential of securities for good government', was one of the driving forces behind the Great Reform Act. For the radicals 1832 was the first step on the path to full democracy; to their Whig allies, whom they regarded as 'squeezable material', the Reform Act was simply the perfecting of existing constitutional arrangements.

It was the break-up of the social homogeneity of the ruling class itself which caused the House of Commons to begin to cease to be 'a closed arena in which the cliques and factions within the ruling class contended for power'. In the 1830s the Duke of Wellington lamented the decline in 'party', and indeed after the election of 1830 so great was the confusion that it was impossible to get agreement as to who had actually won, the government claiming gains of twenty-two seats and the opposition declaring that the government had lost fifty! But there can be no doubt that if parties in Wellington's sense were dying other kinds of party were taking their place. The House of Commons was regularly being divided into two camps on major issues. Governments were beginning to pursue policies with more consistency than hitherto, and as royal patronage declined after 1832 it was not long before governments were going to the electorate, still only about 5 per cent of the population, with a specific set of measures which they promised to implement if elected. This happened most notably in 1835, when Sir Robert Peel addressed his electors at Tamworth – the famous Tamworth Manifesto.

If something resembling a modern two-party system was emerging, or re-emerging, by the late 1830s, it was not destined to last long, for in 1846 the prime minister Sir Robert Peel, in repealing the Corn Laws which his government was pledged to maintain, smashed the historic Tory party, sending some of the more progressive Conservatives finally into the new Liberal party.[14] In the shorter term this measure destroyed not only his own party but also that coalition of Whigs, radical and middle-class representatives who had defeated the Tories, for these had no need to stay together any longer and did not in fact do so. 'Parliament', according to Ostrogorski, 'ceased to exhibit its old consistency because society had lost it. The constant multiplication of degrees in the social scale, the variety of new aspirations, the change of social relations from the concrete to a generalized standard, all found their way into the House, narrow as the entrance to it was at that time.'[15]

But we are running ahead of ourselves. There are other aspects of the 1832 Act to be considered. At the time the duty of preparing lists of voters belonged to the overseers of the poor in every parish and any qualified elector could have his name included in the register (and indeed object to names already on the list). Shortly after the Act was passed registration societies began to be formed with the purpose of ensuring that all known supporters of the party were registered to vote. Sir Robert Peel quickly appreciated the significance of registration, describing it as an element more powerful than king or Commons. 'The registration', he said, 'will govern the disposal of offices, and determine the policy of party attack; and the power of this new element will go on increasing as its secret strength becomes better known and is more fully developed.'[16] Peel prophetically predicted the 'systematic organization' of registration, because he grasped the new reality that in order to win, candidates would have to gain the votes of a large number of people to whom they were not personally known and they could do so only on the basis of outlining what they proposed to do if elected. This is precisely what he himself did in the Tamworth Manifesto, which may be regarded as both the first modern election address and the first party manifesto.

Peel's prediction was justified: registration societies multiplied and in 1861 the Liberals established the Liberal Registration Association with the task of co-ordinating constituency registration and establishing societies or associations where none existed. The name of this body was later changed to the Liberal Association. Characteristically the registration societies formed after 1832 were not in any sense representative but self-elected and self-perpetuating and it was only with the passage of time that pressures towards greater representativeness made themselves felt. Conservatives in Liverpool, for example, organized originally in 1832, reorganized themselves in 1848 into a representative constitutional association, based upon wards with elected officials, each holding positions on the association committee. But this early example was not followed by more than a handful of Conservative associations before the second major electoral reform of the century, in 1867, which produced a plethora of Conservative associations of all kinds.

The Liberals had generally been slower off the mark but they were to respond to the changes ushered in by the Second Reform Act in a spectacular fashion. The 1867 Act created four three-member constituencies, Leeds, Manchester, Liverpool and Birmingham. During the passage of the bill, the House of Lords had successfully added an amendment to the effect that voters in these cities would be allowed only two votes. Now, the Liberals of Birmingham believed that there were enough Liberals in their city, if properly organized, to ensure the election of three Liberal MPs. In order to achieve the necessary organization the Birmingham Liberal Association reformed itself on a democratic basis at ward and city level. The number of Liberal voters in each ward was ascertained and each was advised how he should use his two votes. The upshot was that three Liberals were returned for Birmingham in the next election. In 1873 the association appointed as its secretary Francis Schnadhorst who, together with Birmingham's favourite-son-to-be, Joseph Chamberlain, sought to gain control of municipal government for the Liberals. That year Chamberlain was elected mayor and the party was massively successful in the council elections. The Birmingham association was clearly a shining example for municipal political associations throughout the country, an example which the Conservatives would ignore at their peril.

The 1867 Act also stimulated organization at the national level. Within a year the National Union of Conservative and Constitutional Associations had been formed and annual conferences were established. These became important when at the Crystal Palace in 1872 the party leader Disraeli chose the occasion to make a major speech. By 1878 the National Union had grown sufficiently to establish provincial bodies. The Conservatives had also established a Central Office in 1870, pretty much under the control of the party whips. This was to grow to the extent that in 1911 the post of party chairman was created to co-ordinate the organization and liaise with the National Union.

It is generally considered that the Conservative's electoral success of 1874 was attributable in some considerable measure to the activities of the National Union and the Central Office, and the lesson was not lost on the Liberals. At a conference held, appropriately, in Birmingham the National Liberal Federation was formed, with Chamberlain as its president and Schnadhorst its secretary. There was an important difference, though, between the Liberal Federation and the Conservative National Union. The federation sought to take on the mantle, to use Chamberlain's words, of being a 'Liberal parliament', formulating by open democratic debate the policies to be followed by future Liberal administrations. It was this aspiration which earned for the Federation Disraeli's dismissive description, 'the Birmingham caucus'. But the value of the caucus was undeniable: it was instrumental in the party's triumph in 1880. All the same, its overwhelmingly radical character put it at odds with the parliamentary leadership. Indeed the deadlock was not broken until an open breach formed between Gladstone and Chamberlain over the issue of home rule for Ireland in 1886, after which Chamberlain and the Liberal Unionists left the party and formed a separate association. Thereafter, with the fear of Birmingham radicalism removed, the great majority of local associations affiliated to the National Federation.

Another feature of the 1880 election had been the national tour undertaken by the party leader, Gladstone. This development was said to have filled Queen Victoria with some alarm but it was, of course, to become a standard feature of subsequent election campaigns. Taken together with the organizational changes outlined above, this development gave to the late Victorian party system much the shape of our modern system.

One major development, though, still remained: the arrival and establishment of the Labour party. It was becoming clear to a number of labour leaders by the 1880s that the existing party framework did not take the interests of labour much into account. Working-class males had been enfranchised in 1867 or in 1884 (the Third Reform Act) but only a few were able to become parliamentary candidates because some measure of personal wealth or patronage was usually necessary to enter politics. For example, the Liberals supported only eleven successful working class candidates in the 1880s, the so-called Lib-Labs, though miners' candidates also secured election and these too took the Liberal whip. Moreover, the Liberal leader, Gladstone, 'the people's William', was focusing his party's attention more on Ireland than on domestic politics, resulting in the breach with Chamberlain. So during the last twenty years of the century the Liberal party took insufficient note of the rise of two phenomena related in the modern mind but not in the Victorian mind: working-class politics and socialism. They came together officially only in 1893 at a conference in Bradford which included representatives of trade unions and socialist societies and which established the Independent Labour party. Little followed directly but in 1899 the Trades Union Congress called a meeting in London to which representatives of seventy trade unions, the ILP and socialist societies were invited. This conference established a Labour Representation Committee (LRC) with the declared purpose of seeking a distinct Labour group in parliament with its own whips and its own policies, ready to co-operate with any party which showed itself interested in 'promoting legislation in the direct interest of labour'. The LRC's first secretary was later to become Britain's first Labour prime minister, James Ramsay MacDonald. Shortly the LRC fought its first election, putting forward fifteen candidates of whom two were elected. More important, though, was a decision taken in 1903 that successful parliamentary candidates should sign a pledge restraining them from identifying with any section or interest within the major parties. To be independent, however, was to be independently financed, and the same conference took a decision to make a levy on all members of affiliated bodies to provide MPs with £200 per annum. (In 1911 all MPs were to receive an official salary.)

The rise of the Labour party, in parenthesis, indicated that another major change in the nature of party politics had taken place. We observed that the fierce inter-party competition of the earlier part of the nineteenth century, exemplified by the hustings, did not much correspond to a pattern of expectations amongst the people, most of whom did not have the vote. As the century wore on, though, parties began to strive for power on the basis of appeals to the growing electorate that they and not their opponents could better manage the interests of the nation. At much the same time, these interests became more diverse and yet more interdependent, and managing them became a much more complex task. Indeed, it became increasingly difficult finally to state what those interests were, though they became more or less synonymous with managing the economy. The original purpose of parties, of canalizing conflict into constitutional channels, of agreeing to stop fighting at dinner time, had become transformed by the complexities of the modern economy and the expectations aroused by democracy, into a purpose far more positive and sophisticated. It was in this atmosphere of expectation and confidence that socialism flourished.

For their part, there can be little doubt that the Liberals, severely weakened by the loss of Chamberlain and his radical Unionists in 1886, exhausted by their attempts to solve 'the Irish problem', had not responded to this new challenge on the left. It was also damaging for a Liberal party to find itself in government at the time of war when, almost by definition, illiberal measures would be essential. Worst of all for the party, though, was the split occasioned by the leadership crisis in 1916 when Lloyd George replaced his party leader H. H. Asquith as prime minister and head of the wartime coalition. The split between the 'Squiffites' and the Lloyd George Liberals was never to be effectively healed; indeed after the death of both, their daughters continued the struggle until Megan Lloyd George left to join the Labour party in the 1950s.

The struggle between the Liberal and Labour parties as to which was to be the major opponent of the Conservatives continued for most of the interwar period. The first battle occurred in 1922 when the Conservatives withdrew from the post-war coalition and forced Lloyd George to fight an election which the Conservatives easily won. More significantly perhaps, Labour overtook the Liberals as second party, to the extent of forming a minority government in 1924. Though MacDonald's ministry was short-lived his party's achievement in gaining power in so short a time was remarkable. In 1929 the party again came to office, this time as the largest single party. The Liberals by contrast, unified superficially by Asquith's death the previous year, managed to win only fifty-nine seats. The battle for supremacy between the two was over, at least until the modern era.

Success over the Liberals, however, was not matched by success in managing the economy, for in 1931 prime minister MacDonald found it necessary to establish a national coalition government with himself at the head, and as a consequence the bulk of his party left him to his new friends. The depleted Liberals split once more when the National government introduced protectionist measures in 1932, thereby losing the support of the Liberal free-traders. The Coalition or National Liberals continued in what was to become a permanent alliance with the Conservatives and eventually they lost their separate identity during the 1950s; the independent Liberals managed to survive but only with a handful of seats. The Labour party, on the other hand, achieved its greatest success in 1945, forming the government with one of the largest non-coalition majorities of the century. A period of over twenty years of Conservative dominance, either independently or as the major partner in a coalition, had come to an abrupt and unexpected end.

If the distinctive feature of the postwar party system was overwhelming domination by two parties, an equally important if less immediately obvious feature was the considerable amount of agreement that existed between the parties over a wide variety of policy issues for approximately a quarter of a century. The framework of the party system seemed to have acquired a stability, not to say rigidity, of which, probably, the best indication is that between 1945 and 1959 only thirteen seats (including two university seats and two Northern Ireland seats) changed hands at by-elections out of a total of 168, and five of these were in the pre-election year of 1958. No doubt one of the reasons for the 'me too-ist' character of British politics during these years was the attempt made by the Conservative party to acclimatize itself to the aspirations of a postwar electorate and by the time of the next election in 1950 the Conservative party had undertaken a series of organizational and policy reforms which revitalized the party machine and 'modernized' its policies, principally by emphasizing the party's commitment to interventionist politics. Although the Labour government contrived to win the 1950 election it did so with a majority of only six and managed to survive for just eighteen months. In the 1951 election, although gaining more votes than the Conservatives, Labour lost and their opponents began thirteen years in power.

By the early 1960s, however, Britain's economy began to falter and the Conservative government became increasingly unpopular until, in 1962, it suffered a startling by-electoral defeat in the safe seat of Orpington at the hands of the Liberal party. This event was a turning-point in the history of the postwar Liberal party and was very harmful to the government. In 1964 the Labour party under Harold Wilson took office, though with only a slender majority. In 1966 Wilson sought to strengthen his hand and went to the country again. For only the second time in its history the Labour party came to power with a substantial majority. By this time, however, the economy was in serious decline and Labour's inability either to manage the economy successfully or to convince socialist supporters of its ideological good faith led to a series of confidence-sapping by-electoral defeats. In 1967, for, example of eight by-elections in constituencies held by Labour no fewer than five were lost. A pattern rapidly became established of the electorate's moving decisively against a government it had elected only a year or so before: this was quite new.

In 1970, somewhat against the odds, Labour was defeated at the general election and Edward Heath became prime minister and inaugurated a legislative programme which moved decisively away from the consensus politics of the postwar period. Heath initiated a reform of industrial relations the aim of which was to restrict the power of the trade unions and he pursued an industry policy designed to eliminate government intervention in industrial affairs; 'lame ducks' would no longer be supported by public funding. Heath's abrasive style of leadership offended many within and without the party and his mid-term conversion to interventionism, some said to a form of corporatism (including a statutory incomes policy), offended many more. In 1972 and 1973, of eight by-elections in constituencies held by the Conservatives four were lost. Significantly each of the four was won by the Liberals who also won a seat from the Labour party.

The Heath administration had also to contend with major industrial disputes, notably with the power workers and the miners. In 1974, in the face of a miners' strike which resulted in power cuts and industry's working a three-day week, the Conservatives decided to hold a general election to strengthen their hand. The election was lost, though in fact the Conservatives polled more votes than Labour. Heath sought to hold on to power by offering a coalition pact to the Liberal party, which had returned fourteen members, but no agreement was possible and Labour eventually came to office with a majority of four. Eight months later Wilson turned to the electorate once again but his position was not greatly improved. A substantial increase in the Liberal vote in the February election seemed to have been largely responsible for the ensuing stalemate, and although the 'wasted vote' argument was deployed by the major parties subsequently, the Liberal vote stood up surprisingly well ensuring another hung parliament.

The Labour government of 1974–9 was beset by a number of major problems amongst which rampant inflation and a poor and worsening economic performance were the most important. The government sought support for its economic and industrial strategies through a concordat with the Trades Union Congress (TUC) and for a time this approach was successful. But the small and diminishing parliamentary majority put a constant strain on ministers and this became particularly trying when the government felt obliged, in the face of the relative success of the Welsh and more especially Scottish Nationalist parties, to pursue legislation to grant some measure of devolution of power to assemblies in Scotland and Wales. In the event referendums in both countries failed to produce a large enough majority in favour and the legislation was lost. By 1977 the Labour government sought and obtained a pact with the Liberal party to sustain it in office. Sensing a general election in the autumn of 1978 the Liberals ended the pact (which seems anyway to have given them little beyond some extra political visibility and some nearly disastrous by-election results), but in fact the election did not come until 1979 and the intervening winter witnessed the breakdown of the government's compact with the unions, and the resultant so-called 'winter of discontent' produced a plethora of strikes which seemed to indicate that Labour's claim to be the natural party of government precisely because it could work with the unions was no longer tenable. In the spring of 1979 the Conservative party led by Mrs

Thatcher won a clear victory and once more a Labour leader was borne down under a torrent of recrimination from the party's left wing to the effect that the government had reneged on its commitment to socialism.

It would be difficult to overestimate the change that took place in 1979. In many senses this was a traditional British election in which a conservative administration emphasizing its managerial skills took on a radical opposition seeking to transform society; in this case, however, the conservative administration was Labour's and the radical would-be transformers were the Conservatives. Committed, like Heath in 1970, to rolling back the state, the new Conservative government initiated a policy designed to cut inflation, limit public expenditure and revitalize British industry. Apparent success with the former, coupled with Labour's internal divisions which became so pronounced that a prominent group of right-wingers departed to found the Social Democratic Party, and with the kudos which Mrs Thatcher gained from the military successes of the Falklands War, enabled the Conservatives, despite high unemployment, failure to control public expenditure and an unexampled decline in the nation's manufacturing base, to gain a second and even more impressive electoral victory in 1983. The election of that year was also contested by a new political grouping, the Alliance, comprising the Liberal and Social Democratic parties fighting together on one manifesto. Alliance intervention helped to produce Labour's worst performance at a general election since 1935, arguably since 1918. Britain's party system, based upon two parties since 1945, had changed, with the Alliance taking over 25 per cent of votes cast. In 1987 the Alliance was unable to improve upon its position. Nevertheless it remained a major electoral force, securing seven and a half million votes (twenty-three per cent of the total), thereby helping to secure a third successive defeat for Labour. For much of the last 300 years British politics have been dominated by two parties and yet the nature of that dominance, and of the parties themselves, indeed of the tasks they have set themselves, has varied considerably. True, parties have always possessed an identifiable leadership commanding a measure of loyalty in parliament; parties have always pursued group interests, be they religious, economic, regional, ideological, or social-class; parties have always sought and, to varying degrees, secured a measure of public support. But the rest of the pattern has changed with time.

But what of the party system? There is considerable basic

agreement among writers on British politics as varied as Jennings, Mackenzie, Birch and Punnett, for example, that Britain has traditionally enjoyed the benefits of a stable, consistent, two-party system, and they also broadly agree on what the phrase signifies, though Sartori's is probably the best working definition.[17] According to him a two-party system implies the existence of the following four features:

1 Two major parties are in a position to compete for an absolute majority of parliamentary seats.
2 One of these parties succeeds in winning a workable majority.
3 This party is prepared to govern alone.
4 That both parties may reasonably expect to hold power alternately.

Politics being an imperfect science, it would be unreasonable to expect these features to correspond precisely to reality. Even so, it will be instructive to discover to what extent the history of British parties approximates to Sartori's model. Before we test the model, however, it is worth considering an essential precondition of its functioning: that the strength of the two major parties should reflect the division of public opinion, not in any precisely arithmetical or proportional sense (that would be too much to ask) but roughly. In a two-party system, that is to say, we should expect that if party A wins an election, this would be the consequence of its having secured the support of the majority of voters; and that government policies would consequently reflect the wishes of the majority of people (more realistically that the drift of government policy would reflect the disposition of the majority). It is appropriate to bear this precondition in mind when assessing the salient features of British party history. Now on to Sartori.

Sartori's first criterion for a two-party system stated that two parties must be in a position to compete for the absolute majority of seats. Apart from the obvious caveat that, for long periods of time, third and fourth parties such as the Irish, the Liberal Unionists, the Labour party and finally the Liberals and their Social Democratic allies, have commanded substantial support, it is often forgotten that a large number of seats in the House of Commons were simply not contested during the nineteenth century. Although it was not uncommon before the Second Reform Act of 1867 for uncontested seats to comprise a majority, even much later they were an important factor, comprising for example over 36 per cent of all seats as late as the general election of 1900. So much for partisan rigidity in the nineteenth century and for Sartori's first criterion.

Sartori's second criterion argued the necessity of one party's winning a workable majority. It would clearly be quite inappropriate to include the period before, say, 1880 in considering this criterion. Even so, Jorgen Rasmussen shows that about 30 per cent of elections in the twentieth century have failed to produce a majority in the House for one party. He concludes: 'Taking a very lenient definition of working majority – one party has at least twenty seats more than its combined opponents – only about half of the elections have produced such results.'[18] One general election, that of 1964 when Labour came to power after thirteen years, produced an overall majority of four. Roberts points out that if only 350 voters in four specific consituencies had stayed at home on election day, Labour would have had no majority at all. So much for strong government based on working majorities and for Sartori's second criterion.

The third of Sartori's criteria for the two-party system was the willingness of a party with a majority to govern alone and this has certainly been a feature of the British system. The basis of this willingness might at first sight appear to have been the parties' ability to command the votes of their supporters, but not necessarily so; historically speaking this is a relatively recent phenomenon. A. L. Lowell, for example, who defined a party vote as one where nine tenths of a party voted together in a division in the House, discovered that in 1836 party votes comprised only 23 per cent of all divisions and that, indeed, in 1860 they comprised only 6 per cent. Not until the early twentieth century is it possible to describe the party vote as normal. In 1906, for example, Beer speaks of the Liberals voting as a party in 88 per cent of divisions. It seems clear, then, that during the major part of the nineteenth century parties did not assume power on the understanding that their supporters would sustain them but rather that they could win support for their policies in the House from persuasion or accomodation. Moreover, the idea of idiological confrontation is inappropriate not only to the nineteenth century but also to those periods in the twentieth when coalition governments held office, which is to say for about twenty years. So much for adversarian politics and Sartori's third criterion.

Arguably the most important feature of the two-party system is the rotation or alternation of power between the two parties. A party which has reason to believe that it has no possibility of achieving power constitutionally is unlikely to be a strong supporter of the party system or the constitution. In the long run, we like to believe, British parties share power more or less equally. History clearly shows that this is not the case. The parties of the left, both Liberal and Labour, have held power for much shorter periods than the Conservatives and almost always have gained smaller parliamentary majorities. Indeed there have been only three occasions in the last century when parties of the left have enjoyed substantial majorities; their years in office with such majorities have amounted to no more than thirteen. In contrast, the Conservatives have enjoyed substantial majorities on eleven occasions and their years in office under such conditions have amounted to fifty-six (including eighteen years when they were the dominant party in a national coalition). History shows a very considerable disproportion between the chances for power of the Liberal and Labour parties on the one hand and the Conservatives on the other. Modern psephologists who invented the 'swing of the pendulum' theory of alternating power were bad historians; their perspective went back only to 1964, or arguably to 1945. Before then the clock case tilted decisively to the right. So much for the pendulum theory and for Sartori's final criterion.

Of equal interest are the results of a survey of electoral support for the major parties over the last hundred years. On only four occasions has an incoming government secured more than half of the votes cast and on each occasion there were extenuating circumstances. On the first two occasions, 1886 and 1900, the Conservatives were in alliance with the Liberal Unionists and on the second two, 1931 and 1935, they were the major partners in a national coalition. It is worth reflecting on this fact for a moment. It was stated previously that the strength of the two major parties should reflect the division of public opinion, but the truth of the matter is that on only these four occasions in twenty-six general elections was the majority public opinion reflected in the choice of government. Moreover, on three of the four occasions the majority in question was marginal. Only in 1931, with the election of a national coalition, was a substantial body of opinion – 61 per cent – nominally behind the government. Only once in a hundred years could a government's claim to represent 'the people' be taken seriously. So much for mandate theories.

The history of British political parties indicates a complexity and capacity for change which renders the label 'two-party system' misleading and to be applied only with great caution. Sartori's criteria are clearly applicable to the British party system but only with a margin of tolerance and only, as he is the first to accept, during the last thirty years. Moreover, the nature of parties has changed profoundly over the years and not in a unilinear manner. There is no reason to believe that they will not continue to change equally profoundly in the future and no reason to suppose that the two-party system, so called, will not continue to develop from its present (and very recent) rigidity back to a condition in which party discipline is less dominant and less intransigent.

It has been part of the British tradition to believe not only in the historical validity of the two-party system but also in its geographical validity, so to speak. It has been held by writers like L. S. Amery that the strongest democracies, the Anglo-Saxon democracies, have two-party systems, and that continental multi-party systems are somehow aberrant, and carry 'a certain opprobrium' as Drucker says.[19] The evident success of systems such as the Swedish and West German deals a considerable blow to traditional British self-confidence but a similar blow may be dealt if one examines the Anglo-Saxon democracies themselves. American parties, for example, bear a much closer resemblance to nineteenth-century British parties than to the modern ones in the sense that they are weak and owe their periodic unity principally to the personality of the leader. Canadian government has had to contend with three and more parties and several minority governments. In all there have been fourteen postwar Canadian governments; six of these have been minority governments. Moreover, the pendulum has swung in a lop-sided way, with the Liberals forming ten governments and the Conservatives only four. Since the war the Liberals have been in power for thirty-three years and the Conservatives for only eight.

Australia has a two-and-a-half party system which has given that nation predominantly right-wing coalition governments since the war. The Liberal/Country (now National) party coalition (Conservative) has formed the government on twelve occasions, the Labor party on only four. The coalition has been in office for thirty-one years to Labor's ten. Moreover it has enjoyed sound majorities on nine occasions to Labor's one. South African politics, since shortly after the second world war, have been dominated by a single party: the Nationalists have won every election.

Only New Zealand has a predominantly two-party system

broadly similar to the British, though here too right-wing governments have been far more common. Since the war the National party
(Conservative) has won ten elections compared to Labour's four and
has been in power for twenty-nine years compared to Labour's
eleven, enjoying strong majorities on eight occasions compared to
Labour's two.

In short, far from being grounded in a long history and offering a
model to which others should aspire because it produces stable
government to which two parties contribute more or less equally, the
present British party system is the lop-sided, somewhat aberrant
product of a continuing process of evolution, the direction of which,
as this chapter indicates, has chiefly been the product of historical
exigency. As Ian Gilmour suggests: 'The two-party system . . . is the
result neither of the wishes of the British people nor the foresight of
British statesmen. Like Tristram Shandy it was begotten in a fit of
absence of mind.'[20] History shows that its subsequent career has
been as muddled, unpredictable and as generally undistinguished as
was that gentleman's, and its future as uncertain.

Notes

1 L.D. Epstein, *Political Parties in Western Democracies* (London, Pall Mall, 1967), p. 5.
2 Alan R. Ball, *British Political Parties* (London, Macmillan, 1981), p. 3.
3 See S. B. Chrimes, 'Before 1600', in S. D. Bailey (ed.), *The British Party System* (London, Hansard Society, 1952).
4 Quoted in H. R. Williamson, 'The Seventeenth Century' in Bailey, *The British Party System*.
5 Ibid., p. 18.
6 David Hume, *History Of Great Britain*, vol. II (London, 1824), p. 532.
7 T. F. T. Plucknett, *Taswell Langmead's Constitutional History*, 10th edn (London, Sweet and Maxwell, 1946), p. 692.
8 K. Feiling, *The Second Tory Party* (London, Macmillan, 1938), p. v.
9 See G. K. Roberts, *Political Parties and Pressure Groups in Britain* (London, Weidenfeld & Nicolson, 1970), p. 18.
10 M. Ostrogorski, *Democracy and the Organization of Political Parties* (London, Macmillan, 1902), p. 6.
11 Ibid., p. 22.
12 Ernest Barker, *Reflections on Government* (London, Oxford University Press, 1967), p. 86.
13 Ian Gilmour, *The Body Politic* (London, Hutchinson, 1969), p. 24.
14 Information on the changing of party names will be provided in the relevant chapters.
15 Ostrogorski, *Democracy and Organization*, p. 57.
16 Quoted in Ivor Bulmer Thomas, *The Party System in Great Britain* (London, Phoenix House, 1953), p. 14.
17 G. Sartori, *Parties and Party Systems: A Framework for Analysis* (Cambridge, Cambridge University Press, 1976).
18 See 'Was Guy Fawkes right?', in Isaac Kramnick (ed.), *Is Britain Dying?* (London, Cornell University Press, 1979).
19 See H. Drucker, *Multi-Party Britain* (London, Macmillan, 1979).
20 Quoted in Gilmour, *The Body Politic*, p. 33.

2   What is Conservatism?

The purpose of this chapter is to establish an understanding of the nature of conservatism and then to consider the history of the Conservative party in an attempt to discover the extent to which the party's policies have been motivated by its guiding principles. The first task, then, is to discover whether conservatism constitutes a recognizable and identifiable way of thinking about politics.

'Conservative belief', says Anthony Quinton, 'becomes explicit only in reaction to a positive, innovative attack on the traditional scheme of things. What exists speaks for itself simply by existing.'[1] It is wise to underline the significance of this statement, for it suggests that the particular nature of conservatism at any historical period will be shaped at least partly by the nature of the attack upon the 'traditional scheme of things'. To put it another way, we should not be able to state with any precision what conservative politics amounted to in, say, the early 1900s unless we knew what liberal politics were. But what could be said independently about conservatism in that period, indeed in any period, is that its proponents believed in 'what was' rather than 'what might be', though, as we shall see, even this minimalist position presents some problems for conservatives. The basic reasoning behind Quinton's assertion is that, after all, 'what is' only has to be justified when it is under attack; thus most historians of conservatism locate its origin in the period immediately after the French Revolution when writers like Edmund Burke sought to defend the established order in Britain against the criticisms of the radicals inspired by the revolution in France and the principles of 1789.

There can be little doubt that although the French Revolution was the most positive and innovative attack on the traditional scheme of things it certainly was not the first. Indeed Quinton himself looks back much further for the origins of conservatism, and with obvious good cause. He begins his account with the Puritan attack upon the 'traditional scheme of things'; that is to say, monarchical control of the church through the bishops. Conservatives reacted to defend the episcopacy; indeed Dr Johnson defined a Tory as one who 'adheres to the ancient constitution of the state and the apostolic hierarchy of the Church of England'.[2] Such a Tory was Hooker who wrote his celebrated *Law of Ecclesiastical Polity* to justify the close relationship between the church and the Elizabethan state. We have already seen that a party system of sorts existed at the time of the debate upon episcopal succession in 1640, so there are strong grounds for accepting Quinton's point of departure. All the same, the argument in which Hooker participated was eventually settled not by political accommodation but by civil war, after which came a lengthy period when there was no major challenge to the traditional scheme of things and hence no philosophical defence was required: until, that is, the French Revolution. So although we may accept Quinton's argument about the origins of British conservatism, simply for reasons of time and space we will concentrate on the post-1789 period.

If conservatism is to be understood as the defence of the established order, does this imply that the established order is to be defended under all circumstances? If not, when and according to which principles is it to be defended? We may hope to be able to answer this question later in the chapter but for the present the task is to investigate conservatism in theory and in practice.

Quinton adduces three chief principles of conservatism which will provide as good a beginning as any. He speaks, first, of traditionalism, a strong emotional attachment to existing procedures and institutions. A system which evolves over a long period of time will surely come to represent the accumulated wisdom of the community, or at least of that part of the community habituated to making decisions. So a fixed constitution may be seen as representing the composite outcome of innumerable compromises, struggles and adjustments; it may be regarded as a kind of residuum of practical political wisdom, capable of adaptation but not of sudden and major change. The practical political implication of this reverence for tradition is the fundamental conservative belief in the rule of law, a belief reinforced as we shall see by conservative views of human nature.

Quinton's second major principle is what he calls organicism, which holds that society is analogous to a natural living body and not a machine or other man-made structure. Citizens are social beings connected to each other in a complex pattern of mutually beneficial relationships. It is precisely because of the complexity and mutuality of these relationships and, crucially, because they arise naturally that they are not amenable to wholesale change. Even minor changes must be considered carefully because of their possible effect upon other parts of the living body of the state.

Some conservative thinkers have seen the existing social order as representing a reflection of divine intention, a view which they shared with medieval thinkers like Aquinas. It makes little practical difference whether society is hierarchical – a place for everybody and everybody in his/her place – at the behest of God or as a consequence of natural design. What follows is that things should not or cannot (or both) be other than they are.

Other conservatives, as O'Sullivan[3] tells us, see the existing social order as representing the culmination of an historical process, a 'more complete and more profoundly rational expression of the human spirit then any deliberately contrived social order could ever be'.[4] O'Sullivan locates this version of conservatism in the German romantic movement, whose exponents were greatly influenced by Hegel's dialectical view of history. Its influence on British conservatism was mediated by writers like Samuel Taylor Coleridge and Thomas Carlyle.[5] Whatever its philosophical origin the organic view of society has had a profound influence upon conservatism, tending to stress the mutuality of duties and obligations. In the well-known ninenteenth century hymn 'All Things Bright and Beautiful' we are told:

> The rich man in his castle,
> The poor man at his gate.
> He made them high and lowly,
> He numbered their estate.

That the rich have obligations to the poor is central to the organic view and gives to conservatism its paternalistic aspect found, for example, in Coleridge's idea of a national church dedicated primarily to the welfare of the poor or Disraeli's 'One Nation' philosophy or, most recently, in the compassionate conservatism of so-called Tory 'wets' such as Sir Ian Gilmour. For all its compassion, however, organicism implies the retention of hierarchy, as Dr Johnson told his friend Boswell: 'You are to consider that it is your duty to maintain the subordination of civilized society; and where there is gross or shameful deviation from rank, it should be punished so as to deter others from the same perversion.'[6] This is precisely the fate of Thomas Hardy's Jude, a man who tried to 'rise above his station' and suffered accordingly. He came to regard himself as a 'frightful example of what not to do'.

Quinton's third major principle is that of scepticism, which holds that life is not very amenable to 'improvement' by the application of social and political theories. H. G. Wells said that socialism was based upon the same principle as all scientific work: the assumption that 'things may be calculated upon, may be foreseen'[7] The conservative, on the other hand, believes pretty well the opposite: that in the end things may not always be calculated upon, not always foreseen. As far as the conservative is concerned it is certainly far better to put one's faith in established institutions and customary procedures than in political theories.

Underpinning Quinton's principle of scepticism and traditionalism is the overpowering certainty of human fallibility. As Quintin Hogg[8] argues, this belief has traditionally been associated with the Christian concept of original sin which holds that since the fall of Adam we have all of us been tainted with sin, or to put it more prosaically, none of us is capable of moral perfection. Such a belief is not restricted to Christianity, however. There are important secular theories (none more so than Freud's) which stress man's moral limitations. The consequence of this belief is clearly to make conservatives suspicious of any utopian scheme and strongly supportive of institutions which, though far from perfect, have stood the test of time. Moreover, it is not merely man's moral imperfection which disposes the conservatives against grand designs but also man's intellectual limitations. Believing, in Kant's words, that nothing straight could be built from the crooked timbers of humanity, conservatives have tended to disregard abstract theories of progress and settle for the piecemeal redress of proven grievances.

Given man's moral and intellectual limitations, conservatives believe that life only becomes tolerable to the extent that man is constrained by customs and institutions with which he is familiar and which are broadly acceptable to him. O'Sullivan's thesis, put briefly, that the lynchpin of conservative politics is the belief in limited government seems to be entirely consistent with the arguments above. He adds another consideration, however, of great importance. Politics, he points out, is after all about choices; now, to the extent that they advance the interests of one person or group, these choices are likely to injure the interests of another. Not merely this but in securing a benefit for himself a man will often forfeit some other, presumably lesser good, from which he had previously benefited. 'No advantages in this world', said David Hume, 'are pure and unmixed', from which it follows that governments ought to advance in a spirit of compromise and moderation which emphasizes individual liberty, the rule of law and constitutional government. In Aldous Huxley's novel *Eyeless in Gaza*, the pacifist Miller argues a similar line. English politics, says Miller, have not traditionally been an arena of large-scale plans or of thinking in terms of first principles but rather of dealing with problems as they arise: thus politics in a limited system are simply a matter of higgling.

'Now higglers lose tempers but don't normally regard one another as fiends in human form. But this is precisely what men of principle and systematic planners can't help doing. A principle is, by definition, right; a plan, for the good of the people. Axioms from which it logically follows that those who disagree with you . . . are enemies of goodness and humanity.'[9]

Government by grand design, says Miller, is, *ipso facto*, government by machine gun.

These are the main ingredients of conservatism. Conservative tradititionalism stresses the importance of adhering to traditional institutions and customs which represent the accumulated wisdom of society over the ages; conservative organicism stresses the complexity and mutuality of social arrangements, which are either natural or God-given or the result of long historical development (or indeed any combination of the three). A crucial ingredient of this organicism is the obligation it lays upon the wealthy to further the interests of the poor. Conservative scepticism recognizes that man's ability to reshape his environment by design is strictly limited by his own moral and intellectual limitations, and that moreover any gain accruing to some elements of society as a result of 'progress' is likely to result in an equal loss for others. Therefore all grand designs for improving man's lot, his institutions, or his customs, are to be taken with a pinch of salt. Conservatism may be summarized, to paraphrase O'Sullivan, as the defence of a limited style of politics based upon the idea of imperfection.[10]

It was said at the beginning that conservativism was a reactive or responsive ideology and it is this aspect which, according to O'Sullivan, has been responsible for creating a crisis of identity for modern conservatives. In the nineteenth century the principle threat to 'the traditional scheme of things' was posed by the individualistic doctrines of liberalism. These doctrines threatened the existence of even a limited form of government, for in stressing above all the rights of the individual, liberalism called into question the very notion of government by consent. If a man chooses only to obey those laws and institutions which directly reflect his values he sows the seeds of anarchy. In the twentieth century, however, the threat came not from individualistic liberalism but from collectivist socialism which, in order to achieve its objectives, invariably sought to aggregate substantial state power at the expense of invidual liberty. Now conservatism can only be fully understood at any historical period by reference to the policies of its political opponents. In the modern era conservatism has had to react to challenges from 'anarchistic' liberalism and 'statist' socialism. Hence O'Sullivan's claim of an identity crisis, with conservatives defending the state against the individual and the individual against the state. This may seem a somewhat precious argument especially since O'Sullivan readily admits that without any single dominant theme or thinker, conservatism is a far more flexible ideology than either socialism or indeed liberalism. In government, political parties often undertake considerable about turns within the space of a week without any obvious identity crisis. Conservatives are probably somewhat more resilient than O'Sullivan would have us believe.

There are other problems with the ideology of conservatism which need more detailed investigation, however. The first is a major one: how to distinguish between conservatism as a political ideology and as an attitude of mind. In his classic work *Conservatism* Lord Hugh Cecil[11] speaks of 'natural conservatism' which is to be found in most people. It amounts to little more than a 'distrust of the unknown and a love of the familiar'. It makes little sense to the majority of men, says Cecil, to depart from the known. Taking any risks is clearly dangerous and requires considerable forethought. 'Why not let it alone', he advises, 'why be weary instead of at rest?' The implicit problem here must now be made explicit. If we assume that even in a sophisticated democracy parties other than the conservatives will come to power (although this does not happen very often in Britain), and if, when in power, they implement certain liberal or socialist policies (and this happens even less often), then the problem for an incoming conservative government is: is it radically to undo what the past government has done or is it to conserve what has become 'the traditional scheme of things'? Clearly the radical course of action will invite uncertainty and perhaps danger: why not follow Cecil's advice and 'let it alone'? If conservatism is an ideology and not simply an attitude of mind it will not do for conservatives to hide behind their belief in limited government, for their political opponents are not likely to be so modest. Speaking in the 1960s the Liberal party leader Jo Grimond made just such a point when he said of the Conservative government that at the time it was conserving socialism whereas previously it had conserved liberalism. This paradox represents a major tension within conservatism.

We come now to a graver difficulty for conservatism, and in discussing it we return to one of the questions posed at the beginning of this chapter. Under what circumstances should conservatives support the 'traditional scheme of things'? The conservative writer T. E. Uttley believes that in the modern world a conservative government must embody the social disciplines of capitalism, maintaining the unequal distribution of property necessary to that discipline and backing it up with an emphasis on law and order.[12] A limited government perhaps, but a strong one. But Uttley ducks the real issue: is the social order based upon capital accumulation to have any regard for social harmony as well as social order? Peter Walker poses the same question and answers it. The test of capitalist inequalities, he declares, is the contribution they make to the general welfare of society. If they make no contribution there would have to follow 'drastic and radical reforms to secure a socially responsible capitalism in which inequalities do contribute to public welfare'.[13] It is hard to reconcile drastic and radical reforms with limited government. It is hard not to see a conflict between the view that hierarchy is natural or God-given or the gift of some inexorable historical development and the view that hierarchy must be assessed by some Benthamite-like measure of utility, with drastic and radical reform threatened if it falls short. Walker's tests, moreover, seem to be largely economic and not to take account of the argument of writers like George Santayana whose concern is chiefly cultural: hierarchy must be preserved because it has provided 'the source from which all culture has hitherto flowed'.[14] There can be little doubt, though, that Walker has exposed a tension within conservatism between the view that hierarchy or, more generally, 'the traditional scheme of things' is inherently worth preserving, and the view that it is worth preserving only in so far as it serves the interests not merely of the rich man in his castle but also those of the poor man at his gate.

Norton and Aughey, aware of this tension, declare: 'Conservatism may be deemed the intellectual justification of inequalities in society and the preservation of the privileges that such inequalities entail. It is the justification of the authoritative relationship based upon these inequalities . . . This is the essence of the Conservative Party's role – to formulate policy that conserves a hierarchy of wealth and power and to make this intelligible and reasonable to a democracy.'[15] Yet when the authors go on to discuss the kinds of policies likely in a democracy to make inequalities seem reasonable to the less favoured they come exactly upon Walker's problem – the perennial problem for conservatism – when should conservatives support the 'settled order of things' and when should they not? At the conclusion of the Napoleonic Wars, when conservatism was said to be defining itself as a political ideology, the British Foreign Secretary, the Tory Castlereagh, refused to give support to the establishment of a permanent international force for the suppression of revolution. Nothing would be more immoral, he said, than to support established power without considering the extent to which that power was being abused. This was the same Castlereagh who supported the brutal suppression of unarmed English radicals at Peterloo and of whom Shelley wrote:

> I met Murder on the way –
> He had a mask like Castlereagh.

That there are major inconsistencies and tensions within conservatism, then, is certain. It follows equally certainly that these inconsistencies and uncertainties will have shaped the history of the Conservative party, to which we shall shortly be turning. It is worth considering, first, the sense that historians of the Conservative party have made of them. Maude is not at all defensive, refering to the inconsistencies as 'archaeological strata, specimens from all its historic stages'[16] but, adds Gilmour, with 'common characteristics imposed by the geography and topography of the site'.[17] Inconsistencies and tensions, then, tend to be regarded by conservatives as simply a rich diversity within a common theme. For practical purposes, though, these tensions may be rendered down to one single choice: to change or to preserve. The guiding principles for changing and preserving will vary – organicism versus limited government for example – but in the real world of politics the actual decision will be what to change and what to preserve '. . . which interests to defend and which expectations to disappoint.'[18] This is the tension that has shaped the history of the party.

The history of the modern party opens with a resounding defeat: the Great Reform Act of 1832. The unreformed constitution embodied each of the four dominant conservative values – traditionalism, organicism, scepticism and limited government. Tory leaders fought strongly to prevent reform but were eventually forced to give ground and the reform marked a decisive move away from the aristocratic dominance exemplified by and institutionalized in the House of Lords. It soon became obvious that the Conservatives would have to live with the change since to reverse it was impossible.

The party leader whose task was to accomodate the Conservative party to the new world was Sir Robert Peel. For Peel the tension between change and stability was intensified by the emergence of a new wealthy class whose interests were in many respects opposed to those of the landed aristocracy. The focal point of this opposition was the Corn Law question. The Corn Laws had been enacted to protect British agriculture from the importation of cheap foreign wheat, and many Conservatives had come to see them as somehow representative of the traditional, organic, hierarchical society which needed to be protected from further blows from destructive radical forces. For the new wealthy class of mill and factory owners, moral arguments about cheap bread apart, clearly the availability of cheaper food would be a disincentive for their work-forces to press for higher wages. But there were other important factors in the equation. The 1840s witnessed a series of failures of the Irish potato harvest with mass starvation as a direct consequence. It was argued that the availability of cheap bread in England would release other foodstuffs such as potatoes for Ireland. It is not clear how logistically convincing these arguments were, though it was important not to leave undone anything which might ease the suffering across the Irish Sea: paternalistic organicism demanded no less.

Here was the classical problem for a Conservative leader:[19]: how to 'sell' necessary change to the landed interest so as not to arouse what Norton and Aughey call a 'blind emotional reaction' which could actually damage their cause even further. History shows that Peel was not suited to his task; the man with a smile like the silver plate on a coffin was quite unable to carry his party with him: the Corn Laws were indeed reformed but in the process the new Conservative party was shattered. It is interesting to note that the judgement of conservative historians has been far kinder to Peel than was the judgement of many of his contemporaries, especially Lord George Bentinck and the waspish Mr Disraeli.

Peel's failure to sustain the Conservative party may have been a failure of tactics, but after all the Corn Laws were central to the maintenance of the domination of the landed aristocracy, or so members of that class believed. Norton and Aughey descibe Peel as a statesman; he was not. Neither was he a skilled and adroit politician. He was a far-sighted and very able administrator of considerable integrity confronted by a task which needed statesmanship of a high order and great political guile. He had to convince the landed aristocracy that its interests were best served by coming to terms with the claims of the new industrial owners and the needs of the industrial working class. He failed to resolve the tension between change and stability.

That the Conservative party managed to reassert itself so successfully after its period in the wilderness was thanks in no small measure to the leadership of the second of its great men, Benjamin Disraeli. It would be difficult to overestimate the importance of Disraeli in the history of the Conservative party – the only party leader, says Gash, to whom the Conservative young of successive generations have turned to for inspiration.[20] Gilmour attempts to account for Disraeli's prominence by suggesting that he was one of the few Conservative leaders able to 'bring warmth to conservatism and to add to its basic common sense a degree of romance, generosity and excitement'.[21] This was certainly not the judgement of his contemporaries however, many of whom viewed him with deep distrust.[22]

Disraeli's great achievement was to detach much of the moderate support from the Liberals, thus securing a base for future

Conservative governments, and the most important single step by which he managed this was the Second Reform Act of 1867. Much has been made of Disraeli's opportunism in seizing upon a Liberal bill, making it more radical, and thereby earning the lasting gratitude of the workers. The truth seems to be that Disraeli was always reluctant to become enmeshed in electoral reform; indeed Ward urges that Derby had to press the case for reform upon Disraeli.[23] It is certainly true that the radical nature of the 1867 bill was not a question of design but of concession; Disraeli needed the support of the radicals to get the measure passed at all. Norton and Aughey conclude that 'As an act of long-term political strategy the passage of the Reform Bill proved that the Conservatives were no longer bent upon reaction but could accommodate the demands of the day and do so competently'.[24] In fact it was not so much a strategy as a stratagem, a piece of political opportunism, though Disraeli clearly believed it could only be beneficial to the Conservative interest in the long run. If there was a direct pay-off to the Act it came not in the next election in 1868 but in the following one of 1874. It is certainly impossible to assess the extent to which the passage of the Second Reform Act actually did help to achieve the victory of 1874, still less the extent to which it laid the foundation of the long-term support which the Conservative party has continued to enjoy among the working class, but it certainly could not have done any harm. It is interesting to note that the party which had opposed parliamentary reform so vehemently thirty-five years before should itself introduce a measure of further reform. Clearly the party had learned to live with the reformed system and equally clearly its interests were not so directly affected by the second Act. Nevertheless, it was, as was remarked at the time, a 'leap in the dark', a move quite out of character with conservative traditions.

The Second Reform Act may have been important to the development of conservatism principally for symbolic reasons but Disraeli's six-year ministry from 1874 to 1880 was a more substantial development in terms of its organicist 'social harmony' programme of domestic reforms which equalled anything attempted by the Liberals. Moreover, Disraeli gave an added dimension to conservatism which was so appropriate that it is difficult now to imagine conservatism without it: empire. It is not generally remembered that the main thrust of conservative thought in the nineteenth century had been anti-imperialist; Disraeli himself once refered to the colonies as 'millstones around our necks'. Colonies cost money to defend and were likely anyway to prove ungrateful to the mother country as they developed towards political maturity, as the example of the American colonies clearly showed. To extract economic advantage from colonies was the job of independent commercial companies rather than governments, and the case of the United States, and indeed of the South American continent, showed that trade did not necessarily follow the flag. The idea of an imperial 'mission' cut very little ice with Conservative politicians until well into the second half of the century, but Disraeli was one of the first to recognize its electoral value. By 1872 he was publicly extolling the virtues of empire and in his famous Crystal Palace speech of 24 June he claimed that 'no minister in this country will do his duty who neglects any opportunity of reconstructing as much as possible of our Colonial Empire, and of responding to those distant sympathies which may become the source of incalculable strength and happiness to this land'.[25] Moreover, Blake rightly points out that the association of conservatism with empire was also in part due to the far less enthusiastic attitude adopted by the Liberals under Gladstone.

Disraeli's contribution to the development of the Conservative party was profound. He incorporated the traditional support for property and hierarchy (extended to include the new owners of industrial wealth) with a paternalistic concern for the well-being of the industrial poor. The thrust of Disraelian conservatism is rightly remembered as having been to stress the unity of the nation. In *Sybil* Disraeli wrote the following dialogue between Egremont and a young radical journalist:

'Well, society may be in its infancy', said Egremont slightly smiling; 'but, say what you like, our Queen reigns over the greatest nation that ever existed.'

'Which nation?' asked the younger stranger, 'for she reigns over two.'

The stranger paused; Egremont was silent but looked enquiringly.

'Yes', resumed the younger stranger after a moment's interval. 'Two nations; between whom there is no intercourse and no sympathy; who are as ignorant of each other's habits, thoughts and feelings, as if they were dwellers in different zones or inhabitants of different planets; who are formed by a different breeding, are fed by a different food, are ordered by different manners, and are not governed by the same laws.'

'You speak of –' said Egremont, hesitatingly.

'THE RICH AND THE POOR.'[26]

Disraelian conservatism seeks to replace this division with unity, with a new sense of organicism; One Nation, a true community. 'There is no community in England; there is aggregation', Egremont is informed, 'but aggregation under circumstances which make it rather a dissociating, than a uniting principle.' A true community, then, is based upon hierarchy, but with the wealthy classes taking a compassionate concern over the conditions of the poorer classes. Needless to say, the interests of this national community could only be secured by the governance of the truly national party, the Conservatives. Moreover, the Conservatives would also protect the interests of the national organic community overseas by building up the empire and calling into being an imperial community of kith and kin. This was the thrust of Disraelian conservatism.

If it is right to picture the task of Conservative leadership as attempting a balance between change and stability, then it is clear that Disraeli had tipped the scales towards the side of change. Inevitably upon Disraeli's departure there were forces within the party keen to redress the balance; equally inevitably, forces were aroused which sought to tip the scales even further towards change. Such a force was the Fourth Party, a smallish but influential ginger group led by Lord Randolph Churchill. The Fourth Party aimed at nothing short of democratizing the management of the Conservative party. In much the same way that Chamberlain attempted to make the parliamentary leadership of the Liberal party more accountable to the party membership, so too Churchill sought to play off the party organization (stronger now since the Reform Act) against the 'old identity', the traditional ruling groups within the party.

The next two decades were years of Conservative dominance, the result more of Liberal disunity than Conservative strength. One important consequence of this disunity, caused principally by Gladstone's growing preoccupation with Ireland and the strength of radicalism within the Liberal party, was the inexorable transfer of middle class opinion from the Liberals to the Conservatives, as James Cornford has demonstrated.[27] But not just middle-class opinion. The Whigs, too, had seen their party drifting towards the dangerous rocks of radicalism. Warnings to alter course had not been heeded by the bridge; as the century drew to its close the Whigs decided to abandon ship. More surprising, though, was the defection of another part of the crew who saw danger only in the swirling currents of Gladstone's

Irish policy. The defection of Chamberlain's radical Unionists and their eventual merging with the Conservatives was a major event in British party history in its own right; in a more immediate sense Chamberlain's group outflanked Churchill's Fourth Party, making the latter expendable for the Conservative leader Lord Salisbury.

Salisbury's leadership produced only marginal readjustment in the balance of change and stability, though specific reforms in the field of social welfare were made. In the early years of the new century, however, a policy issue was to emerge as injurious in its consequences for the party as Irish home rule proved to be for the Liberals: the issue which later became known as imperial preference.[28] Imperial preference implied the creation of an empire-wide tariff barrier, important in its own right for British industry, but which was seen as a first step on a long road which led through a common defence strategy and on to nothing less than imperial federation. As such, although the policy was pursued principally by Chamberlain the Unionist it can be seen as fitting in with the Disraelian concept of an empire-wide organic community of kith and kin. All the same, imperial federation was not achieved and the only palpable consequence of Chamberlain's campaign was to 'cast the Conservative party into confusion and internecine strife and help to achieve what had seemed inconceivable in 1900 – a Liberal government'.[29] Once again a Conservative leader had failed to sustain the balance between change and stability.

The years before the first world war were to witness another policy stance taken by the Conservatives which gives considerable cause for comment: the stance on Irish home rule. With the advent to the leadership of Bonar Law, of Ulster Presbyterian stock, to whom the prospect of Irish home rule was anathema, the party's natural reluctance to see the Union weakened was greatly intensified to the extent that it offered support to Ulstermen prepared to take up arms to prevent the implementation of constitutionally enacted legislation (i.e. a Home Rule Act). 'Ulster will fight and Ulster will be right' was an unequivocal message whose implication was support for the gun against the ballot box and the dispatch box. True, the passage of a bill through a House of Commons in which the Irish held the balance of power and a House of Lords whose constitutional powers had recently been severely clipped by the Liberal government (so that it could only delay but not kill proposed legislation) hardly provided the best example of constitutional legality. On the other hand, most conservative thinkers are quite clear about the primacy of the constitution and the rule of law; to pick and choose which laws a man will and will not obey is, as O'Sullivan pointed out, simply not compatible with conservatism. Winston Churchill, a minister in the Liberal government, remarked that Bonar Law's motion of censure on his government's Irish policy constituted support for an attack by the criminal classes upon the police.[30] Where all of this might have led is a matter for conjecture because events on the continent of Europe in 1914 were to take precedence over Irish affairs. All the same, the Conservative claim to support the constitution, to put faith in laws above men, about which a great deal has been made by conservative thinkers, looked less convincing after these events.

The first world war was won by a coalition under the leadership of the Liberal David Lloyd George and such was his dominance that the Conservatives were willing to continue the coalition government after the war. In fact the government that came into office in 1918 was predominantly a Conservative one. Blake argues that the alliance between the Lloyd George Liberals and the Conservatives could have become permanent,[31] though this hinged almost entirely upon Lloyd George's continuing popularity, which proved to be a diminishing asset. At a meeting of Conservative members of the coalition at the Carlton Club on 19 October 1922 the party decided to drop the Welsh wizard and to opt for a safer if more prosaic leadership. This they achieved in the unimposing person of Stanley Baldwin.

Baldwin contributed little to the development of conservative thinking as leader; he responded to the problems of his time within the organistic paternalist tradition which was later consciously to be aimed at by Harold Macmillan. 'He is out to develop a democratic Conservatism', said Haldane, 'and has a great deal of sympathy with the aspirations of labour.'[32] Baldwin was clearly a 'One Nation' man who sought to minimize social conflict, and the measure of his achievement, ironically, was his handling of the General Strike of 1926. Although he was unable to prevent the strike, and indeed was absolutely adamant that no industrial action should be allowed to dominate the parliamentary process at whatever cost, he made it plain both to right-wingers in his own party and to employers in the country at large bent on retribution, that no advantage was to be wrung from the workers in the shape of wage reductions or increases in working hours after the end of the strike. This stand was in the best traditions of conservative organicism. It was also a triumph for Baldwin's moderation.

In a sense it was precisely this moderation, maintained and extended by Neville Chamberlain,[33] leader of the Conservative-dominated national coalition governments of the 1930s, which helped to blind successsive governments to the threat posed by German rearmament. War found Britain unprepared but Churchill's wartime leadership proved to be truly inspirational: hence the Conservative disbelief at losing the 1945 general election. Not only was the election lost but lost to a socialist party with a massive majority. So stunning was the defeat that it provoked a major reappraisal of Conservative ideology. Once again the balance between stability and change appeared to need readjustment. The party was fortunate to possess men like R. A. Butler, Harold Macmillan and others who were committed to 'convince a broad spectrum of the electorate', as Butler said, ' . . . that we had an alternative policy to socialism which was viable, efficient and humane, which could release and reward enterprise and initiative but without abandoning social justice or reverting to mass unemployment'.[34] The task for the reformers was made easier by the fact that Churchill was not particularly interested in such matters and gave his lieutenants a free hand. The research department and industrial policy committee, under Butler's guidance, rehabilitated the party to a considerable extent, especially through the promulgation of the new Industrial Charter, committing the party to a policy of full employment and Keynesian demand-led economic management. The charter and the others which followed provided the party with modern policies on which to fight and at the same time restored confidence among the shell-shocked party faithful, giving them the determination and confidence to defeat socialism.

The public was ready to respond to a modern non-socialist party: the austerities of the late 1940s were beginning to sap morale. Between 1945 and 1950 the Labour government had built the foundations of postwar Britain; perhaps no other party could have done this. And it had built well. But it was no fun living on a building site and after a while the new occupants hankered after better amenities, landscaping and the like. So it was that in 1951, after Labour had found it impossible to sustain itself in government following the very narrow victory of 1950, the Conservatives came into power for thirteen years. These were to be the years of deregistration, of the burning of ration books, of growing affluence among the working class, of the spread of material benefits among all classes in a way never seen before. The benefits were not equally spread but on the other hand nearly everybody was better off. For ten years and three successive electoral victories there was no serious challenge to Conservative domestic and economic policies and the comment attributed (erroneously) to prime minister Harold Macmillan that the people had 'never had it so good' seemed entirely appropriate.

The foreign policies of the Conservatives were not so successful, however. The party of empire found it almost impossible to face up to the reality of declining British military and economic power in the postwar world and sought to sustain a British military presence on a world-wide scale. Yet within ten years or so British colonies would be achieving independence with almost indecent haste and the dominions of the 'white Commonwealth' were soon to become very much their own men. But this did not happen without an ill-advised struggle: in 1956 British and French troops invaded Egypt in order to regain control of the Suez Canal which the Egyptians had nationalized. Although in military terms the operation was successful it was a huge failure in all other terms.[35]

The prime minister of the day, Sir Anthony Eden, who became seriously ill soon after, chose to resign. His successor, Harold Macmillan, had to restore national pride and at the same time to educate the nation to the inevitability of the loss of empire. At least he managed to heal the rifts within his party and to soothe the bruised national temperament sufficiently skilfully to win the next general election in 1959 by a very large margin. However, Macmillan was far-sighted enough to realize that Britain's future lay in sloughing off the vestiges of empire as quickly as possible and pressing her case for membership of the European Economic Community with equal speed. These two processes were by their nature so radical that they hardly seem to fit into the framework of Conservative ideology: dismantling of empire is obviously against the post-Disraeli Conservative tradition and to become part of Europe, despite Churchill's immediate-postwar enthusiasm, had no real pedigree in conservatism. In fact the strongest opposition to entry into the EEC came from the Labour party whose leader Gaitskell spoke of Britain's 'turning its back on a thousand years of history'. In the event Macmillan was far more successful in wrapping up the empire than in joining the EEC.

Macmillan's leadership probably represents the fullest expression of conservative organicism since Disraeli. The policies of his government sustained the privileges of the wealthy and yet improved the lot of ordinary people. Moreover, Macmillan saw the necessity of the most fundamental changes in British foreign policy and managed to make many of them, though his failure to gain British membership of the EEC was humiliating.

Not surprisingly these changes in Britain's international role made Macmillan unpopular with the party and the country; worse, though, were the blows discussed in chapter 1 which caused the loss of the 1964 general election. The party was out of office for six years and when it returned to power it was with a new leader and a new brand of conservatism. Edward Heath had his own ideas on the proper balance between stability and change. In many respects Heath represented a departure for the Conservatives; although he was not the first non-patrician to lead the party by any means, he was the first lower-middle-class leader, the first 'man of the people'. Not only this, but his whole approach to politics, the ethos of his cabinet, was optimistic, 'managerial' and almost utilitarian rather than sceptical, organicist and traditional. In his book *The Making of the Conservative Party* Ramsden quotes a letter from a middle-aged industrial manager and lifelong Conservative which sums up the expectations which Heath aroused in certain kinds of Conservative. The manager writes: 'We are sick of seeing old men dressed in flat caps and bedraggled tweeds strolling about with 12 bores . . . The nearest approach to our man is Heath . . . He is our age, he is capable, he looks like a director [of the country].'[36] That phrase 'he looks like a director' sums up the new managerial balance in conservatism that Heath sought to build. If he had a picture of an ideal Britain before him when he came to office it was of a meritocratic society built upon the successes of the technological revolution.

Heath was nothing if not a pro-European and he it was who piloted Britain through the dangerous waters towards membership of the EEC. Not for Heath the nostalgia for empire or Powell's belief in national sovereignty, both more plausibly traditional conservative policies.[37] Heath's over-riding concern was for the efficiency and competitiveness of British industry, a laudable but not specifically Conservative goal. British industry was seen to be bedevilled by three continuing problems: the strength of militant trade unionism, government intervention to support inefficient companies which allowed them to escape the consequences of their inefficiency, and a disastrous investment profile. Heath believed that if the first two problems could be tackled successfully the third would solve itself. His approach, nicknamed the politics of 'Selsdon Man' (after a conference at Selsdon Park in January 1970 from which this general approach emerged), was opposed to macro-planning, noting the failure of Labour's national plan, opposed to statutory incomes policies – Labour's had failed – and in favour of the statutory limitation of trade union powers, which Labour had backed away from. What Britain needed was resolute business management to bring it out of economic stagnation.

By mid-term Edward Heath's policies had not provided the expected up-turn in the economy. More particularly the centre-piece of Heathite policy, the Industrial Relations Act of 1972 which sought to constrain the power of the unions, was acknowledged to have failed. These early years were marked not only by failures of measures but also failures of men. Chief among these failures was the Secretary of State for Trade and Industry, John Davies. Davies had been brought into politics straight from the Confederation of British Industry (CBI), where he had been Director General. He had no background in politics but his business acumen was exactly congruent with the needs of Heathite conservatism. Davies had enunciated a policy of no support for industries which were proving unprofitable – lame ducks he had called them – and this was a policy well tailored to Heath's general approach. But by 1972 the government had committed a series of complete about turns including the injection of public funds into the 'lame duck' Upper Clyde Ship Builders and the nationalization of Rolls Royce. The Industry Act of 1972 constituted a complete rejection of the politics of Selsdon Man; it gave governments unprecedented powers to aid and – worse – to regulate private companies. The bracing air of the market economy was thought not to be invigorating British industry but killing it off and even the commitment to free wage bargaining was dropped in favour of a statutory policy of wage and price control.

Heath may be accused of reneging, Peel-like, on party commitments; alternatively he may be applauded for having learned from his mistakes. He certainly may not be congratulated on having convinced his party of the necessity of change: indeed he hardly attempted to do this. Within the space of a year Heath was transmogrified from Selsdon Man to neo-corporatist man, a change as complete as that from Jekyll to Hyde (or vice versa!). If these brands of politics had one thing in common it was that both were difficult to accommodate within the framework of traditional Conservatism. In any event the phase-two Heath government proved no more successful than had phase one and the party was defeated in 1974 and did not return to office until 1979 under the leadership of Margaret Thatcher.

Margaret Thatcher described herself as a 'conviction politican', a leader 'not for turning', whose aim was to beat back the growing tide of interventionism and allow market forces to shape the development of British industry to the widest possible extent through policies such as privatization. The title neo-liberal has frequently been used to define Thatcherite politics: clearly their economics owe more to the Manchester School theories of the early nineteenth-century Liberals than to the neo-Keynesianism of the Macmillan Conservatives; equally clearly its morality owes more to Samuel Smiles than to Benjamin Disraeli.

Hackneyed though it has become, the proper word to describe Thatcherite conservatism is reactionary: it seeks to recreate a world whose values changed half a century or more ago. In its evocation of such symbols as 'Victorian values', 'traditional family life', the 'inventiveness' and 'entrepreneurial skill' of the small businessman, Thatcherite conservatism rejoices in its reactionary nature and clearly recognizes that its endeavour must also be a radical one. The Conservative general election manifesto of 1987 provided so un-equivocal a testimony of the radical intent of the party that, whatever its strengths and weaknesses, Thatcherite conservatism, reactionary in purpose, radical in action, cannot be accommodated within the mainstream conservatism.[38]

Similarities between Thatcherite conservatism and Heath's Selsdon conservatism are too obvious not to have been commented on by a number of writers but there is a fundamental difference. Heath was simply trying to run the country more efficiently; Thatcher is trying to create a new spirit of self-reliance and enterprise in the British people.[39] All the same, Mrs Thatcher has been sufficiently concerned by the similarities to stress time and again that her government will pursue its policies resolutely until they bear fruit, whatever the short-term hardship.

We will have occasion to discuss the Thatcher government in a little more depth later but for now it is enough to point out that Thatcherite conservatism has pursued the objectives of bringing down inflation and controlling the money supply with the greatest vigour, exhibiting a willingness to allow inequalities to increase, presumably so as to improve incentives.[40] The Thatcher government, like Heath's, has also extended state interference in industrial relations through legislation and has substantially altered the balance of power between central and local government in favour of the former. Successful or not, these have little to do with the ideals of traditionalism, organicism, scepticism, or limited government (though certainly this last is claimed as an ultimate objective) and much more to do with reaction, radicalism and neo-liberalism.

What emerges from this brief history of the Conservative party is that the policies of various Conservative governments show little more than a random relationship with the principles enunciated at the beginning of the chapter. If we were to accept Norton and Aughey's argument that neo-liberalism is part of the conservative tradition then the relationship becomes stronger though no more consistent, and it is the lack of consistency that characterizes the history of conservatism. Several commentators have stressed that one of the marks of conservatism is its pragmatism, what Gilmour refers to as the over-riding importance of 'circumstances', about which nothing has been said in this chapter. This is because pragmatism is in fact a residual category; when a government's actions cannot be explained in terms of first principles they are said to be 'pragmatic'. But we can only discover what precisely this means after the event. All the same, we could, if it was considered helpful, say that Conservative leaders have exhibited a healthy pragmatism when attempting to build a balance between stability and change, and that this pragmatism provides a measure of consistency.[41]

There is another measure of consistency, though, which is worth considering. Suppose we take conservatism to represent – substantially though by no means entirely – a rationalization of the interests of the advantaged; conscious political actions taken by the socially privileged classes.[42] The principles we have considered are certainly not injurious to those interests. Traditionalism, for example, favours the retention of institutions and customs which, by definition, have allowed the advantaged to dominate the polity. Organicism, too, favours the advantaged. After all, it is far easier to believe that the hierarchical society is natural, God-given, or the product of history when one is nearer the top than the bottom of the hierarchy. The argument is clearly more appealing to the rich man who is in his castle than to the poor man who is at his gate. Again, we should be more inclined to be dismissive of large-scale plans for human betterment, more inclined, that is, to be sceptical, if our own interests were already well catered for in society. Finally, it is safer and more comfortable to argue that man's moral and intellectual imperfections commend strict limits to government when, because of good fortune or wealthy forebears, we are quite capable of maximizing our own interests in society as it exists. For the poor man at the gate any injury to individual liberty of government intervention probably seems secondary when his family is hungry; indeed he might consider his 'liberty' to be a blessing that he could manage without. This same man may also be less likely to enthuse over the possibility that his condition is the natural and necessary outcome of some historical process.

These arguments, if we accept any of them, do not deny an independent validity to conservative principles but they suggest the context in which these principles might operate most effectively and also offer a possible explanation of the apparent inconsistencies of Conservative governments' policies. The constant tension between conserving and changing could be described as maintaining the privileges of the advantaged and yet conceding some of these privileges when the pressures become too great. A marxist would argue that in sustaining the interests of the capitalist class as a whole the Conservative party finds it expedient from time to time to sacrifice a fraction of capital. The socialist propagandist Bernard Shaw put the point more simply, saying the rich were prepared to give up anything for the poor except the theory and practice of robbing them.

It may be fairly concluded that to portray conservative ideology as no more than a rationalization of the interests of the property-owning class would be absurd. On the other hand, to believe that this assortment of principles, only randomly related to the policies of Conservative governments, could have survived as an ideology were it not for its suiting the interests of the advantaged, would be equally absurd. This is why we may be certain that, like the poor, the Conservatives will always be with us.

Notes

1 Anthony Quinton, *The Politics of Imperfection* (London, Faber and Faber 1978), p. 24.
2 Samuel Johnson, *Dictionary of the English Language.*
3 N. K. O'Sullivan, *Conservatism* (London, Dent, 1976).
4 Ibid., p. 24.
5 See F. J. C. Hearnshaw (ed.), *Social and Political Ideas in the Age of Reaction* (London, Harrap, 1932).
6 Frank Brady (ed.), *Boswell's Life of Johnson* (London, Signet Classics, 1968), p. 297.
7 Quoted in W. Wagar (ed), *H. G. Wells: Journalism and Prophecy* (London, Bodley Head, 1965), p 277.
8 See *The Conservative Case* (Harmondsworth, Penguin, 1959).
9 Aldous Huxley, *Eyeless in Gaza* (Harmondsworth, Penguin, 1972), pp. 150–51.
10 O'Sullivan, *Conservatism*, p. 12.
11 Lord Hugh Cecil, *Conservatism* (London, Home University Library, 1912).
12 T. E. Uttley, 'The significance of Mrs Thatcher', in M. Cowling (ed.) *Conservative Essays* (London, Cassell, 1978), p. 51.
13 Peter Walker, *Ascent of Britain* (London, Sidgwick & Jackson, 1977), p. 20.
14 Quoted in Philip Norton and Arthur Aughey, *Conservatives and Conservatism* (London, Temple Smith, 1981), p. 37.
15 Ibid., p. 47.
16 Angus Maude, 'Party paleontology', *Spectator*, 15 March 1963.
17 Sir Ian Gilmour, *Inside Right* (London, Hutchinson, 1977), p. 144.
18 Norton and Aughey, *Conservatives and Conservatism*, p. 92.
19 He had been persuaded to support Catholic Emancipation, for example, twenty years before. It is interesting to recall that in his political novels Disraeli spoke of Peel's 'conservatism' as a betrayal of what he termed 'true toryism'.
20 N. Gash, 'From the origins to Sir Robert Peel', in R. A. Butler (ed.), *The Conservatives* (London, Allen & Unwin, 1977), p. 125.
21 Gilmour, *Inside Right*, p. 86.
22 R. J. Feuchtwanger, *Disraeli, Democracy and the Conservative Party*, (Oxford University Press, 1968), p. 10.
23 See J. T. Ward 'Derby and Disraeli', in D. Southgate (ed.), *Conservative Leadership 1832–1932* (London, Macmillan, 1974).
24 Norton and Aughey, *Conservatives and Conservatism*, p. 107.
25 Quoted in Southgate, *Conservative Leadership*, p. 181.

26 Benjamin Disraeli, *Sybil* (Harmondsworth, Penguin, 1980), Book ii, ch. 5, p. 96 (first published 1845).

27 See James Cornford, 'The transformation of conservatism in the late nineteenth century', in *Victorian Studies* (Vol VII, No 1, September 1963) pp 35–66.

28 See R. R. James, *The British Revolution 1886–1939* (London, Methuen, 1978), for a full account of this issue and its consequences.

29 Norton and Aughey, *Conservatives and Conservatism*, p. 117.

30 Quoted in Southgate, *Conservative Leadership*, p. 246.

31 See Robert Blake, *The Conservative Party from Peel to Churchill* (London, Eyre & Spottiswoode, 1972), p. 197.

32 Quoted in K. Middlemas and J. Barnes, *Baldwin* (London, Weidenfeld & Nicolson, 1969), p. 177.

33 For a full account see K. Feiling, *Life of Neville Chamberlain* (London, Macmillan, 1946). See also K. Middlemas, *Politics in Industrial Society* (London, André Deutsch, 1979).

34 Quoted in Norton and Aughey, *Conservatives and Conservatism*, p. 128. For a full acount of the work of this group see Lord Butler, *The Art of the Possible* (Harmondsworth, Penguin, 1973), ch. 7.

35 See Anthony Nutting, *No End of a Lesson* (London, Constable, 1967).

36 J. Ramsden, *The Making of Conservative Party Policy* (London, Longman, 1980), p. 226.

37 See D. E. Schoen, *Enoch Powell and the Powellites* (London, Macmillan, 1977).

38 This is not the conclusion that Norton and Aughey reach. Having extended the definition of conservatism to include various forms of 'whiggery' – indeed having given that category pride of place in the conservative panoply – the present government, according to them, is clearly conservative 'by definition'. It is also true that a number of writers such as Uttley, Howell and Lawson have found little difficulty in accomodating Thatcherite conservatism within the conservative tradition.

39 The title of her pamphlet for the Centre for Policy Studies in 1977 captures the flavour of Mrs Thatcher's ambition: *Let Our Children Grow Tall*.

40 The most substantial wage rises during the Thatcher administration have been at the top end of the scale whereas the bottom 10 per cent have suffered cuts (see *The Guardian*, 11 April 1985); tax changes have followed a similar pattern (see *The Guardian*, 29 January 1987).

41 Lord Salisbury's paradoxical assertion that the only absolute principle in politics is that there are no absolute principles indicates the limited utility of pragmatism as an explanatory concept in analysing conservatism.

42 See H. G. Schumann, 'The problem of Conservatism', in *Journal of Contemporary History*, 13, no. 4 (October 1978), p. 807.

3 Leadership and Organization in the Conservative Party

Many who write about the relationship between the Conservative leader and his/her party seek to provide some analogy to clarify the relationship, presumably because it is not formal and so may not be stated in strictly constitutional terms. The most common is probably the monarchical analogy, with the leader surrounded by a court from among whom advisers will be chosen. The monarch will necessarily give attention to the aspirations of the people in order that his/her rule remains unchallenged. A second analogy is that of the baronial system, with more emphasis on bargaining and coalition-building.[1] A third analogy may be described as Hobbesian,[2] with the leader as Leviathan, to whom absolute power is surrendered so long as the interests of the supporters are protected (by electoral victory). If the covenant is broken (by electoral defeat) then the obligation to obey is no longer binding; hence the rather precarious hold that incumbents to the Conservative leadership appear to have had. In Winston Churchill's words: 'The loyalties which centre upon number one are enormous. If he trips he must be sustained. If he makes mistakes they must be covered. If he sleeps he must not be wantonly disturbed. If he is no good, he must be pole-axed.'[3] These Leviathans, however, seem to make covenants of clay which they are continually breaking; only Churchill among postwar Conservative leaders retired at a time of his own choosing and even he had been under great pressure to do so earlier.

Norton and Aughey prefer a more homely analogy, though, for the leader–party relationship: that of the traditional family. 'As in most families', they tell us, 'there may be occasional discord, but the members remain bonded to one another by ties of loyalty, respect and kinship.'[4] This analogy stresses the 'naturalness' of the hierarchical structure; but there are important aspects of the model which vitiate its appropriateness. Heads of household are not elected nor are they bound by obligations beyond what the law imposes (which are minimal) and which they themselves choose to adopt. Moreover, they cannot be held to account – outside the law, that is. In short, the model is cosy but misleading, though its emphasis on mutuality is important. We shall attempt to describe this relationship without the aid of analogies or models; they seem to create as much confusion as clarification.

We will begin at the centre, with the king, the Leviathan, the most powerful of the barons, the head of household, or more simply, the leader of the party. No Conservative leader was elected by his party until 1965; prior to that date Conservative leaders were judged to have 'emerged'. The great advantage to this system was that it provided continuity without any overt struggle for the succession; the disadvantage occurred when there was no natural successor and no compromise candidate acceptable to senior figures in the party could easily be found. At the resignation of Harold Macmillan in 1963, for example, no natural successor emerged. Contenders for the leadership used the party conference as a launching pad for what amounted to a public 'selection campaign', not unlike an American party convention. It is difficult to see how the traditional procedures could have coped with this kind of pressure, and in the event the decision to select a compromise candidate, Lord Home, was so generally unpopular and his short period of leadership so unhappy as to provide the *coup de grâce* for the traditional method. Though the system was generally considered to be outmoded there was litle enthusiasm for more overtly democratic procedures. A system was needed which would provide a leader able to command the confidence of the parliamentary party and to appeal to the modern voter. What finally emerged was election by the parliamentary party in which an overall majority plus 15 per cent was required for victory on the first ballot. Additional candidates could join the second ballot but if no overall majority was obtained the three top candidates would proceed to a third ballot using the alternative vote method.

This system remained unaltered for only a decade when an important and apparently democratic limitation was placed upon the leader's powers: re-election. Again this limitation was the consequence of a practical problem; that of removing Edward Heath, the first elected leader, from office. Not only had he lost an election but he had become generally unpopular with the parliamentary party because of his alleged indifference to backbench opinion. A committee was set up to draw up rules for re-election of leaders. In brief, the 15 per cent above an overall majority in the first ballot now became 15 per cent above an overall majority of all eligible voters; provision was also made for elections at the beginning of each new parliament and thence at the beginning of every new session. Much to his own suprise Edward Heath lost the leadership of the party to Mrs Thatcher, thus becoming both the first elected leader of the party and then the first to be de-elected.

The election and re-election issues were not part of a principled campaign to democratize the party. They emerged because the party did not always get the leader it wanted and could not always get rid of a leader it did not want. All the same, the relationship between the Conservative leader and the party inside and ouside parliament had hardly been transformed. No major parliamentary party can hire and fire its leader like a soccer club; no major parliamentary party can immunize itself against the necessity of electing compromise candidates to the leadership or against all the consequent problems. Moreover, Edward Heath, who had lost three general elections out of four, whose abrasive style of leadership had alienated many backbenchers, whose 'U-turns' in government had been notorious, who had led Britain to a three-day working week and a State of Emergency, lost his re-election battle by a mere eleven votes. So much for the Tory pole-axe. Indeed it is possible to argue that re-election has strengthened the hand of the party leader because a leader under threat may well risk re-election, banking on the instinct to loyalty of the average Conservative backbencher. In the event of a challenge being beaten off the leader's position clearly becomes stronger. In general terms the traditional relationship between leader and party has not been much changed; Mrs Thatcher's continued dominance over her parliamentary party, for example, is well illustrated by the effect of her last-minute decision, in November 1985, to vote against televising House of Commons debates. Although the whips were off, numbers of Conservative backbenchers, about to cast votes in favour of televising, rushed over to the 'No' lobby so as to be seen to be voting with their leader.

It is accepted wisdom that a Conservative prime minister is required to achieve a balance when constructing his/her cabinet in which the principal ideological strains and sectional interests are represented. In the case of Edward Heath it is argued that his original appointments were unduly weighted towards colleagues known to be personally loyal to him. Norton and Aughey clearly believe this to have been a major source of weakness for Heath, not a source of strength because he 'deprived himself of any means of communication between the pro- and anti-marketeers. The latter feel dispossessed. They are on the other side of the tracks.'[5] Norton and Aughey contrast Heath's attitude to Mrs Thatcher's, who, they claim, rated parliamentary ability higher than personal loyalty. One commentator, writing six months after the 1979 general election, declared that on certain issues Thatcher supporters were actually in a minority in the cabinet. He spoke of a 'solid line-up of Carrington, Gilmour, Whitelaw, Pym and Soames', to whom one could add St John Stevas, Carlisle and Walker as representing what came to be called the 'wet' wing of the party. Her inability to persuade cabinet to accept a second round of public expenditure cuts in 1981 convinced Mrs Thatcher that balanced cabinets were not always a good thing. A cabinet reshuffle produced a swing to the right. Indeed after the 1983 election, of all these senior figures in the party only Walker (and to a lesser extent Lord Whitelaw) retained positions of influence. Shirley Williams commented that Mrs Thatcher had replaced her cabinet with an echo chamber (indeed when receiving *The Spectator's* Backbencher of the Year award in 1984 Nicholas Budgen, on the liberal wing of the party, actually called for a return to cabinet government).[6] After the electoral victory of 1987, with the removal of John Biffen, the demotion to the Welsh Office of Peter Walker, and the advancement of a number of younger 'drys' – especially John Moore to Social Services – the traditional Tory wing of the party was largely unrepresented in the cabinet.

It was said of Heath and is now being said of Thatcher that their desire to surround themselves with like-thinking people is a sign of intolerance of opposition; but perhaps it is a sign of something more fundamental. Both leaders felt themselves to be leading a crusade, Heath to take Britain into Europe and Thatcher to transform Britain's way of life. Both rightly felt that important sections of the party were hostile to their ambitions and perhaps as a consequence felt the need to surround themselves with strong supporters. If at first commentators remarked upon the differences between the Heath and Thatcher approaches it became more common to see the similarities, for as the general climate grew more hostile to Thatcher so she has tended to withdraw more into the neo-liberal camp.

tended to withdraw more into the neo-liberal camp.

The most severe test of Mrs Thatcher's leadership and judgement occured in 1985/6 when her Minister of Defence, Michael Heseltine, resigned because he claimed that the prime minister had prevented full discussion in cabinet of the future of the Westland helicopter company. His allegations of autocratic rule were disavowed by his critics who argued that an autocrat would have dismissed the Minister upon his refusal to accept a collective decision rather than allow him the luxury of public opposition. It later became clear that more than autocracy was at issue when Leon Brittan, Minister for Trade and Industry, also resigned because it was felt that he had misled the House. It was argued that unconstitutional and indeed improper means had been used to discredit Heseltine's position and that, by resigning, Brittan took much of the pressure off Mrs Thatcher, who was also implicated. Autocrat or no, these events illuminated the animosities within Mrs Thatcher's cabinet. Perhaps the well-balanced cabinet is a sign of more relaxed days, when the Conservative leadership's approach was more pragmatic than ideological and when, perhaps consequentially, there was a greater consensus within the parliamentary party.

If the relationship with senior members of the parliamentary party is one key indicator of the power of the Conservative leader, another is surely the relationship with the party bureaucracy. In fact this relationship is quite unequivocal: the party chairman is appointed by the prime minister, and the main organ of the party bureaucracy, the Central Office, has been referred to as the leader's personal machine.[7] Although the leader must make symbolic gestures towards the effective two-way transmission of views, a chairman who saw it as his/her main task to act as a tribune for the broader movement, seeking to modify the policies of the leadership according to the perceived wishes of the rank and file would not be in the interests of the party leader. Accordingly when a party chairman is chosen he/she will be a well-known party figure, preferably on the frontbench, with proven administrative skills, a good ability to mix with and inspire the party faithful, and above all, a loyal supporter of the party leader. Pinto-Duschinsky has pointed out that it is by no means always easy to find people with the requisite skills or to persuade them to take on the job. Leaders have sometimes been obliged to make appointments they would probably have preferred not to make, though the appointment in 1985 of Norman Tebbit indicates as perhaps nothing else could the importance which the present party leader attaches to the post.[8] A party leader about whose policies the rank and file have misgivings must seek to retain the loyalty of the party – Heath's failure to do so was a lesson not to be forgotten – and the best way to do this is by the appointment of a popular, active and loyal colleague to the post of party chairman, whatever the limitations of that office. The appointment of the ex-MP and novelist Jeffrey Archer as deputy chairman reinforced the impression that it is the transmission of views dowwards rather than the receipt of signals from below which most interests Mrs Thatcher. Publicity rather than exchange seemed to be the object of the exercise. Indeed Archer's concentration upon public relations persuaded Mrs Thatcher to appoint a second deputy chairman in 1986 with responsibility for the organization at Central Office.

The third area we need to explore when assessing the power of the Conservative leader is that of policy. We shall shortly be considering the machinery of policy-making within the party but policy selection is something different. It is a function of the Conservative leader to provide a policy context within which priorities may be established and this context will affect policy-making at two levels. First, at the level of policy options. Under the present leader, for example, it would have been unthinkable for policies favourable to reflating the economy to have emerged from the machine at least before 1986. Second, at the level of selecting policy priorities when the party is in office. At this level the powers of the Conservative leader are quite formidable and he/she is able, indeed expected, to imprint his/her personality upon government policy in a manner to which Labour leaders could seldom aspire. Yet it is essential for Conservative leaders to sustain contacts with the party at all levels, so that a process of consultation is believed to operate. 'To impose a policy, however good it may be,' say Norton and Aughey, 'without adhering to the accepted "form" can constitute an affront to [party] sensibilities.'[9] This may be too sanguine: a leader whose policies are generally considered successful will have greater scope regarding party sensibilities; but there will be very little sympathy if the policies begin to fail. This is where the pole-axe might be found useful.

It would be inappropriate to conclude this discussion on the powers of the Conservative leader without some general comment on prime ministerial power in general. First, unlike Mozart's Papageno, whose magic bells had the capacity to transform situations, incoming prime ministers have to deal with precisely the problems responsible for the demise of their predecessors. Not only this, but much of the financial independence of an incoming government will have been eaten away by the commitments of previous governments. If these contraints were not sufficiently limiting there are also those arising from the nature of cabinet government. A cabinet comprising men and women of ability and some independence of mind will prove difficult for a prime minister to dominate especially in the early years, and the kind of unity based upon regular personal contact and a common ideological approach which tends to characterize shadow cabinets can soon disintegrate in government. Ministers become the advocates, indeed sometimes the creatures, of their departments; spending ministers compete both with each other and, collectively, against Treasury ministers, and there is little time for discussions of medium- and long-term strategy, leave alone ideology.

What emerges from the pages of Crossman's diaries[10] is the clear message that it is the prime minister's task to provide the drive, the unity and the sense of mission which a successful government must possess and for which no institutional framework or relationship can provide. From what has been said about the nature of leadership in the Conservative party it is arguable that his or her 'training' is far better suited to this kind of role than a Labour leader's. It is the tradition of loyalty and mutuality which provides such a suitable context for that 'training'. Given all that, it is not surprising that Conservative administrations almost invariably bear the stamp of their leader, though few have sought to promote their personal domination of the party and, with it, their public image as remorselessly as Mrs Thatcher. On becoming leader she appointed a public relations expert to advise in the projecting of her public image. The strategy was to improve Mrs Thatcher's image with working-class voters; thus her more revealing interviews took place on the *Jimmy Young Programme* not *Panorama*; with *Woman* rather than *The Times*. The selling of the leader was given great priority; her hair was restyled, her clothing made smarter (if still traditional), her voice modulated (speaking closer to the microphone gave her voice a less strident quality).[11] The 'personalization' or 'Americanization' process reached its apogee in the 1983 election campaign during which a series of filmable 'events' were contrived to keep the leader in the limelight. Mrs Thatcher clearly sees herself, and takes pains to be seen, as actually embodying her party's principles. Her adviser's success in helping to achieve this objective was later recognized by a knighthood.

So far in this chapter we have been exploring the nature of leadership within the Conservative party and in the process have referred to the main constituents of the party. Now we shall be considering these constituents in their own right and in more detail.

The Conservative party comprises three separate entities: the parliamentary party, the National Union of Conservative and Unionist Associations together with the consitituency organizations, and finally Central Office. There is no doubt in Conservative history and mythology which body dominates: the parliamentary party is 'the party'. It is the task of 'the movement' (the National Union) and 'the bureaucracy' (Central Office) to support and sustain the party and its leader. Their task is aided by a number of groups which, though not officially part of the structure, nevertheless play an important part and must not be omitted from our discussion.

Traditionally such party structure as existed at Westminster allowed the leader to communicate with the backbenchers, transmitting instructions downwards. Yet in the same way as the ideology of conservatism developed in response to changing circumstances and events, so did the party in parliament. By far the most significant development occurred as a reaction against Lloyd George's continued dominance of the post-1918 coalition government: it was the founding of the '1922 committee'. This committee took its name from the meeting of Conservative backbenchers at the Carlton Club in that year when opposition to the coalition was so strong as to oblige the compliant Conservative leader, Sir Austen Chamberlain, to resign. Backbenchers in the next government formed a permanent committee to 'enable new members to take a more active interest and part in parliamentary life'.[12] The new committee elected officers and an executive committee. Official recognition followed and a whip began regularly to attend meetings to give details of business for the following week. Within a few years membership of The 1922 was extended to any Conservative private member and as it grew so its activities became more institutionalized and a structure of permanent and ad hoc committees, with their own officers, began to emerge, eventually with frontbench spokesmen as chairmen. Party whips began to attend the meetings of these committees and so a comprehensive structure had developed by the 1950s allowing for the transmission to the leadership of advice and opinion, with the chairman of The 1922 having ready access to the party leader. There has been no major change to this structure since. One recent chairman, Sir Edward Du Cann, held the office for twelve years. It befitted his role that one commentator felt able to observe: 'No one, least of all Mrs Thatcher, knows whose side he is on.'

The oil which keeps the party machine running smoothly is provided by the whips of whom there are fourteen in all. The chief whip has a deputy, seven whips and five assistant whips. Their tasks are often thought of as being to 'organize' the backbenchers so as to maximize support for the leader. This is not surprising for the word finds its origin in the world of fox-hunting where the 'whippers-in' keep the hounds in good order. Nowadays, though, the whip system has as much to do with informing the leadership of the feelings of the backbenchers. Nevertheless, it is an important task of the whips to attempt to persuade disgruntled backbenchers to support the leadership, for example by arranging for them to meet the relevant minister, or spokesman, to whose policy they are objecting, but they have few sanctions at their disposal should this fail. The written whip is no longer withdrawn from members, though they may find the party leadership less enthusiastic about their prospects for promotion. One Conservative backbencher has written of the events that followed his voting against the party. On the first occasion an appointment was made with the chief whip who 'plied him with whisky' and advised him that it would be a great shame to jeopardize his growing reputation in the party by lack of loyalty. A second such vote was received far less cordially and he was advised to forget about trying to build himself a parliamentary career. 'Wait until your constituency chairman hears!' he was warned.[13] On major issues very considerable pressures are put on reluctant government supporters. Some backbenchers, though, are beyond threat. In the first eighteen months of Mrs Thatcher's second term of office Mr Heath supported the government on only six occasions out of a possible 129. Individual rebellions, though, are small beer compared to the formation of groups, such as that founded by Francis Pym in May 1985, known as Centre Forward. This group of about twenty was regarded by the leadership with what Hugo Young described as 'condescending ridicule', though he believed that it represented a growing disunity within the party. Centre Forward was not the first backbench group to be formed after the 1983 election; this was a more amorphous association of 122 like minds in a group known as

Care, dedicated to more radical policies to combat unemployment.[14] Centre Forward has clearly been seen as potentially more dangerous by the leadership but its influence has not been significant.

Although far less exciting than 'rebellions', the weekly meetings of the full 1922 Committee still provide an invaluable forum for the discussion of general issues, though more detailed policies are the prerogative of the twenty-four subject committees or perhaps the seven geographical area committees which also usually meet on a weekly basis. These meetings attract those with a specialized interest but are open to all, and guest speakers are commonly invited. It is not in a minister's interest completely to ignore messages from the troops. When this does happen it can have unexpected consequences. For example, in 1984 the Secretary of State for Education Sir Keith Joseph sought to increase the parental contribution to the cost of university education. Some 180 backbenchers signed a motion of protest – reacting, said one, to months of irritation and frustration. At question time Sir Keith faced 'one of the most concerted onslaughts ever experienced by a Tory Cabinet Minister from his own side'. A few hours later he met the 1922 and more hostility; of thirty speakers only three supported the minister. In what was described as 'one of the swiftest and most effective assertions of backbench power over the executive' in many years, Sir Keith felt obliged to give his tormentors most of what they wanted.[15] It is worth observing, though, that the respected chief whip, John Wakeham, was in hospital at the time of this revolt, recovering from the Brighton bomb attack. His might otherwise have been a crucial restraining influence on both ministers and backbenchers.

It would be inaccurate to conclude discussion on the party in parliament without saying something about the House of Lords and about the European parliament. The organization in the Lords is a pale reflection of that in the Commons.[16] The whipping system comprises a chief and deputy whip and five whips but contact with backbenchers is fairly perfunctory except on major issues, such as the debates in 1985 on the bill to abolish the Greater London Council. There is an association of independent Unionist peers which meets weekly with a role similar to that of The 1922 but it possesses no permanent committee structure. Surprisingly little contact exists between the party in the Lords and the Commons. Finally, although Conservative peers have no vote in the election of the party leader they continue to sustain greater cabinet representation than their

Labour colleagues, with such senior posts as Foreign Secretary and Minister for Employment being held by Conservative peers in recent years.

In the first direct elections to the European parliament held in Britain, shortly after the general election of 1979, no fewer than sixty of the eighty-one seats fell to the Conservatives. In the second such election in 1984 the Conservatives won forty-five seats. This group, together with one Ulster Unionist and three Danish MEPs, formed the European Democrats, with a chief and two deputy whips. This has become a fairly cohesive group but its contacts with the party in Westminster are few, chiefly because dual membership of both institutions was discouraged and only a handful of MPs successfully contested the European elections in 1979 and 1984. All the same, until the British electorate takes a greater interest in European affairs MEPs are unlikely to play an important part in the activities of their party. So much for the Conservative party in parliament.

We turn now to 'the movement'. As we have seen, the National Union was set up in 1867 to orchestrate the activities of existing local associations and to help create new ones. One of its chief activities was the dissemination of information, but from the beginning its role was entirely supportive of the party at Westminster; it was never considered to be a means by which to assure accountability of the party to its supporters. Robert MacKenzie quotes the chairman at the inaugural meeting as declaring that members had not met to discuss Conservative principles because they were all in agreement as to what these were; their task was 'to consider by what particular organization we may make these Conservative principles effective among the masses'.[17] The modern National Union caters for all local associations in England and Wales, with separate bodies catering for Scotland and Northern Ireland. Its central council comprises representatives of the associations, all MPs, MEPs, prospective candidates and peers, representatives of the area councils and national advisory committees (about which more in a moment) and affiliated bodies. The central council meets annually to elect its officers and to debate resolutions from the local associations. An equally representative but far smaller executive committee has been established, with a general purposes committee, which tends to be dominated by the elected officers of the executive. The chairman of the executive committee, usually a prominent Conservative business-man, holds an influential position, having the ear of the chairman especially regarding 'what the party membership would take or wouldn't take, and what the members would like and wouldn't like'.[18] The main activity of the National Union is to organize the annual conference of the party, an event which, in a sense, encapsulates the objectives of the National Union.

The essence of the Conservative party conference is consolidation, of rallying the troops and inspiring them to greater efforts; in the words of one Conservative backbencher, 'to repay party workers for the tedious business of selling endless raffle tickets'. It is an opportunity for the faithful to see and perhaps actually to meet their leaders, and for the leaders, if they are wise, to listen to the grumbles of their troops.

The consitutional status of the annual conference as a 'primarily deliberative and advisory' body was formally acknowledged by the 1948 Maxwell Fyfe committee on the party organization. In terms of policy formulation Balfour's much-quoted comment that he would as soon take advice from his valet as from conference may be considered somewhat colourful though not inappropriate. On the other hand, as an exercise in public relations, both within the party and with the outside world, the conference fulfils a function of considerable importance. And whilst there will be little open criticism of the party leadership at conference, the leadership will leave the conference with a good idea of what is the mood of the party, and this mood may well have an influence in the general direction of policy, as happened, for example, over issues like immigration and law and order in the late 1970s and early 1980s. No sensible leadership will ignore the mood of the party, though it may certainly seek to 'manage' it. Indeed motions from local associations are carefully sifted by the conference organizers so as to produce debates which are unlikely to over-excite conference or embarrass the leadership. All the same, at least since the time of Edward Heath, conference has become somewhat less reticent. Ballots are more frequently called for when there is substantial disagreement and nowadays two motions for debate are selected by a ballot of conference attenders. Yet one backbencher cynically observed of the 1985 conference: 'with luck the hierarchy should be able to manipulate things so that, at worst, they are debates on Aids or heroin'.[19]

The importance to the leadership of this public relations exercise is indicated by the fact that the party leader who, before Heath, did not actually attend any of the debates but simply addressed conference before it broke up, is now a regular attender. Frontbenchers or ministers sit on the platform in full view of the faithful and are keen to make a good impression. Their own contributions to conference debates can be crucial to their standing in the party, and a number of very able ministers have progressed less far and less fast than they might otherwise have done because of lacklustre conference performances. Indeed such a performance is said to have been decisive in Maudling's failure to achieve the leadership in 1965; only two years earlier Quintin Hogg had similarly destroyed his chances of the leadership by his general behaviour at the 1963 conference. Other ministers, though, have greatly enhanced their standing in the party, none more so in recent years than the ex-Minister of Defence, Michael Heseltine, a 'darling' of the conference.

In the days of televised conferences it is arguable that the somewhat bland and packaged Conservative conference is more appropriate than its rumbustious Labour counterpart. It is one thing to believe in internal party democracy but quite another to parade party divisions remorselessly before potential voters. The objectives of Conservative conferences, though they are not always achieved, are more limited than those of their opponents': in Gilmour's words, 'The conference now has to cheer the faithful and to impress the infidel . . . and much of the proceedings are more of an exercise in revivalist enthusiasm than a serious discussion of issues and policies'.[20] There comes a point, however, when 'packaging' becomes counter-productive. Hugo Young believes that the conferences can become merely a 'marketing event', with form and substance merging. 'The image will not prettify the message, it will be the message', he warned.[21]

The National Union comprises eleven areas, each with an office staffed by a professional area agent and one or two full-time officials appointed by the Central Office. An area council, with an executive committee, comprising MPs and candidates and constituency officers and representatives manages the business of each area. Advisory committees also exist at the area level, their organization, too, following the established pattern. Beneath the areas are the constituency associations, where are to be found the formal party associations together with branches of the Young Conservatives (YCs), Conservative Women and, where appropriate, trade unionists, and the Conservative Political Centre (CPC). This group is responsible for such intellectual and ideological activity as takes place at the constituency level. The local association meets once a year for the purpose of electing officers and apppointing an executive council which will run the affairs of the constituency together with the chief executive officer, normally the agent. Most of the voluntary input into the work of the constituency comes at branch level. More than half of the constituencies have full-time, professional agents, paid by the local parties. These have general administrative functions and co-ordinate fund-raising and general publicity activities. A good agent is crucial to a sitting MP and very important to any prospective candidate, and a sound working relationship between the two is essential for the health of the party locally.

Membership of the party requires only the payment of a constituency membership fee, though in reality it is common for constituencies to fix a minimum fee in the expectation that members will be prepared to contribute more if they are able. It has been calculated that the average membership of a constituency association is 2,400, which would give a national membership in the order of 1,500,000. This compares with a claimed membership in the 1950s of almost twice that number and there can be no doubt that however imprecise the figures there has been a substantial fall-off in party membership. Obviously membership varies from constituency to constituency but there are also clear regional differences. In safe constituencies membership is usually high and in Labour-held constituencies usually low. This generalization does not always hold good. When the Conservatives fought a by-election in 1984 at Portsmouth South, a southern constituency and Conservative held (though not safely), the constituency association was discovered to be almost literally non-existent. The by-election was lost. Nevertheless, since the majority of safe Conservative seats are in the south-east of England this region compares favourably with all others. The same pattern of membership holds for the Young Conservatives. Here the fall-off has been from a high of approximately 160,000 in the late 1940s to 30,000 by the late 1970s, though this fall-off is partly explained by transfer to the party proper at an earlier age following the lowering of the age of maturity.

With a declining membership and rising costs the Conservative party has considerable difficulties in keeping its electoral machine operating at maximum efficiency. Indeed in 1986 the party began a mail-order and discount shopping service to boost funds, with special offers on some of Jeffrey Archer's (signed) books. It has been estimated that the party was over £1,000,000 in debt in 1986.[22] Relatively speaking, though, the Conservatives are rich and efficient; indeed it has been calculated that the organizational and financial advantage traditionally enjoyed by the Conservative party is probably worth somewhere between six and twelve seats,[23] enough to have won at least four postwar elections. Constituency associations see themselves principally as electoral machines; certainly this is how they are seen by the party at Westminster. The model rules set up to guide constituency associations list eleven functions of which only one is not expressly and directly related to optimal electoral efficiency, and that is to spread the knowledge of Conservative principles and policy.

It is not surprising, therefore, that a number of constituency associations attach little importance to ideology and a lot to fund-raising, which recent research suggests was a crucial factor in as many as thirty constituencies in 1983. Ideological debate within the party is the responsibility of the CPC, which operates what it calls a contact programme in which issues are regularly selected (at national level) for local debate and a contact brief is prepared outlining various questions for discussion. Reports on these local discussions are then forwarded to the CPC at party head-quarters where a collating exercise takes place, with summaries sent on to the party leadership. Replies to specific points may then be prepared and circulated. Norton and Aughey give figures of the number of members participating in this exercise and the number of reports submitted but they do not suggest that this process has any effect on party policy, neither do they suggest that it is supposed to. They consider the process a success because it can 'serve as a reinforcement to a sense of belonging'.[24]

It may well be that nothing more 'bottom loaded', exists because there is no demand for it. The 1972 Chelmer report on party organization recommended an increase of discussion of policy within the party and the institutional changes required for this were simply never implemented. There exists among the rank and file a group, known as the Charter movement, with its own newsletter, which regularly campaigns for greater democracy within the party. ' "Traditional party democracy" is not democracy', says the Charter. 'It is a substitute for the real thing, intended to divert the unwary into believing that no further scrutiny is necessary. Nothing could be further from the truth . . . '.[25] Yet Charter is small and ineffectual and most members remain quite unconcerned about their lack of involvement in policy-making, a point made by MacKenzie[26] and re-iterated almost thirty years later by Gamble who spoke of a 'largely sleeping membership'.[27]. But only as far as policy-making is concerned; in other respects party members are actively committed to what most see as their prime task and their patriotic duty: to secure the election of a Conservative government. In performing this task there is nothing sleepy about the Conservative membership.

Although much is made of the contributions to party funds made by 'big business', about one-third of party funds come from contributions by the local associations. Norton and Aughey declare that contributions from private companies account for only one-twentieth of income, but they cannot be so certain, for local associations do not generally attempt to distinguish between a private contribution from the managing director of a local business and one from a local housewife, and contributions in the former category are made throughout the country. All the same, each constituency is given a quota based upon votes won locally at the previous election and is expected at least to achieve this quota; some of the more wealthy home counties constituencies exceed the quota by several times.

Second of the most important functions of the local party is the selection of parliamentary and local government candidates. The latter may be dealt with rather summarily, for it is sometimes a question of endorsing the candidature of whoever is willing to stand. Many local hierarchies, though, will tend to have favourite sons and daughters (or more usually, fathers and mothers) whose candidature is very difficult to resist. Parliamentary candidature, however, especially in safe seats, is a very different story; hundreds of applications may be received. Usually the local party will appoint a selection committee which will draw up a short list and submit this to the council which may either recommend one name for approval by a general meeting of the association or simply submit two or three names and leave it to the general meeting to decide. Research on candidate selection in the Conservative party[28] indicates that policy considerations do not normally figure very highly; more important are such factors as knowledge of and sympathy for constituency problems, style and presentation, potential as a national figure, and so on.

Candidates must either be on the party's approved list or secure

acceptance by the party's standing advisory committee on candidates, but direct attempts to persuade local parties to adopt
candidates favoured by central or area office are usually strongly
resisted. There have been several attempts by the party headquarters
to persuade constituency parties to try to encourage candidatures
from sectors of the community generally underrepresented, the most
recent of which, headed by vice chairman Emma Nicholson, has
sought to encourage the selection of more women candidates and the
inclusion of more women on the official candidates' list. These
problems will be considered more fully in the next chapter; it is
enough to point out here that candidates tend to be middle-class,
middle-aged, white and male. History shows that constituency
parties have always been reluctant to broaden the base of candidate
selection. Despite exhortations from Central Office only about 10 per
cent of constituencies formed local trade union councils or labour
committees, and those that did made no attempt to integrate these
bodies into the association proper; hence the paucity of working-class
Conservative candidates locally and nationally.[29]

Before leaving the National Union it is appropriate to say
something about the system of national advisory committees, such as
the Young Conservatives (YCs) or the Women's National Advisory
Committee. The structure of these groups is modelled upon that of
the National Union, each holding an annual conference along similar
lines, though the leadership does not seek the same degree of control
over proceedings. The YCs' conference of 1985, for example,
dedicated itself to moderation despite opposition from a minority of
right-wingers whose chants of 'pinko' and showers of paper darts
punctuated events.[30] Like the National Union, too, each is organized
into areas and, beneath them, usually, constituencies and branches.
National advisory committees exist for Conservative students, local
government, trade unionists, education and the CPC, in addition to
those for the Young Conservatives and for women. The Federation of
Conservative Students, however, being based upon universities and
colleges is organized somewhat differently. This body attained a
certain notoriety in 1982 after alleged ballot-rigging and again in
1985 and 1986 for its rowdy conferences and robustly right-wing
views. Party chairman John Gummer set up an enquiry tasked with
drawing up a constitution intended to curb the powers of the right-
wing leadership, but the new constitution did nothing to weaken
their domination, perhaps because Gummer had by this time been

replaced as chairman by Tebbit.[31] In 1986, against party instructions, the FCS campaigned on behalf of Official Unionist candidates in the by-elections in Northern Ireland which were called to protest against the Anglo-Irish Agreement of the previous year. In this and other ways FCS is seen to be a nuisance to the party, 'losing it valuable support among "ordinary" Conservatives on campus'.[32] Eventually even Mr Tebbit lost his patience and withdrew the party's annual grant of £30,000 to FCS. Further, he replaced FCS executive by a Central Office-appointed Conservative Collegiate Forum. There is some anxiety that the 'Libertarian' right may instead transfer its attention to the Young Conservatives.

We now turn our attention to what we have called the party bureaucracy. Party headquarters actually comprises three separate bodies, the Central Office, the Conservative Research Department and the Advisory Committee on Policy. Each, though separate, is none the less responsible to the party leader. Established under Disraeli in 1870, the Central Office was soon fully committed to all the professional supportive work required by the party both nationally and locally and, despite some lean periods, its position has become stronger over the years. Initally the Central Office was run by the chief whip but by the turn of the century such had become the work-load that it was felt necessary for the party leader to appoint a chairman (and later two deputy chairmen).

We have already seen, from the constituency level, what services the Central Office provides; it does so through various departments and units most important of which is the organization department, with officers responsible for trade unions, community groups, youth and small businesses. Other departments in the Central Office include the publicity department and the CPC, which services the consituency groups and the national advisory committees. The Research Department, established in 1929 and reorganized in 1948, currently services the advisory committee on policy and the various policy groups, as well, of course, as the party in parliament. The head of the department has traditionally been a senior politician and the most celebrated was R. A. Butler, who was head from 1945 to 1964. Ten years later Ian Gilmour became chairman, though he was quickly replaced by a parliamentarian more of Mrs Thatcher's persuasion, Angus Maude. On Maude's apointment to cabinet in 1979 the post was abolished and the department is now run by a full-time director. In the past the research department earned a reputation as the party's 'think-tank' and as offering a home for young men of intellect and promise who were later to make a name for themselves in the House; for example Maudling, Macleod, Powell and, more recently, Patten. It also earned a reputation for being somewhat to the left of centre and its influence in policy formulation has declined consequently in the last decade, its role being increasingly taken over by the Centre for Policy Studies, an independent body established by, among others, Sir Keith Joseph and Margaret Thatcher. The centre sees its task as being to provide the 'policy sciences' and 'scientific method' to guide those attempting to transform political and administrative structures.[33]

The advisory committee on policy was established in 1949; its chairman is chosen by the leader and its membership represents the various sections of the party. The committee generally meets once a month while parliament is sitting and its task principally is to co-ordinate the various research activities of the party, such as the summaries of the CPC discussion papers, reports from policy groups, developments within government departments (when the party is in power) and so on. The policy groups themselves usually comprise a mixture of interested backbenchers, members drawn from other sections of the party and outside experts. It would be easy to overemphasize the impact that these groups, working through the advisory committee, have upon policy but, as King has indicated, it is not negligible. When the party is in power, though, King sees the system more as 'a sounding board – as one way of keeping party leaders from getting too far out of step with their followers'.[34]

Gamble has described the whole headquarters edifice as 'antique and ramshackle',[35] Norton and Aughey regard its antiquities as 'understandable' to a Conservative. Its basic role has traditionally been to give advice on how to achieve power when the party is in opposition and to provide loyal though largely uncritical support for the leadership when in office. Whatever its shortcomings the head-quarters, especially Central Office, has usually been considered as superior to its Labour counterpart. The general election of 1987, however, exposed a dramatic reversal of roles; Central Office managed an ill-coordinated and poorly directed campaign.

Finally, mention must be made of the various groups which, though not part of the official structure, are none the less important elements of the party. The most important of these is probably the Bow Group, founded in 1951 by a number of Oxford graduates who wished to create a rough Conservative equivalent of the Fabian Society. Though the group has a number of branches it is strongest in London and includes about seventy MPs in its ranks. The group organizes itself into a number of policy committees roughly paralleling government departments and involves itself in research programmes the fruits of which are often published as discussion pamphlets. The group also produces a quarterly journal, *Crossbow*, which helps to sustain a radical image.

Originally thought of as a right-wing counterbalance to the Bow Group is the Monday Club, founded in 1961. Traditionally the group has tended to concentrate on foreign and defence matters, being strongly supportive of the regimes in South Africa and white Rhodesia. During the late 1960s it attracted considerable publicity by attempts to unseat certain Conservative MPs whom it considered to be too liberal, though without success. Its influence within the national party has always been limited, and there have never been more than around fifteen MPs among the membership. Moreover, the election of Mrs Thatcher 'helped to take more wind out of its sails'[36] because her general attitude was substantially further to the right than that of her predecessors. The Monday Club has exercised considerable influence in some south-eastern constituency parties and has been charged with acting as a vehicle for infiltration from the National Front. However, the 'infiltration' has chiefly comprised ex-Conservatives who have returned to the fold from the Front, some of them actually becoming parliamentary candidates.[37] In 1983 the leadership investigated claims that the YCs were also being infiltrated by right-wing groups but found that only a handful of members gave cause for concern. Cecil Parkinson dismissed them as the 'tip of the ice-cube'.

Other less important ideological groups include the Primrose League, founded in 1883 (in honour of Disraeli whose favourite flower the primrose was), to sustain Disraelian social democracy. Important in its early days, the league became less so as the official party organization grew. Its activities nowadays are rather more social than political and the cutting edge of Disraelian conservatism tends to be provided by the Tory Reform Group, established in 1975 and frequently labelled as 'anti-Thatcher', a charge it strongly denies. Its membership, though, which includes only a handful of MPs, has never sought to act as more than a research group. There are a number of branches throughout the country and the group publishes a journal, *The Reformer*.

Balancing the Tory Reform group is the Selsdon Group, founded in 1973, to support the kind of neo-liberal policies inaugurated only to be later abandoned by the Heath government. The Selsdon Group's chief focus has been economic and it has tended to act since 1979 as a small but dedicated ginger group, with only a handful of MP members. It has attempted to influence thinking at senior levels within the party by organizing meetings and discussions and distributing pamphlets. It co-operates with a number of like-minded groups outside the party such as the Centre for Policy Studies and the Institute for Economic Affairs. Another like-minded group is the Salisbury Group, founded in 1979 to defend the neo-liberal cause in intellectual terms. It, too, publishes a journal, the *Salisbury Review*, which gained a vicarious notoriety in 1985 for publishing allegedly racialist articles by a Bradford headmaster, whose case subsequently became a *cause célèbre*. Generally the group has not sought wide publicity but is concerned to act as an intellectual spearhead for the Conservative right in social policy matters and specifically the neo-liberal right in economic matters.

It might appear reasonable to conclude that these groups on the left (Disraelian social democrats) and the right (neo-liberals) of the party constitute a balance. In fact this is not strictly true. It is true in the sense that the groups talk to each other and listen to each other: they see themselves as planets in orbit around the same sun. It is not true, though, that left- and right-wing pressures on the leadership cancel each other; at least from the leadership of Macmillan to that of Thatcher, the influence of the Disraelian social democrats was substantially greater and conversely since then the neo-liberals have been more influential. As with all other aspects of Conservative ideology and policy the balance is decided by the preferences of the party leader.

A brief conclusion to this discussion of leadership and organization within the Conservative party is to suggest that it reinforces Mackenzie's treatise on power within the Conservative party written thirty years ago. We can be more assertive than he about the formal and informal constraints upon the powers of the Conservative leader, which are real and not inconsiderable; but we have still to acknowledge the fundamental strength and considerable personal prestige throughout the party enjoyed by the Conservative leader. When all is said and done, this pre-eminence remains the defining characteristic of the Conservative party today.

Notes

1 Richard Rose, *The Problem of Party Government* (Harmondsworth, Pelican, 1976), p. 154.
2 R. T. McKenzie, *British Political Parties* (London, Heinemann, 1955), ch. 3.
3 Quoted in Sir Nigel Fisher, *The Tory Leaders* (London, Weidenfeld and Nicolson, 1977), p. 3.
4 Norton and Aughey, *Conservatives and Conservatism*, pp. 242–3.
5 Ibid., pp. 250–52.
6 *Observer*, 16 December 1984.
7 M. Pinto-Duschinsky, 'Central Office and "power" in the Conservative party', *Political Studies*, 20, no. 1 (March 1972).
8 Hugo Young, *The Guardian*, 7 March 1986.
9 Norton and Aughey, *Conservatives and Conservatism*, pp. 258–5.
10 R. H. S. Crossman, *Diaries of a Cabinet Minister*, published in four volumes jointly by Jonathan Cape and Hamish Hamilton, from 1976.
11 See 'Image maker to the prime minister', *Observer*, 12 June 1983.
12 Philip Goodhart, *The 1922* (London, Macmillan, 1973), p. 15.
13 Michael Brown, 'Confessions of a Tory rebel', *The Guardian*, 2 August 1985.
14 See *The Guardian*, 21 May 1985.
15 Ian Aitken, *The Guardian*, 7 December 1984.
16 See Nicholas Baldwin, 'The House of Lords: Behavioural changes', in P. Norton (ed.), *Parliament in the 1980s* (Oxford, Blackwell, 1985).
17 McKenzie, *British Political Parties*, p. 151.
18 *The Guardian*, 26 June 1986.
19 Michael Brown, *The Guardian*, 4 October 1985.
20 Sir Ian Gilmour, *The Body Politic* (London, Hutchinson, 1971 edn), p. 80.
21 *The Guardian*, 8 October, 1985.
22 *Sunday Times*, 24 August 1986.
23 See F. W. S. Craig, *British Parliamentary Statistics 1918–70* (London, Political Reference Publications, 1971), pp. 65–6.
24 Norton and Aughey, *Conservatives and Conservatism*, p. 218.
25 *Charter News*, Spring 1985.
26 McKenzie, *British Political Parties*, p. 244.
27 Andrew Gamble, 'The Conservative party', in H. M. Drucker (ed.), *Multi-Party Britain* (London, Macmillan, 1979), p. 40.
28 Michael Rush, *The Selection of Parliamentary Candidates* (London, Nelson, 1969).
29 See John Greenwood, 'The Conservative party and the working classes – the organizational response', University of Warwick Working Papers no. 2, 1974.
30 *The Guardian*, 11 February 1985.

31 *The Guardian*, 15 December 1985.
32 *The Guardian*, 5 April 1986.
33 Sir Alfred Sherman, co-founder of CPS, writing in *The Guardian*, 11 February 1985.
34 Anthony King, 'How the Conservatives evolve policies', quoted in Norton and Aughey, *Conservatives and Conservatism*, p. 231.
35 Gamble, 'The Conservative party', p. 39.
36 Norton and Aughey, *Conservatives and Conservatism*, p. 235.
37 Martin Walker, 'A prodigal rush back to the fold', *The Guardian*, 11 October 1983.

4 Who are the Conservatives?

One of the most striking features of the Conservative party, according to Burch and Moran, has been its 'extraordinary ability . . . to combine electoral success with social elitism',[1] with the proportion of ex-public school boys in the party's ranks being higher in 1970 than at any time since the first world war. Since that time, though, there appears to have been a radical change on the Conservative backbenches, a change likely to have considerable consequences for the style and perhaps the policy preferences of the party; arguably it has already done so.

The most authoritative work on the background of members of the House of Commons remains Colin Mellors's *The British M.P.*,[2] which considered each new wave of MPs from 1945 to 1974. The Conservative party was seen to be remarkably resistant to social change. In 1945 the typical Conservative MP came from a privileged background, over 80 per cent having been to a public school. More than 25 per cent had been to Eton and almost exactly 50 per cent had gone on to Oxbridge from their public school. Mellors says that the Conservatives, in choosing their parliamentary candidates, 'concern themselves more with rank and achievement than party political experience. Breeding and educational attainment are customarily seen as the two most important qualifications . . . for recruitment to the political elite.'[3] He went on to say that the 'old school tie' remains the single most important qualification for would-be Conservative MPs. 'As a guarantee of success it ranked with sponsorship from the mineworkers' union in the Labour party.' It would be difficult to overstate the preponderance of public school-boys in the Conservative party since the second world war: more specifically three schools, Eton, Harrow and Winchester, produced over 25 per cent of all Conservative MPs between 1945 and 1974.

This represents an unusually narrow channel of recruitment implying a tight network of old school friends. Moreover, Mellors indicated that this preponderance of public school backgrounds found an echo at the university level. It was not simply that Oxbridge products similarly dominated the Conservative party but that the products of four Oxford colleges (Christchurch, Balliol, New and Magdalen) and four Cambridge Colleges (Trinity, Trinity Hall, King's and Gonville and Caius) dominated the party. As far as educational background is concerned the Conservative parliamentary party has been homogeneous to an unparalleled degree.

Education is often an indicator of social class and it may be stated quite simply that the postwar Conservative parliamentary party has been overwhelmingly middle class. It has, as we shall see, strong aristocratic connections, but since the war has produced only two MPs who could be classified as working class. So educational homogeneity has tended to reflect an underlying social homogeneity. Moreover, the careers from which Conservative candidates have tended to come reinforce this homogeneity to a remarkably high degree. It may be true, as Robert Louis Stevenson once wrote, that politics is the only profession for which no preparation is thought necessary, but it is clear that Conservative candidate selection committees believe that some professional backgrounds are eminently more suitable for an aspiring politician than others. This is not unique to the Conservative party or indeed to Britain. Lawyers, lecturers, teachers and journalists tend to be found in every legislature in the free world. In the House of Commons lawyers form about 19 per cent of the membership of the House, but the proportion in the two Houses of the American Congress is nearer 55 per cent. Mellors characterized the parliamentary Conservative party as representing 'law, land and business' but acknowledged that it was in fact business and not the law which provided the preponderance of MPs, the corner-stone of the parliamentary party. Again, we can be more specific and say that a certain category of businessmen provided the overwhelming majority of these MPs: company directors.[4] In the thirty years after the second world war 273 company directors were elected to parliament of whom no fewer than 245 were Conservatives. As Mellor righly concludes, 'it is by far the largest single occupation group represented at Westminster'.[5] Perhaps making a virtue of necessity, Winston Churchill once defended an unhealthily close correlation between public and private interest when he pointed out to the committee of privileges, 'everybody here has private interests: some are directors of companies, some own property . . . We are not supposed to be an assembly of gentlemen with no interests of any kind and no association of any kind. That might happen in Heaven, but not, happily, here.' It seems abundantly clear, then, that for a substantial majority of Conservative MPs 'training' has traditionally consisted of having succeeded in a previous career, usually business, a finding supported by the fact that 75 per cent of MPs of both parties do not enter the House until they are in their thirties or forties.

There is ample evidence, none the less, that the Conservative party has actively sought to broaden the social base of the parliamentary party so as to counter the charge of privilege, not merely because it is assumed to be electorally disadvantageous but also because it is politically limiting. When Lord Woolton became party chairman after the war he initiated a review of party organization under Maxwell-Fyfe which turned its attention to the general problem of the party's unrepresentativeness. It recommended, among other things, that the entire election expenses of candidates should be the responsibility of the constituency association and that candidates should be permitted to make no contribution; that candidates should be required to subscribe no more than £25 per annum to constituency funds (MPs not more than £50); that in no circumstances should the question of an annual subscription be mentioned during the selection interviews.[6] The aim of the recommendations, which were accepted by the annual conference and by the central council, was to remove the financial considerations which might deter ordinary people from standing as Conservative candidates or, more likely, might dispose constituencies to prefer more wealthy candidates. The prewar selection procedures were described as being exercises in plutocracy, with three categories of potential candidate: those willing to meet all their election expenses and contribute handsomely to local association funds, those willing to pay half their election expenses and able to contribute modestly to funds, and those unable to do either. Needless to say, those in the first category stood the best chance of being selected as candidates.[7]

Recognizing the problem and attempting to solve it does not guarantee success. Butler and Pinto-Duschinky point out that 'all these developments have had very little effect upon the social composition of the party, either within or outside the House of

Commons'.[8]The Conservative party remained as elitist and as hierarchical as ever, though the influence of the aristocracy and of rich businessmen has been replaced to a considerable extent by that of professionals and managers.

It was in 1979 that the changes in the party started to become obvious. The 175 successful candidates selected in 1979, 1983 and 1987 are a different group from those whom they joined. For the first time in 1979, and again in 1983, the proportion of those following what Burch and Moran call the meritocratic route, that is, state education followed by university, outnumber those who followed the traditional public school followed by Oxbridge route. What is more, Etonians counted for only 6 per cent of these new intakes. In 1979, 1983 and 1987 there were more new members educated in the provincial and London universities than there were from Oxbridge.

Before we can consider seriously the possibility of a major transformation however, we need to remember that in 1979 and 1983 many marginal constituencies were won, where the selection precedures might have been somethat more relaxed. Burch and Moran have attempted to examine this possibility and conclude that although it may have provided a partial explanation for the 1979 intake it could not explain what happened in 1983. They compare the 1983 intake with that of another landslide, 1959. Of the latter over 80 per cent of the new MPs were from public schools, with 20 per cent from Eton. The 1983 election, repeated in 1987, produced 47 per cent from public school and only 6 per cent from Eton. Morever, when they compare safe seats (i.e. a majority in excess of 15 per cent) with the whole group they find no disproportionate differences.

When they seek to account for this change Burch and Moran suggest not only that the wider opportunities of the Butler Education Act were making themselves felt but that also the appeal to the privileged of a parliamentary career was diminishing. Such a career can no longer easily be coupled with a long-term career in the law or in industry. It can be argued that the House of Commons will be the poorer for having deprived itself of this experience, but the move towards full-time politics has been going on for some time and as specialist committee work takes up more of the backbenchers' time and energy, so the move is likely only to gain pace.

Not only are the new intakes distinctive socially but they are also recognizably different in so far as many of them were already, in effect, full-time politicians. In 1983 over half of new Conservative

MPs had local government experience, in Burch and Moran's words 'the most striking index of the change'. They continue: 'They would have been amongst the ablest councillors. As chairmen of committees, they would influence budgets worth millions of pounds. Articulate, experienced and opinionated councillors do not make good lobby fodder in Westminster.' The difficulties the modern Conservative whips are experiencing 'spring in part from the party's success in broadening its social base in parliament'. This is not so plausible an argument as it sounds, though, when we remember that those whom the new group have replaced were also successful in influential careers, no doubt also being involved in transactions worth millions of pounds or in important legal cases. On the face of it they would be even less amenable to party discipline; at least the ex-local councillors would recognize the importance of such discipline and be thoroughly familiar with its demands. More important, surely, is the fact that this group came to a House of Commons which had just gone through a decade of well-documented dissension. Moreover, since 1983 the size of the goverment majority has simply lessened the need not merely for Conservative backbenchers to be tightly disciplined but even for them to be physically present at the House for much of the time. For these reasons the new wave of backbenchers are altogether less amenable to the old-style party discipline than were their predecessors.

It is worth pointing out, too, that selection precedures have changed since 1980[9] and these have had some effect upon the quality of candidates being chosen. Since that year residential selection boards have operated a system rather like that of the civil service. Prospective candidates are assessed in groups in a number of different situations over a period of forty-eight hours by a team including an MP, an industrialist and a member of the National Union. About 25 per cent fail at this hurdle; the remainder are scrutinized by the party vice chairman in charge of candidates; about 40 per cent fail here. Competition for places on the resulting approved list has increased substantially over recent years and we can assume that this has helped to improve the quality of candidates. However, it is worth remembering that no gains are made without losses. Like the Maxwell-Fyfe reforms, these new procedures have tended to replace men with considerable varieties of background, interest and ideological persuasion who had chiefly one thing in common, their wealth, by candidates who correspond most closely to an amalgam of all desirable Conservative qualities; the day of the Conservative candidate clone may be coming.

There are, however, countervailing pressures. It is in the nature of a large majority that many of the new MPs will represent a number of normally Labour seats, with a more working-class electorate than Conservative MPs will usually represent. The logic of these MPs' situation, says David Thomas,[10] is that, to survive, they should be more attentive than usual to constituency needs and hence (because of the nature of their constituencies) to concerns not traditional to Conservatives.

It is easy to exaggerate the extent of these changes. After all, about 75 per cent of the present parliamentary party went to public school and there are still virtually no manual workers. All the same the changes are real enough, producing not simply a more independent party but also a more able one. 'The standard of professionalism and intellect among Conservative MPs', said Sir David Price, MP for over thirty years, 'is infinitely higher than when I first came here.'[11] Moreover, members new to parliament after 1987 were by no means dissimilar to those whose places they had taken: of over forty new members nearly half were educated privately (only four at Eton or Harrow); a smaller proportion had been to Oxbridge (almost twice as many as went to a provincal university); half had local government experience and the great majority were successful businessmen. Only five were women. Those hoping for revolutionary changes may welcome the election of the great-grandson of the socialist agitator Tom Mann.

'The most striking social feature of the modern Conservative leadership is . . . the fact that the two most recent Conservative Prime Ministers have been . . . meritocrats of modest social origins.'[12] Mrs Thatcher has used her origins to considerable political advantage. For example, she defended grammar schools by declaring: 'People from my sort of background need good schools to compete with children from privileged homes like Shirley Williams and Anthony Wedgwood Benn.'[13] She may well regard herself as typical of a new wave of Conservatives, and we shall shortly test this belief. There is little doubt, though, that the cabinet as a whole has not yet been affected by the same social change as the backbenchers. The proportion of cabinet ministers born to working class families or with only an elementary or secondary education actually fell during the period 1955–87 compared to earlier periods.[14] Whilst on the one hand it is true that the proportion of ministers with an aristocratic background has declined, their places have not been taken up to any noticeable extent by meritocrats from the state schools or by self-made businessmen. Burch and Moran examined new entrants to Conservative cabinets after 1970 (thirty-four in all) and discovered no great break with the past: over 80 per cent were from public schools and 75 per cent were Oxbridge educated. There was, however, one noteworthy change: whereas between 1916 and 1955 Eton and Harrow supplied about half of the membership of Conservative cabinets, they have since supplied only 15 per cent and the trend, confirmed in 1987, is downward. In general, since 1885 the percentage of Conservative cabinet ministers with an aristocratic background has varied from 44 per cent in that year down to 22 per cent in Heath's 1970 cabinet, with the principal fall-off occuring during Churchill's last government in 1955. Over these years aristocrats have provided an average of 37 per cent of Conservative cabinets.[15] Burch and Moran went further and examined the backgrounds of non-cabinet ministers who were under forty-five years of age on appointment in 1983. This group, it could reasonably be expected, would comprise those from whom future Conservative senior figures would emerge. Of these (twenty-nine in number), ten had an aristocratic background, twenty-four were public school educated and seven were old Etonians. Not only has cabinet failed to follow the trends obvious in the party at large but if anything it has moved in the opposite direction. The only significant change in line with general party trends is a decline in the number educated at Oxbridge. In short, Heath and Thatcher remain atypical among the Conservative leadership; Conservative administrations are not becoming more socially representative, nor even noticeably more meritocratic.

There are a number of critics who would claim, though, that the Conservative parliamentary party has already changed in character. In her unprecedented third term of office Mrs Thatcher will have the opportunity, should she wish, to reinforce these changes, making the party increasingly less like the traditional Tory party. In a previous chapter we considered recent developments in Conservative ideology; we return to them now to explore them in the context of the parliamentary party and its personnel.

The question of 'new' and 'old' Conservative parties has been raised on a number of occasions since 1979 but perhaps never more forcefully than in 1983 when Francis Pym established his ginger group Centre Forward. 'The Pym faction . . . unlike any other in British politics . . . is a ginger group not at the extreme but at the centre. 'So said *The Guardian*'s Ian Aitken who saw Pym as the true heir to the Tory tradition.[16] Critics attacked Pym's group as 'squirearchs and landed gentry from another era' but defenders drew consolation from its traditions. Anthony Howard, for example, wrote: 'backbench knightage and baronetage with its roots in the soil provided the Tory party with its ballast – and some of them at least . .. were markedly enlightened and modern-minded in their outlook . . . their successors have tended to be young, thrusting professional politicians, for whom party, if not faction, means all'.[17] Pym's group sought a more compassionate and less radical approach to government, hence his claim to be in the Conservative tradition. The historian Lord Blake seems also to favour the idea of such moderation being central to that tradition. He quotes Salisbury with approval, who saw the role of the Conservative party of his days as providing a kind of purgative to cure the excesses of Gladstonian liberalism. 'I rank myself no higher in the scheme of things than a policeman – whose utility would disappear if there were no criminals.' Blake built upon this argument by pointing out that many people over the years have voted Conservative out of fear of a more radical alternative. The Conservatives, he concludes, have no business engaging in radical change or social transformation. Being at least partly a man of politics as well as history Blake was careful not to tar the Thatcher government with a radical brush, reminding us that undoing other parties' radical measures was not the same as being radical oneself.[18] The Conservative MP Julian Critchley was not so circumspect, describing the 1975 leadership which brought Thatcher to power as 'the Peasants' Revolt'.[19] What Thatcher had done, he said, was to change the Conservative party into a Liberal party. Far from being a party of conviction and crusade the Conservative party was properly 'the non-political political party', eschewing ideology, tempering belief with scepticism, and flying 'by the seat of their pants'.

What was causing concern to Pym and his colleagues was the fact that the new intake of MPs tended to be on the Thatcherite wing of the party. According to Andrew Roth the new MPs are 'more aggressively business minded. They are the sort for whom capitalism doesn't have an unacceptable face'.[20] John Curtice undertook a survey comparing the attitudes of the 1983 intake with those of the pre-1983 members, and found new members and old to be similarly disposed on issues such as curbing the power of the unions and privatizing nationalized industries, but the new were noticeably tougher on some others: for example, 78 per cent were against increasing public borrowing even to boost the economy.

The character of the parliamentary party has changed, then, since the advent of Thatcherism. Burch and Moran have established changes in the background of MPs, changes that have gathered momentum since 1979. Sixty years ago around a fifth of the party had 'private means'; now just about every Conservative MP works for a living. Butler and Pinto-Duschinky conclude: 'The relatively dumb knight of the shire is said to be a dying breed, replaced by the thrusting city banker or the advertising man.'[21] Under the present government's policy of mass enoblement it might be simpler to say that the knights of the shires are being replaced by the knights of the suburbs. One senior backbench MP declared that these changes had made the party less gentlemanly. He said of new members: 'Their behaviour is boorish and they don't have any real sympathy for the place [parliament].' Another experienced member took a similar position, adding: 'They're mostly hard-nosed businessmen who are here for their own reasons, and that includes quick promotion come what may. But they've no time for party loyalty unless it happens to suit.' A third backbencher felt, 'They're a pretty disaffected lot, by and large, with the whole set up, actually. Their attendance at the House is pretty dismal . . . one of the disadvantages of such a big majority I suppose.' One final comment from a backbencher of long standing: 'They may be a clever lot – everybody says they are – but they're not my idea of gentlemen. I think they behave as badly as the other side personally.'

These 'new' Conservatives, though, claim to be articulating the interests of the majority of people, and in some senses they clearly are. Rhodes Boyson, for example, has written: 'There is a very large centre group in Britain making up possibly 80 to 90 per cent of my fellow countrymen and women who have firm views on law and order, morality, personal initiative and responsibility, educational standards and discipline, and national pride. The Conservatives lose elections only when they lose contact with this central group.'[22] According to Boyson this combative form of Toryism reflects the wishes and anxieties of the majority of ordinary people. Crewe and Sarlvik have considered Boyson's claim and have concluded that he is basically right.[23] On issues such as law and order, education and morality (populist-authoritarian issues as they term them) a pugnacious stand substantially to the right is electorally popular. Crewe and Sarlvik conclude: 'In a large number of policy areas – foreign affairs, defence, crime, minority rights, sexual morality – the majority view aligns with Conservative rather than Labour instincts.'[24] As Sir Alfred Sherman has said, 'Margaret Thatcher achieved her predominance primarily because she articulated the feelings of a majority of people'.[25] The Thatcherite revolution was based, he tells us, upon the conviction that neo-Keynesian economics, trade union domination and the permissive society had failed. Mrs Thatcher represents a 'deep felt though incoherent hunger for change and a new sense of national purpose which go well beyond the economic, social and electoral stereotypes'.

Norman Tebbit, too, identifies the 'new' Conservatism as representing the aspirations of the majority.[26] The public, he claims, 'are demanding stiffer sentences for criminals – and in the end they will get them. They will demand that television producers will think about the effects of what they broadcast upon impressionable people – and in the end it will happen. They will insist upon traditional style in schools – and more parental influence.' What this amounts to, says Tebbit, is in fact not a 'new' conservatism at all, but a campaign for a return to traditional values, and this is pre-eminently a Conservative task.

New or old, Thatcherite conservatism set about trying to build a revolution. The entire structure of the welfare state was to be reconsidered so as to stress a commitment to family life and to voluntary effort. Indeed, cabinet set up its own family team in 1983 including eight ministers whose task was to promote 'self-respect and a sense of individual responsibility based upon family life'. There was to be a revolutionary transformation of the relationship between the 'ordinary citizen' and the 'expert' involving teachers, doctors, social workers and architects. Taking the example of education, parental power through boards of governors was substantially to be increased, but more significantly parental choice was to be enriched through the introduction into secondary education of a system of vouchers which parents could spend at the school of their choice. Confidential documents leaked to and published in extract form in *The Guardian* indicate the breadth and depth of proposed change. Some changes, indeed, have happened; the revolution has not. Indeed, within two years half of the ministers involved had left or been thrown out of the cabinet family.

Anthony Howard sought to test the strength of the 'new' conservatism. He regarded the issue of capital punishment as his yardstick. In 1979 Mrs Thatcher, who had previously voted in favour of the cane and the birch, allowed the party a free vote on the issue of restoring the death penalty. Roughly two-thirds of the parliamentary party followed their leader and five of her cabinet colleagues into the pro-death-penalty lobby; the others followed Whitelaw and eleven other cabinet colleagues into the anti lobby. The motion was defeated by 362 to 243. Howard was convinced that the issue would be debated again after the subsequent election and that the Thatcherites would win. He was right about the debate, wrong about the result. Amongst the new intake of Conservative MPs, fifty voted in favour of restoration and nineteen voted against. In the 1979 parliament 33 per cent of the party had opposed the death penalty; approximately 29 per cent of new members in the 1983 parliament voted the same way. In 1987 a third unsuccessful attempt to restore capital punishment was mounted. On this occasion an additional four Conservatives supported restoration. There is no indication that the new House will behave differently.

Clearly there is no strict correlation between an MP's social background and his/her ideological beliefs. Moreover, evidence suggests that the average voter is more concerned with a candidate's perceived ideological disposition than his or her social background.[27] In more global terms, though, parties have been traditionally perceived by the majority of voters as representing the interests of one or other of the social classes. 'There can be no doubt', say Butler and Pinto-Duschinsky, 'that the Conservatives are damaged by being seen as a class party.'[28] Moreover, any social prejudices amongst the electorate are only likely to be exacerbated by those symbols of privilege commonly associated with traditional Conservative candidates, style and accent. It will be no electoral disadvantage that the Conservative party is becoming somewhat more like the rest of the nation.

More important than the electoral disadvantages of privilege, which may be alleviated anyway by giving media coverage to major figues in the party like Mrs Thatcher herself or Tebbit who are clearly from 'ordinary' backgrounds, is the restricted frame of reference which the social homogeneity of privilege can give, thus distorting the party's perception of problems. There may be a wealth of knowledge amongst the backbenches on matters of finance, commerce, agriculture and the law, but there is an absolute dearth of first-hand experience of poverty, unemployment, the sharp end of the welfare state, the problems of living in the inner cities, and so on. It is true that the electoral successes of 1979 and 1983 have brought into the House a number of MPs with a vicarious knowledge of some of these problems through their constituents, but these, for the foreseeable future, will be backbench MPs and thus unlikely to play any major part in the shaping of party policy.

The nature of this disadvantage and the voters' perception of it are shown by the following extract from a tabloid newspaper. Entitled 'School Report' it tells of the decision of Bob Dunn MP to send his son to a local fee-paying school. Nothing very unusual in that, comments the journalist, except that Dunn happened to be a junior minister in the Department of Education and Science. 'Perhaps if it were his child whose future depended upon how he came through the state system, his child who came home semi-literate, rude and uninterested, he might get off his backside and do something to improve it.'[29] But ordinary working people are not the only ones whose interests may be ignored by Conservative ministers. We have already had cause to look at Sir Keith Joseph's ill-fated attempt to increase the parental contribution to the costs of university education. It provoked an 'unholy alliance of some 180 Conservative backbenchers . . . from left-wing soppy to right-wing nasty'[30] whose common denominator was constituency pressure. One such MP, Keith Hampson, wrote tellingly: 'Possibly Ministers never really appreciated how difficult it is to find an extra £200 or more after tax. But for the upwardly-thrusting lower-middle classes . . . in their mid-forties, living in inner suburbia, it means a considerable sacrifice, possibly over several years.'[31] Hampson went on to point out to ministers that these parents were already committing 10 to 20 per cent of their income to their children's higher education and that the extra burden was simply too much. Through its insensitivity to their plight the Conservative government had brought upon itself 'the revolt of the "Yuppies" '.

One short final example of the Conservative parliamentary party's difficulty in seeing the world as ordinary people see it. Norman Tebbit tells the story of one Tory grandee who, prior to cabinet discussion on the subject, had to ask his senior civil servants what mortgages were and how they worked . . .[32] We may summarize this discussion of the parliamentary party since the 'Thatcher revolution' as follows: the party today is less homogeneous, more factious, more abrasive, and less deferential. There have been changes but there has been no revolution. When Pym founded Centre Forward his constituency party was shocked. A statement to the effect that the move did not constitute a bid for the leadership was accepted by 140 votes to 2, though few endorsed their MP's action. Nobody thought the MP was being deliberately divisive: nobody, said the constituency chairman, could believe Mr Pym capable of 'such a dastardly thing'.[33] There will be few 'new' Conservatives whose constituency chairman would be able to say that of them.

Mention of constituency parties leads us to consider the nature of the extra-parliamentary party. Has it, too, been subjected to change? Biographical information about party activists is more difficult to obtain than it is for MPs but some generalizations are nevertheless possible. Research shows,[34] for example, that relatively few working class people become active in local Conservative associations; it is middle-class territory. Taking the key position of constituency chairman, survey material indicated that 9 per cent were farmers, 24 per cent could be described as professionals (with solicitors and chartered accountants being the most numerous), and that no fewer than 66 per cent could be described as businessmen (more or less equally divided between large and small businesses). Butler and Pinto Duschinky have compiled information comparing Conservative supporters with constituency members, the latter category being broken down into ordinary members, activists and chairmen. The comparison is characterized by a diminishing working-class component (social categories C2, D and E) and an expanding upper-middle-class component (social categories A and B) as one moves up the scale of involvement. The authors refer to this as a filter pattern, with each level more socially exclusive than the last. Branch chairmen, too, fit into the pattern somewhere between activists and constituency chairmen. In terms of education a discrepancy was found between constituency parties in Labour-held and Conservative-held seats: approximately half of constituency chairmen in Conservative-held seats had been to public school whereas less than a quarter in Labour-held seats had enjoyed that privilege; conversely whereas only about 5 per cent of chairmen in Conservative-held seats had been to elementary school only, the comparable figure for

Labour-held seats was 25 per cent. It needs only to be added that the overwhelming majority of chairmen (94 per cent in 1969) were male, though recent evidence suggests that this position is changing substantially.

As in the parliamentary party so in the constituencies, the influence and participation of local aristocrats and landowners, and of substantial businessmen, has declined. In prewar days these people had virtually employed the local agent and generally provided the funds for the constituency's activities. Nowadays leadership in the local associations concerns skills and know-how rather than money. Butler and Pinto Duschinsky conclude: 'They are normally well-established, respectable professionals – solicitors, accountants, executives and proprietors of small and medium-sized companies. But they are a different breed from the landowners and business magnates who controlled many associations before the war.'

Ideologically speaking constituency activists tend to be right-wing almost by definition. Some older activists regard their membership as one of the few forms of patriotic duty still open to them but some younger and middle-aged people see the local association as a vehicle for the pursuit of their own self-interest; directly, in the form of making useful business contacts in the community, and indirectly, in the sense of helping to return a government which might be expected to create the kind of conditions in which their businesses might flourish. There is in the constituencies a deeply ingrained loyalty to the party leader which is almost entirely absent in the Labour party. One MP suggested that a poll amongst activists in early 1975 would have found more than three-quarters enthusiastic about Heath's leadership; an even higher proportion, he added, would promptly have supported Thatcher after she supplanted Heath in the leadership contest.

Several Conservative MPs have expressed deep anxiety about the ideological composition of some local association leaderships. 'There are a fair number of constituency parties in the commuter belt which are run by peole who, frankly, might quite properly be labelled neo-fascists', said one. Another described some constituencies in the Home Counties as 'simply nightmarish'. 'What concerns me', said another, 'is that with the kind of robust "call-a-spade-a-spade" leadership that the party has now, all sorts of class and racial prejudices, which had always been there in some constituencies, locked away in the cupboard under the stairs, is now coming out into the open – and we could do without it.' These comments are impressionistic, but they are, after all, the impressions of knowledge-able constituency MPs. Moreover, the party itself has become concerned about the activities in the constituencies of certain fringe groups, such as Tory Action.[35] This is an extreme right-wing group headed by George Kennedy Young which comprises activists and (it claims) about two dozen MPs. It is a rather shadowy body, membership of which is by invitation only. The group is active in candidate selection and tries to imitate the tactics of the far left in the Labour movement. It infiltrates, it encourages constituencies to propose model motions for debate at the annual party conference, and so on. It has had its successes, claiming six of the 1983 intake of MPs; certainly it managed to get immigration debated at the 1983 conference in an atmosphere which, leaders felt, reflected little credit on the party.

Philip Tether has examined in detail the structure of the local party in the city of Kingston upon Hull.[36] He argues that local parties provide a framework for aspirations which are only tangentially connected to politics. Tether distinguishes two levels of membership, the total and the visible. The first comprises all who pay a subscription, the second is restricted to activists and comprises, in the constituencies he looked at, between twenty and fifty members (though in more successful constituencies the figure would be substantially greater). He continues: 'The party is seen by much of this visible membership as a social organization. It serves the function of a social club for a limited type of clientele – middle-aged to elderly, predominantly female but not exclusively so and completely middle-class in origin.' This visible membership sets the tone of the association. 'They tend to regard the party proprietorially since they are all long-established members. Membership of the group is by co-option through evolution . . . '[37] The social goals which this group set up are straightforward: the maintenance of an agreeable and congenial coterie and the domination of the organiza-tion of all social events. The status goals of the 'visibles' are provided by office, which is seen as confirmation of local social prestige. Office thus becomes personalized and is granted not by election but by acclamation, and any elective challenge would be seen in personal terms, not policy terms.

In this environment, says Tether, recruitmentof new members and the maintaining of the existing membership tend to be given low priority. 'There are clearly grave dangers for the party in areas like Hull', he concludes, 'if it relies on the "social shell" theory of mobilization. The "social shell" thesis is probably applicable in safe seats where the electorate needs, and expects, only minimal servicing. It may be adequate in marginal seats where the importance of public goals is permanently on view . . . It is certainly not adequate in hostile seats where – if Hull is anything to go by – it merely facilitates the retreat from public goals and encourages the complete privatization of the local party.'[38]

Tether emphasizes the point that local associations differ one from another, but his comments on the personalization, or what he calls 'privatization', are clearly applicable to all but the best-organized and most active of constituencies. One final point on constituency activists. Tether highlights the importance of women in the local structure, though we have established that they do not normally hold the chair. A number of MPs have also emphasized the role of women. One explained that the housewife whose children were no longer a full-time responsibility was an invaluable asset to the local party, the more so since, in his words, 'if you get the woman you'll often get the husband too'. Constituency parties are beginning to notice, though, that women in this category are becoming rarer as more of them return to full-time employment; the work of some local associations is beginning to suffer.

The third and final category of Conservative that we need to consider is the voter. The relationship between class and voting has been clear enough at least since 1945 with the middle and upper-middle classes tending to vote Conservative and the working class and the very poor tending to vote Labour. Further, support for the Conservatives has been strongest in the upper-middle class (about 75 percent) and the further down the middle-class the less substantial becomes Conservative support, though these voters are more important because there are many more of them, and many tend to be located in the more marginal constituencies.[39]

Even with this substantial middle-class vote, the Conservatives, to secure election, need the support of a sizeable number of working-class voters. That they have managed this so frequently since universal male suffrage was granted has been described as 'one grand historical paradox'.[40] It is instructive to consider why it should be considered paradoxical for working-class voters to support the Conservatives: the answer is, of course, the relationship between class and voting. But it is important to bear in mind that the relationship cannot logically be established to be causal and is a long way from being exact: we cannot be certain that class *determines* voting at all. In fact the generalization 'class determines voting' (which more accurately should state 'class and voting are related') has never been much more than 70 per cent accurate, and no predictive theory which is wrong about every third time can be taken too seriously. To call the working-class Conservative vote a paradox makes little sense and indeed may be considered somewhat patronizing. Paradox or not, however, the working-class Conservative has always been of interest to the political sociologists who have sought to explain such 'deviant behaviour'. Three theories have been developed in this attempt, those of deference, embourgeoisement and generation cohort.

The theory of deference argues that a number of working-class voters see the Conservatives as the 'natural rulers of Britain – sensitive to her traditions and peculiarities and uniquely qualified to govern by birth, experience and outlook.'[41] Deference theory also speaks of a second category of working-class Conservatives who have a more pragmatic motivation: the Conservatives' record is deemed to show that they are better able than their opponents to run the country. The first category of voters has been called 'deferential' and the second 'secular'; moreoever, although the first category could be relied upon, the second had to be persuaded. According to McKenzie and Silver the second category was younger, larger and growing. This theory has been criticized on the grounds that it describes but does not explain the phenomenon: there are a number of middle-class deferentials and a number of working-class voters who defer to Conservative leadership in much the manner described but vote Labour all the same. Other factors must be at work.

The second theory, generated by the Conservative victories of the 1950s, held that as workers' disposable incomes rose, so they acquired more middle-class attitudes amongst which was support for the Conservatives. According to this, the theory of embourgeoisement, the better-off sections of the working-class were simply becoming middle-class, or bourgeois. This thesis,[42] which was not without influence on the Labour leadership, was generally held to have been discredited by Labour's electoral victories of the 1960s. Yet even the elections of the 1950s, when analysed in detail, show the theory to be less than wholly convincing, for the working-class Conservative voters were by no means exclusively the better-off.

The third and most recent explanation of working-class Conservatism is that of the generation cohort. 'Given the extent to which party loyalties are transmitted in the childhood home', say Butler and Stokes, 'time was needed for historic attachements to the "bourgeois parties" to weaken and for "secondary" processes to complete the realignment by class.'[43] This theory has an obvious potential for self-destruction: if the working-class Conservative vote did not decrease with the years, the theory would have demonstrated its own fallacy. As it was, the elections of the 1960s and 1970s seemed to corroborate the theory but wholesale working class defections to the Conservatives in 1979, 1983 and 1987 seem to have proved it fallacious. Moreover, in the 1983 general election, of the 18–24 age group 42 percent voted Conservative and 33 percent voted Labour[44]. In short, there has been no sign whatever of the permanent collapse of the working-class vote; quite the reverse in fact.

Perhaps we should not regard the working-class Conservative vote as a paradox at all, but as a rational appraisal of self-interest. The lives of a considerable number of people have been changed by totally different patterns of consumption, by social mobility, greater educational opportunities, and so on. This may have led not necessarily to voting Conservative (à la embourgeoisement theory) but to voting instrumentally. When he led the Labour party Harold Wilson actually targeted these instrumental voters by presenting his party and its policies as theirs, and with considerable success, though Labour failed to sustain their allegiance. Instrumental voting is no less, though no more, rational an activity than any other in which ordinary people engage and is by no means paradoxical. Many working-class people, whilst not racist, may feel that large-scale immigration poses a threat to their traditional way of life; though not Draconian, may have come to believe that tougher measures need to be taken in the field of law and order; whilst not prudish, may have come to the conclusion that the permissive society has undermined moral standards. In 1979 and 1983, as Boyson indicated, only one major party promised to redress the balance in these fields; it is hardly paradoxical that many working-class men and women voted Conservative. In 1987 Labour directed its strategy to law and order and other inner-city issues, thus managing more realistically (and successfully) to promote itself as the party of the workers.

Instrumental voting is by no means confined to the working class, neither is it the only characteristic of that group. It is, in fact, another dimension of the process to which Crewe, Sarlvik and Alt have referred as partisan dealignment: that is, the erosion of the class–party correlation.[45] This is a general development, well documented by the authors, in which voters are seen to be less and less tied by traditional party loyalties. The Conservatives were the chief recipients of most of these votes in 1979 but in 1983 and 1987 had to share them with the Alliance parties. If we are right to consider these votes largely instrumental then they are clearly not the Conservative party's as of right; the party must prove its ability to 'deliver the goods'. Of course there have always been instrumental voters amongst the so-called floating voters; what is new is the growth of the dealigned, instrumental vote. 1987 produced a similar picture, with Labour losing three London seats together with two southern seats and winning only two others. In the North only one non-Labour MP represents a constituency in Liverpool, Manchester or Newcastle. In Scotland the Conservatives were reduced to a rump of ten seats.

Moving, finally, from the general to the specific, let us look at the Conservative vote in the 1980s. It comprises around 60 per cent of the managerial and professional groups (though only 55 per cent in 1983), that is, social classes A, B and C1; about 40 per cent of the skilled working-class, social class C2, and between 30 and 35 per cent of the unskilled working-class and the poor, that is social classes D and E. These social differences may also be expressed geographically. In 1979 the Conservatives won 146 of the 193 seats in the south of England (compared to 127 out of 189 in 1970) whilst losing support in the north. In 1983 this apparent re-emergence of 'two nations' was reinforced: the Conservatives won no fewer than 183 of the 186 seats south of a line from the Wash to the Severn (excluding London) whereas there were swings to Labour in the northern cities. The net result of this trend was a voting pattern (when adjusted to a 50 : 50 ratio) of 61.4 per cent Conservative support and 38. 6 per cent Labour support in southern Britain – what Butler and Kavanagh[46] refer to as Tory Britain – and exactly the reverse of this in what they refer to as Labour Britain (Inner London, the former West Midlands Metropolitan County, the North of England and Scotland). This division, replicated almost exactly in 1987, was considered by some commentators to have become permanent; perhaps so, but it should not be thought of as new. The Conservative party has traditionally been the party of the south, with sometimes as many as 80 per cent of its MPs representing southern constituencies. What is new, however, is the extent of the polarization.

If the Conservative party, in parliament and the constituencies, can be said to be the party of the 'haves', Conservative voters cannot be classified so easily. Not only have the Conservatives traditionally secured the majority of their votes from the working class but, in 1979 and again in 1983 and 1987, they actually secured more than half of the working-class vote. Norton and Aughey feel sufficiently confident to conclude that conservatism 'can be seen as the articulation of the interests not only of those who benefit from the present institutional structure and who wish to preserve the privileges they derive from the status quo, but also those who prefer, despite not having these privileges, what is known and predictable in the present system, and who believe that this is how things should be'.[47]

No doubt there is much in what Norton and Aughey say. We have seen, too, something more positive at work: a response by the party, natural and traditional if Boyson is to be believed, to 'populist-authoritarian issues'. But what must not be forgotten, especially bearing in mind electoral volatility, is that a very substantial number of Conservative voters of all classes – no less than 48 per cent in 1983 – are motivated primarily by the fear of a Labour victory; in 1983 only 40 per cent of Conservative voters actually 'liked the Conservatives'[48].

Notes

1 Martin Burch and Michael Moran, 'Who are the new Tories?', *New Society*, 11 October 1984.
2 Colin Mellors, *The British M.P.* (Farnborough, Saxon house, 1978).
3 Ibid., p. 39.
4 Ibid., p. 71.
5 Ibid.
6 *Interim and Final Reports of the Committee on Party Organization* (London, National Union of Conservative and Unionist Associations, 1949), pp. 13–14.
7 Quoted in J. F. S. Ross, *Parliamentary Representation* (London, Eyre and Spottiswoode, 1948), pp. 236–38.
8 David Butler and Michael Pinto-Duschinsky, 'The Conservative elite, 1918–78: does unrepresentativeness matter?' in Z. Layton Henry (ed.), *Conservative Party Politics* (London, Macmillan, 1980), pp. 186–209.
9 Michael Rush, 'The selectorate revisited: selecting party candidates in the 1980s', *Teaching Politics*, 15, no. 1 (January 1986), pp. 99–114.
10 David Thomas, 'The new Tories', *New Society*, 2 February 1984.
11 Ibid.
12 Martin Burch and Michael Moran, 'The changing British political elite', *Parliamentary Affairs*, 38, no. 1 (Winter 1985), pp. 1–15.
13 Quoted by Ronald Butt, *Sunday Times*, 16 October 1977.
14 Burch and Moran, 'The changing British political elite'.
15 See W. J. Guttsman, *The British Political Elite* (London, MacGibbon and Kee, 1963).
16 Ibid., p. 196.
17 *Observer*, 10 February 1985.
18 See Robert Blake, *The Conservative Party From Peel To Churchill* (London, Eyre & Spottiswoode, 1972), pp. 200–201.
19 *Observer*, 22 May 1983.
20 See Andrew Roth, *Parliamentary Profiles* (London, Parliamentary Profile Services, 1984).
21 *Observer*, 10 February 1985.
22 Rhodes Boyson develops this point at length in *Centre Forward* (London, Temple Smith, 1978).
23 Ivor Crewe and Bo Sarlvik, 'Popular Attitudes and Electoral Strategy', in Layton-Henry, *Conservative Party Politics*, pp. 244–75.
24 Ibid., p. 272.
25 Sir Alfred Sherman, *The Guardian*, 11 February 1985.
26 *The Guardian*, 15 November 1985.
27 Butler and Pinto-Duschinsky, 'The Conservative elite'.
28 Ibid.

29 *Today*, 14 August 1986.
30 *The Guardian*, 5 December 1984.
31 *The Guardian*, 7 December 1984.
32 *The Guardian*, 9 February 1983.
33 Quoted by Michael Jones, *Sunday Times*, 19 May 1985.
34 Butler and Pinto-Duschinsky, 'The Conservative elite', p. 196.
35 See Michael Cockerell, 'Maggie's militant tendency', *The Listener*, 2 February 1985.
36 Philip Tether, 'Kingston upon Hull Conservative party: a case study of a Tory party in decline', Hull Papers in Politics, no. 19, December 1980.
37 Ibid., p. 5.
38 Ibid., p. 37.
39 Richard Rose, 'Voting behaviour in Britain 1945–74', in *Studies in British Politics*, 3rd edn (London, Macmillan 1976) pp. 208–9.
40 David Butler and Donald Stokes, *Political Change in Britain*, 2nd edn (London, Macmillan, 1974) p. 181.
41 R. McKenzie and A. Silver, *Angels in Marble* (London, Heinemann, 1968), p. 242.
42 Usually associated with Mark Abrams et al., *Must Labour Lose?* (Harmondsworth, Penguin, 1960).
43 Butler and Stokes, *Political Changes in Britain*, p. 185.
44 David Butler and Dennis Kavanagh, *The British General Election of 1983* (London, Macmillan, 1984). In 1987 however there was a six per cent swing to Labour.
45 I. Crewe, B. Barrington and J. Alt, 'Partisan dealignment in Great Britain 1964–74', *British Journal of Political Science*, 7, no 2 (April 1977).
46 Butler and Kavanagh, *The British General Election of 1983*, appendix 2.
47 Norton and Aughey, *Conservatives and Conservatism* (London, Temple Smith, 1981), p. 175.
48 Butler and Kavanagh, *The British General Election of 1983*, p. 293.

5   What Is Socialism?

Superficially the problem of dating the origins of British socialism seems easier than that of dating the origins of conservatism. The word 'socialist' was used for the first time, we are told, in November 1827 when Robert Owen's *Co-Operative Magazine* advanced the principle that co-operation was superior to competition and that consequently capital should be 'socially' owned. Arguments over forms of ownership, though, were by no means new. Perhaps people have always looked back to a golden age when all property was held in common. Certainly if we are to understand the nature of the desire for equality which this nostalgia implies and which is universally recognized as fundamental to the ideology of socialism we shall have to begin earlier than 1827. Much earlier. The early Christians, we are told in the Acts of the Apostles, sold their goods and shared the proceeds among the community according to need. Later, as the earthly power and wealth of the popes grew, so many religious orders sought to rediscover the egalitarian values of the early Church. Prominent among these were the Franciscans, over one hundred of whom were burned at the stake during the fourteenth century because some of their supporters had begun to 'expropriate the expropriators'. Some, it seems, had always believed that equality was the proper condition of life and that land and wealth should be communally owned. From time to time this belief would appear as a political phenomenon, as with the Franciscans, for example, or with the Peasants' Revolt in 1381, or with the various millennarian movements associated with the English Civil War such as the Diggers and the Levellers. What these movements had in common was a strong moralistic and religious content, based largely on the teaching of Christ, and summed up by John Ball, a hedge priest in William Morris's story of the

Peasants' Revolt,[1] who asked piercingly:

> When Adam dalf and Eve span
> Who was then a gentilman?

And so when the socialist thinkers and activists of the nineteenth century attacked the existing divisions within society they were using not only newly fashioned economic arguments about capitalism but moral arguments of great force and pedigree.

Socialism seemed particularly appropriate to the nineteenth century because of the enormous changes to the structure of society which had occurred during and just before that century. The traditional way of life based upon the village community was swept away because it impeded agricultural productivity and nursed inefficiencies. The English peasantry, quite simply, all but disappeared as a class (the Scottish crofters suffering a similar fate) and individuals and families were forced to emigrate or to migrate to areas of growing urban squalor. Thus the traditional belief in some past golden age took on a new poignancy well captured in the poetry and prose of Wordsworth and Coleridge.[2] The dominant relationship between men became in Carlyle's phrase a 'cash nexus' in which the interests of one class, the owning class, could only be maximized at the expense of the other, the labouring class. Land enclosure was in the interests of the owners and against that of the labourers; new machinery was in the interests of the owners and against that of the labourers. The labourers sought to safeguard their perceived interests by smashing the machines, and gangs of so-called Luddites roamed the North and the Midlands of England intent upon destruction. The owning class sought to use the power of the state to protect its interests and so the breaking of machines became an offence punishable by death. In 1813 eighteen Luddites died on the gallows at York.

These massive problems of dislocation were exacerbated by two further factors: the demobilization of Wellington's army after the defeat of the French and the spread of the revolutionary ideas which had set France aflame in 1789. But the dangers of violent insurrection began to subside and the government to act with greater discrimination, thus encouraging agitation to take a more political form.

In 1816 Cobbett launched his radical journal *The Political Register* which, along with other organs of radical opinion, began to shape working-class opinion into movements for parliamentary reform. Others sought to organize on an industrial basis – Lancashire textile workers struck in 1818, for example. Finally Robert Owen and others sought to organize the workers into co-operative ventures such as his New Lanark Mills. But by far the most significant working-class movement of this period was that of the Chartists, described by Lenin as the first 'broad and politically organized proletarian-revolutionary movement of the masses'. Briefly, the Chartists got their name from a six-point charter of political reform but they pursued two lines of strategy which were not effectively integrated, 'moral force' Chartism led by men like Attwood and 'physical force' Chartism led by O'Connor. On three occasions (in 1840, 1842 and 1848) huge petitions in support of the charter were organized and taken to parliament. On the last occasion so strong was the fear of violence that thousands of special constables were enlisted in London, among them the future Emperor Napoleon III. The petition, containing thousands of fraudulent signatures, was handed over without incident and the movement faded thereafter.

In what sense may these nineteenth-century movements be regarded as socialist? We have seen that the word 'socialist' was in use, though it cannot be claimed to have had wide currency. They may be regarded as socialist primarily for two reasons: they were egalitarian in aspiration and they were working class in membership, both important characteristics of British socialism. They were also failures, and socialism in however partial a form ceased to feature in British political debate for approximately thirty years, as the working and living conditions of the urban poor began slowly to improve. But if the 'hungry forties' soon faded into the memory they were to be replaced before long in the popular imagination by the 'hungry seventies' and socialism, too, in a more clearly defined form, was to reappear.

The anarchist Prince Kropotkin was of the opinion that the individual principally responsible for the re-emergence and popularity of socialism was an American land reformer named Henry George. Properly speaking George was not a socialist at all but his highly successful lecture tours of Britain and even more successful pamphlet *Progress and Poverty*[3] were instrumental in encouraging the establishment of political groups which were soon to become overtly socialist. George was also instrumental in creating a general climate conducive to the growth of socialist ideas. The intellectuals who were drawn to George's theories and who joined one of the many groups which formed to discuss them were soon introduced to another writer of far greater erudition and analytical skill, Karl Marx, though his work was not available in English until 1886. Men and women of genuine intellectual stature, such as H. M. Hyndman, William Morris, Bernard Shaw, Sidney and Beatrice Webb, Annie Besant and Graham Wallas, were drawn towards socialism in one of its many forms. They shared to varying degrees a distaste for contemporary social and political arrangements, a disenchantment with mainstream liberalism and a sympathetic understanding of Marx's economic analysis.

During this period four avowedly socialist groups grew up. First was was the Social Democratic Federation (SDF) which had begun in 1881 as the Democratic Federation. It developed as a marxist group and was dominated by H. M. Hyndman, the best known of the early British marxists.[5] The SDF sought parliamentary representation, to the extent even of fighting a by-election (unsuccessfully) against the Liberals in 1895 with clandestine financial support from the Conservative party (the so-called Tory gold scandal). Second was a break-away group known as the Socialist League (SL), founded in 1886 by William Morris, Marx's son-in-law Aveling, and Belfort Bax. Anti-parliamentarian, anti-authoritarian, the SL quickly acquired a reputation for anarchism and when, in 1891, Morris withdrew to form the Hammersmith Socialist Society, the SL disintegrated into factions. The influence of the SL was slight, that of the Hammersmith Socialist Society considerably greater; but Morris's personal influence was always substantial. One of his 'converts' was the journalist Robert Blatchford whose Clarion movement, based primarily on a newspaper of that name, flourished in the North of England. Blatchford wrote a tract called *Merrie England*,[6] addressed to a symbolic John Smith of Oldham. It was said with justice if not precision that for every convert Marx brought to socialism in Britain Blatchford brought 50,000: 'the most effective propagandist of socialism that England had produced'.[7]

The third group was the Fabian Society, taking its title from the Roman general Fabius Cunctator whose characteristic tactic was to refuse to give battle until he was certain to win. The Fabian began to develop in an expressly political way in 1884. Among its earliest members was one of the foremost polemicists and propagandists of the age, the playwright Bernard Shaw, and he soon introduced his friend Sidney Webb, the future Labour cabinet minister. Intellectually the Fabian was the most influential of the socialist groups, but it always abstemiously avoided a large membership, preferring to see itself as an intellectual vanguard.[8]

The fourth of the groups, founded in 1877 by Stuart Headlam, was the Guild of St Matthew. The guild represented the involvement of the churches in socialist politics. It has often been said that British socialism owed more to Methodism than to marxism but in fact churchmen of all denominations – Headlam himself was an Anglican – were very active in the socialist movement.

This, then, was the intellectual foundation of British socialism. The popular foundation was provided by the trade union movement. During the 1880s unions representing unskilled workers such as the match makers, the gas workers and the dockers undertook successful strike action, thus increasing the confidence of the labour movement generally. Union representatives, moreover, were standing for parliament, the miners (who took the Liberal parliamentary whip) being highly successful. In 1893 a meeting was called at Bradford of trade unionists and representatives of the socialist societies specifically to advance the parliamentary representation and political visibility of labour. The result was the establishment of a group whose task would be to co-ordinate support for labour parliamentary candidates and for socialism generally (though the word was not actually used): the group was known as the Independent Labour party (ILP). The founding of the ILP did not lead to greater ideological cohesion among affiliated groups, neither did it lead to great parliamentary successes, but it was a step in the right direction.

The next step was the creation in 1900 of the Labour Representation Committee, which sought to establish a cohesive unit in parliament, thereby acknowledging the socialists' acceptance of parliament as their main sphere of activity.[9] The Chartists had not sought parliamentary power for the obvious reason that the working classes of the day were not enfranchised; but by the turn of the century the working-class man had the vote; indeed working-class men had already been elected to the House of Commons.[10] The unions, moreover, had made provision for financial support for LRC candidates.[11] These factors tended to reinforce the natural disposition of those who claimed to speak for the British working class to opt for parliamentary influence and not popular agitation, which was never used as a strategy by the LRC or the broader labour movement. The choice was a conscious one, as is illustrated by Keir Hardie's definition of labourism (not socialism) as the 'theory and practice which accepted the possibility of social change within the existing framework of society; which rejected the revolutionary violence and action implicit in Chartist ideas of physical force; and which increasingly recognised the working of political democracy of the parliamentary variety as the practical means of achieving its own aims and objectives'.[12]

So the LRC was precisely what its title implied: a body dedicated to enlarging labour, not specifically socialist, representation at Westminster. The LRC was an alliance between the 'new unionism' (representing generally the less skilled) and the socialist societies who by now numbered, chiefly, three – the ILP, the SDF and the Fabian. As Coates points out, 'from the beginning the Labour Party was a coalition, in which the socialist wing was a minority'.[13] Most historians of the Labour party agree that any formal commitment to socialist policies at this time, especially if they might involve or envisage extra-parliamentary pressure, would have caused a breach in the alliance. It is probably being rather coy, anyway, to imagine that even the socialist societies could have managed to agree to a socialist programme, let alone sell such a programme to their trade union colleagues. As one of H. G. Wells's characters remarked: 'To understand socialism . . . is to gain a new breadth in outlook; to join a socialist organization is to join a narrrow cult.'[14]

It was the electoral pact with the Liberals which occasioned the electoral successes of 1906. Prior to the pact only two candidates had been successful in the 1900 general election, though three by-electoral successes had followed in the next two years. But in 1906 each of the LRC's leading figures was elected – Hardie, MacDonald, Henderson, Snowden and Clynes. The decision of the Miners' Federation in 1909 to take the Labour whip and join what in 1906 had become the Labour party was decisive. In the two elections of 1910 the party returned forty and then forty-two members. It would be a mistake, though, to believe that by 1910 the Labour party had 'arrived'. Although it played a useful role in the repeal of anti-union legislation and supported the Liberals' welfare legislation it was hardly a major force; moreover, in the period between 1910 and the first world war it lost five seats in by-elections. In short, far from having 'arrived', the prewar Labour party represented, in Coates's words, an 'expression of trade union aspirations which involved no coherent programme and no officially accepted socialist commitment'.[15]

And yet within ten years a Labour government was in office. It is possible to ascribe this reversal of fortune to the party's own efforts, as Coates does; to accept with him and Arthur Henderson that 'some sort of socialist faith' was essential to establish the Labour party as the militant class party that Coates feels was appropriate to the post-1918 world. Yet it is only possible to do this if we ignore the Liberal party. Labour's greatest advantage after 1918, surely, was the irreparable split within the Liberal party; Labour's strength after 1918 was, paradoxically, its weakness before. It was too peripheral to be rent by major schisms or personality clashes, too unimportant to feel obliged to empty the pockets of its conscience publicly in the search for justifications for conscription as did the Liberals in 1916. The party survived the war intact; the Liberals, despite (or perhaps because of) Lloyd George's dominance, survived it in tatters.

So far we have explored the origins of the idea of equality, the growth of working-classs and 'socialist' – or what Hardie called 'labourist' – movements during the early part of the nineteenth century, and gone on to discuss the political development of organized trade unionism and the rise of the socialist groups. We have not yet fully examined the ideology of socialism. In 1918 the Labour party felt obliged to state systematically for the first time what it meant by socialism and so it is appropriate at this point that we turn our attention more directly to the ideology of socialism.

Until the fierce internal disputes which shook the Labour party in the late 1970s, there could be little doubt that socialism had won the war of ideologies. Conservatives were apologetic, admitting that conservatism was not really an ideology at all, merely an attitude of mind. Socialism, by contrast, was coherent and certain. It might be argued that such-and-such a Labour politician was not 'really a socialist' but at least we knew, or thought we knew, what he was being measured against. Now nobody is so sure. When we examine the development of socialism closely, though, we see that in fact nobody was ever sure, and a whole industry evolved around the definition and redefinition of socialism.

What all seem agreed on is the key notion of equality, but differences existed in the kind of equality to be achieved and in the manner in which it was to be achieved. The fundamentalist socialist endorses a programme aimed at creating equality by abolishing capitalism through public ownership. His/her aim is to break up the existing state, though not necessarily by violence, and to reconstitute it so that all its assets are communally owned and equally distributed. The social democrat, on the other hand (the phrase is not meant to suggest any connection with the modern party of that name), is concerned chiefly to create equality by alleviating poverty. His/her policies entail a humane concern for the underprivileged but nothing so ambitious as the desire to reconstitute social relations. So far so good, but back now to equality itself. Equality may be taken to refer to material conditions; thus income, education, health, housing, and so on should be available to all at the same level. But equality might also be taken to refer to power: that each should have an equal say in the decisions affecting his/her life. Now amongst the early socialist groups that we looked at, the Socialist League and especially its leader William Morris could be said to favour equality of power. We may refer to these as moralistic socialists because their belief that men and women ought to control their own lives constitutes a moral position. The moralist tradition seeks to allow wider scope to individuals to take part in the decisions affecting their lives, holding that this can only be done in a fundamental-egalitarian society:[16] that is, one in which power as well as material rewards and opportunites are shared. The Fabians, on the other hand, were perfectly convinced that the underprivileged would be incapable of creating and running a state in which power was shared equally. 'If you ask me', said Bernard Shaw, ' "Why can't the people make their own laws?" I shall answer, "Why can't the people write their own plays?".' The socialism of the Fabians we may call scientific because it held that the state had to be controlled in the interests of all by a scientifically trained elite (hence the Webbs' founding of the London School of Economics and Political Science). The scientific tradition holds that government is a specialized task which must be undertaken by a minority or elite on behalf of the majority. It demands the application of scientific techniques to social and political problems. It attacks the wastes and inefficiencies of capitalist society and believes that a centrally controlled socialist state run by a scientifically trained elite would be capable of maximizing welfare for all.

So, we may speak of four kinds of socialist: the moralistic fundamentalist, the scientific fundamentalist, the moralistic social democrat and the scientific social democrat. In fact, because the social democrats were less ambitious in their objectives and less ideological in their pronouncements, the differences between moral-istic and scientific social democrats could for the most part be ignored. The characteristic quality of the social democrat was his/her moderation. British socialism, then, has from its inception been an uneasy alliance between the social democrats and the fundamental-ists, themselves subdivided between the moralist and scientific traditions. The resultant tensions are by no means unique to British socialism. Indeed, according to R. N. Berki, socialism is never and nowhere a 'single thing, but a range, an area, an open texture, a self-contradiction'.[17]

Before we return to the Labour party it is necessary to say something about marxist socialism, for although Marx's influence has been far less significant on British than on continental socialism, any analysis of British socialism which omitted Marx would be incomplete. One concept that Marx made common currency among socialists was alienation. Man, says Marx, is unique among animals in that his self-consciousness takes in the whole species: man is a species being. But under capitalism he is prevented from living as a species being, his consciousness being limited by social divisions (i.e. classes). Man also has a species activity, labour. To find fulfilment man must 'objectify' his labour in an end product (that is, he must produce a solid object). But under capitalism the worker has no control over the product of his labour, especially in a mode of production which divides labour for specialized tasks. Thus the product of man's labour is independent of its creator and in fact comes to dominate him. What a man helps to make becomes more important than what he is. Thus man becomes alienated from the fruit of his labour, alienated from the activity of labour and alienated from his fellow beings, especially from the exploiters of his labour. And the dominating feature of the system which holds men together is capital; men exist only to further the interests of capital.

Why not throw off the capitalist yoke without delay? Here we come to Marx's second major contribution to socialist thought: the concept of false consciousness. As Marx declares: 'It is not the consciousness of men that determines their existence, but their social existence which determines their consciousness.'[18] And what determines man's social existence? The 'relations of production' (that is, the way economic life is organized, especially property relations). This relationship is the foundation, what Marx called 'the base', of all social and political relations; all other institutions and ideas are dependent, part of what Marx called 'the superstructure'. Now, since the relations of production are dominated by the capitalist class it follows that the institutions which help to shape people's attitudes, such as the education system, the churches, the mass media, and so on, are also dominated by the values of the capitalist class. Most people's ideas, then, are the 'ideas of the ruling class'[19] whose true purpose is to perpetuate that class's dominance.

So the workers live in a state of false consciousness, knowing that theirs is a life of poverty and hardship but believing this to be inevitable. Marx did not develop this concept of false consciousness as fully as did later marxists, especially the Italian Gramsci,[20] but its importance is clearly central, especially for British socialists who had to contend with a passive and accepting working class. This is the theme of Robert Tressell's socialist novel *The Ragged Trousered Philanthropists*[21] which captures vividly the attitude of pre-1914 workers who argue: 'It can't never be altered . . . There's always been rich and poor in the world, and there always will be.' The philanthropists of the title are the workers themselves who willingly give their birthright to the owning class, content to live cocooned in their false consciousness.

But this state of affairs would not continue for ever, because, according to Marx, a proletarian revolution would inevitably occur, and this is the next concept which we need to explore. Why was the proletarian revolution inevitable? We need look no further than the opening sentence of the *Communist Manifesto* to discover a clue: 'The history of all hitherto existing society is the history of class struggles.' For Marx and his collaborator Engels the nature of this struggle resides in the inevitable emergence of a contradiction between the factors whose relationship constitutes 'the base': the productive forces and the mode of production. We have already considered the latter; productive forces are simply the processes and tools or machines used in manufacture. Now, the inevitable contradiction between the two occurs because although the productive forces develop continuously and sometimes rapidly, as modern industrial processes clearly show, the mode of production becomes rigid and increasingly inappropriate to the changing productive forces. The resulting dislocations tend to be disastrous for the workforce and so the contradiction must be resolved by struggle: the class struggle which characterizes historical development.

According to Marx the value of any commodity can only be

measured in terms of the labour bound up in it, which he calls 'abstract labour'. The interests of the capitalists inevitably conflict with those of the workers, for the capitalists must restrict the worker to a subsistence wage in order to make a profit. Moreover, as a consequence of the intensity of competition, capital concentrates in fewer and fewer hands. This leads to falling profits, the growing misery of the proletariat and the heightening of class divisions. Any groups trapped between the two antagonistic classes would join the proletarian camp, leading to – at last! – a growth of 'true' consciousness among the workers. From this growth would come the forces of proletarian revolution.

But who would lead the revolution? Marx believed that the proletariat could hardly manage such a grand objective without leadership, and here we come to consider somewhat briefly our last concept, that of the 'dictatorship of the proletariat'. This is not a concept which Marx himself set out with any precision, though it has played a dominant part in the theories of many marxists since. For Marx there would have to be a transitional stage between the overthrow of capitalism and the establishment of communism. After all, the existing state whose express purpose was to protect the interests of the bourgeoisie would need to be destroyed and it was quite clear to Marx that a new society as radically different from anything that had gone before would need a good time to be built up. But when would such a dictatorship end? Marx did not say, but the transitional period would be a long one.

The marxist legacy to socialism is an extremely rich one and we have time only to deal with those aspects directly relevant to present purposes. Its impact on British socialism has been far from unambiguous. Marx's theory of alienation had a profound effect upon what we have called the moralistic fundamentalists, especially William Morris. On the other hand, Marx's emphasis on the scientific management of society had an equally significant influence upon scientific fundamentalists in Britain, especially upon leaders of the SDF like Hyndman, and even on some allegedly moderate Fabians like Bernard Shaw. For the moralist, then, Marx's belief in equality, in revolution and in what was later to be called the 'withering away of the state' made him one of them; the scientists, on the other hand, could simply point out that Marx himself saw his socialism as being scientific and not ideological and, after all, firmly believed in the scientific organization of the economy. Moreover, no moralist could be very happy with the concept of the dictatorship of the proletariat. For their part, most social democrats had little sympathy for Marx whom they generally regarded, and still do regard, as a dangerous romantic.

In contrast to the Conservative party the Labour party is long on ideology and short on history, but we have arrived at the point now where we must turn our attention back to the post-1918 world. It was important, we discovered earlier, for Labour to establish itself as an independent force with an identity separate from the Liberals. Reforms undertaken by the party in 1918 saw the trade union movement rather than the socialist societies becoming the dominant force in party policy-making, both at the annual conference and at the National Executive Committee (NEC) level. Local constituency parties were set up, thus replacing the old ILP branches. The policy that was to be pursued was not one of reconstituting capitalism but of creating a new order; hence the title of the party's policy document *Labour and the New Social Order*. Through this Labour, in Coates's words, 'appealed to the working class electorate for the first time in its history as a socialist party: one, that is, that claimed to be in battle not simply with discrete problems but with a total social *system*'.[22] But Coates would be hard pressed to justify his description of *Labour and the New Social Order* as a 'programme' in any rigorous sense at all. It is true that some specifics were mentioned, such as tax reforms, the nationalization of service industries and the like, but any programme worth its salt would surely have been quite clear exactly how and in what priority these policies would be put into effect. Even the capital levy, said to have struck fear into the middle classes, never really emerged as much more than a shibboleth. Coates himself admits that the programme 'was ambiguous at its very heart'.

In fact in the general election of December 1923 Baldwin's government was returned to office with 259 seats compared to 159 for the Liberals, briefly reunited, and 191 for Labour. Asquith let it be known that the Liberals would not use their votes to keep Baldwin in office nor to deny Labour the right to govern. The prospect of a socialist administration filled many with alarm: red revolution, according to the conservative press, would destroy the army and the civil service. The Duke of Northumberland put the threat in a more general perspective, prophesying the introduction of free love.[23] To others, of course, a Labour government offered the prospect of a new way of life, no less. The Labour party was a working-class party with many working-class leaders uncontaminated by failure.

Baldwin was defeated on a Labour amendment to the king's speech and on 22 January Ramsay MacDonald kissed hands as Britain's first Labour prime minister. To many people's surprise, the sky did not fall in. Although the key cabinet positions went to party stalwarts there was a leavening of experience. The cabinet contained two old-guard Fabians, seven trade unionists (including three ex-miners) but also a former Liberal minister, an ex-Viceroy of India and several middle-class and aristocratic recruits from the two older parties. The new ministry, as Asquith said, constituted no new departure and the great institutions of the state (and indeed the institution of marriage) remained unravaged.

MacDonald's problems were considerable. To maintain a separate identity meant no coalition with the Liberals, no pact, no deal. This still left scope for some informal understanding: after all there was much that the two parties had in common in terms of policy. However, so great were the mutual antagonisms between the leaders that this was not seriously contemplated. Perhaps the Labour leaders believed that if they made a good show of actually administering the nation's affairs and were forced into an election prematurely, the voters would respond by turning on the Liberals. But of course Labour had to do more than this; it had also to convince the fundamentalists (especially the ILP) that it was attempting, within its limited scope, to implement some of the party's socialist programme. In fact each of these objectives was achieved to some degree. First running the country: Haldane, with considerable ministerial experience himself, believed that the cabinet comprised at least six men of 'first-rate administrative ability'.[24] Second, when Labour went to the people in 1924, it was heavily defeated, but the Liberals were totally eclipsed, with only forty MPs. Yes; the voters would turn against the Liberals. Third, the government's major piece of legislation was its budget, described by Roberts as a political master-stroke; Philip Snowden was hailed as a hero by the left.[25] Moreover, the cabinet presided over the establishment of public works schemes, and Wheatley's Housing Act, providing housing for the poor through the local authorities, was also generally popular. Few would suggest that the fundamentalists, especially the militant Clydesiders, were enthusiatic about the government's performance overall but they tolerated it, which is probably as much as could be expected.

The government was brought down finally by a motion of censure on its mishandling of the 'Campbell case', which involved the initiation and then withdrawal of a prosecution for incitement to mutiny of the acting editor of a communist weekly who had urged regular soldiers to lay down their arms. Any hopes of winning an overall majority at the ensuing election were dashed by the Zinoviev letter,[26] which purported to be from a senior Russian leader, calling upon British communists to prepare for armed insurrection. The letter was obligingly published by the conservative *Daily Mail*. MacDonald calculated that no sane voter would take the letter seriously, but he could scarcely have been more wrong. So MacDonald's minority ministry was a short one and in no position to implement fundamentalist policies.

Labour spent five years in opposition. MacDonald maintained his personal dominance over the party despite criticisms from the Clydeside militants, who were acquiring a firm grip on the ILP and turning it into that regular Labour ulcer, the party-within-a-party. But there was no attempt to translate Labour's aspirations into a firm programme for action. True a new recruit to the party, the dashing aristocrat Oswald Mosley, advanced a platform for combating unemployment which drew some support. The ILP, too, had similar proposals. But Mosley was thought by party leaders to be naïve and the ILP proposals were seen as part of a general challenge to MacDonald's leadership. By 1928, though, a new programme *Labour and the Nation* had emerged. If it was more specific than its predecessor, it was no more realistic, with over seventy proposals but no priorities: implementation, according to Attlee, would prove 'nothing short of a miracle'.[27]

For all that, in the 1929 general election Labour won 287 votes to the Conservatives' 260 and formed a minority government for the second time, with the Liberals returning 59 candidates. MacDonald's second spell in Downing Street was to last much longer than the first, though once again there was to be no arrangement of any kind with the Liberals. Unfortunately for the Labour party it was to confront a world slump and a collapse of the international money market which affected all industrial nations and in the face of which it offered nothing more than a conventionally deflationary economic policy. It rejected the Keynesian public works programme of the Liberals and the radical strategy of Mosley. To paraphrase Keynes, the government promised nothing and kept its word. Treasury orthodoxy – no devaluation – together with chancellor Snowden's opposition to protectionism were MacDonald's guiding principles, though none of his advisers could have known what lay ahead. Anticipating a trade deficit in 1931 a deflationary package, based upon massive cuts in public expenditure, the most severe being in unemployment benefit, was discussed in cabinet. The cabinet decided to balance the budget but it could not agree to the proposed cuts; in fact TUC general council declared its oposition to any cuts. A crisis developed. Gold reserves were dwindling rapidly and a foreign loan became a necessity. Such a loan would be granted only on the promise of severe cuts in public expenditure and of course the government could not agree on a package. MacDonald decided to resign but was persuaded by King George V to stay and head a national coalition government instead.[28] The following month MacDonald was expelled from the Labour party and shortly after was fighting a general election against most of his former colleagues. He remained prime minister but the party he had helped so conspicuously to build returned only fifty-two members in the election of 1931.

Critics usually point out that MacDonald had fought unnecessary economic battles because within a year the National government had gone off the gold standard and introduced protection. But what a coalition government with a massive majority can do and what a party government, internally divided and with no majority at all, can do are quite different things. All the same, the government had achieved some successes before its demise. Greenwood's Housing Act of 1930 inaugurated a programme of slum clearances, Addison's Land Utilisation Act helped with the problems of rural unemployment, and the Coal Mines Act provided some sort of *modus vivendi* for miners and owners. A bill to raise the school leaving age was defeated in the House of Lords. But few would say that this second Labour government advanced the socialist cause one jot: the tension between fundamentalism and social democracy had never been resolved because it had never been considered. And now the parliamentary party had been reduced to a rump and the government was dead; dead, as Tawney said, 'neither [from] murder, nor misadventure, but pernicious anaemia . . .'

In how different an atmosphere did the Labour party next come into office! The party's overall majority in the 1945 election was 146. Its leadership was known to the public but was not tainted by the failures of the 1930s. The Labour cabinet was dominated by men with solid ministerial experience, powerful and respected figures from the wartime coalition administration like Attlee himself, Bevin and Morrison; but it contained imaginative appointments too, none more so that the Minister of Health, the mercurial fundamentalist Aneurin Bevan. The war had impoverished Britain, with exports and overseas investments particularly badly hit, and physical destruction of the infrastructure and facilities and buildings of all sorts was widespread. Yet there were also major advantages for Labour. The machinery established during the war to plan and control all major aspects of the nation's economic life was still in existence and people had grown accustomed to it. Investment was controlled by licence, consumer spending severely restrained by rationing and the balance of payments shored up by import controls. This degree of central management was something that early socialists could only have dreamed about. Major programmes of social reform in health, education and housing had been planned by the coalition govern-ment. They were there ready for Labour to amend and implement. These major advantages were buttressed by the goodwill of the majority of the population, who recognized that recovery was dependent upon planning.

A secure platform existed for the implementation of a socialist programme and very soon the Bank of England, coal, electricity, gas and much of inland transport were nationalized. A comprehensive system of insurance, based upon the Beveridge report, was established, the provisions of Butler's Education Act implemented, the minimum school-leaving age raised to fifteen, new controls established over the development of land, a programme of council house building initiated and finally – and probably most important – the establishment in 1948 of a comprehensive health service, free to all at the point of use. In foreign policy the government had taken the first steps towards dismantling the empire by granting independence to India, Burma and Ceylon.

To what extent did this, the most celebrated of Labour governments, resolve successfully the conflicting demands of funda-mentalism and social democracy? The machinery for the central control of the economy was in the hands of the state and most aspects of the nation's public life were planned; most of the major reforms were aimed specifically at improving the quality of life of the citizens. Yet the emphasis of this Labour government was not, as the moralistic fundamentalists would have wished, on providing a framework in which ordinary people could direct their own lives, but on the government's acting on behalf of ordinary people; in George Orwell's terms this socialism was what ' "we", the clever ones, are going to impose upon "them", the lower orders.' The Labour government was pursuing a form of scientific socialism which comprised elements both of fundamentalism and social democracy, resulting in the heavily centralized structure of the nationalized industries. But it is unimaginable that a miner, for example, would have felt that the local pit belonged to him after nationalization. In foreign affairs the dismantling of the empire and the strong support for the United Nations (fundamentalism) was balanced by membership of the North Atlantic Treaty Organization (social democracy) and eventually, with the outbreak of the Korean War, the most costly peacetime rearmaments programme in history. By this time, however, Labour had fought and very narrowly won the 1950 general election and faced many other problems.

The deteriorating economic climate and the rearmaments programme caused the government to increase taxation and to implement charges for spectacles under the supposedly free National Health Service. This was anathema to many fundamentalists as indeed to some social democrats, and it undermined confidence in the party's future. The general public had become tired of scarcity and regimentation, and the government, some of whose leading lights had retired or died, was being harrassed by the opposition in such a way as to make life intolerable. Attlee went to the people and in 1951 Labour's period of office came to an end. Parenthetically, in defeat Labour secured more votes than any party before or since, but the British electoral system gave victory to the Conservatives. Labour leaders must have left office with some anxiety; if Labour could not succeed with the world it inherited in 1945, could it ever succeed? Labour spent thirteen years in opposition and they were years marked by divisions and bitterness. The divisions were generally reported as between the left and centre-right of the party but in reality were rooted in the traditional contradiction. Moralist fundamentalists could not be satisfied with the programme of the previous government; it had not basically shifted the balance of power in society. New and more radical forms of socialization were called for. Popular participation simply could not be provided by any form of nationalization; this was 'state socialism', antithetical to true socialism. Scientific fundamentalists, too, were dismayed that their planning had not been more effective and argued that it had been half-hearted. More nationalization, more control, was the answer. Some scientific social democrats, too, argued for more refined ways of controlling the economy. The new party leader, Gaitskell, basing his case on the writings of Anthony Crosland [29], Richard Crossman[30] and John Strachey,[31] argued that modern industry had produced a new breed of enemies of socialism, managers who did not own the business they managed. This new enemy might be found in state-run industries just as in private industry, so nationalization offered no easy road to socialism. 'The main aim of socialism today', said Crossman, 'is to prevent the concentration of power in the hands of either industrial management or state bureaucracy.' Crosland believed that socialist ideals could more readily be achieved by taxation policy than by further nationalization.

Matters came to a head after Labour's third successive, and heaviest, defeat in 1959. At the party conference of 1960, Gaitskell argued that not to modify the policy on nationalization (embodied in clause four of the constitution) would be to condemn the party to permanent opposition. So began one of the most acrimonious conference debates since the 1930s which was to end in defeat for the social democrats (or revisionists, as they were referred to during this period). In fact Gaiskell was also defeated on another important issue, his (and the executive's) opposition to the policy of unilateral nuclear disarmament. As the next election began to impinge on politicians' thinking, Labour appeared to be a spent force, riven on major issues, indecisively led and pursuing unpopular and outmoded policies.

Within two years the situation had been transformed. Opposition to two government policies brought the party together; Britain's proposed entry into the European Economic Community (EEC) and the 1962 Commonwealth Immigration Act. Party unity was aided by Gaitskell's untimely death and his replacement by Wilson. With considerable acumen, Wilson circumvented the debate concerning the future of socialism, and indeed the whole debate between the fundamentalists and the social democrats, by revamping Robert Owen's faith in science as the panacea. The 'white heat of the technological revolution' would be harnessed; science would be used to create the conditions for the burgeoning of a modern form of socialism which would incorporate the best features of fundamentalism and social democracy. Simply stated, by achieving a rate of

growth in the economy of 20 per cent over a five-year period a
Labour government would transform the lives of all citizens. It was
on this policy that Labour won the 1964 general election, though by
the slender margin of five seats overall.

Simple to state, 20 per cent growth proved more difficult to
achieve. A Department of Economic Affairs was created with the task
of drawing up and implementing a five-year plan. Labour intended
to involve the trade unions and the employers in collaborative
planning with the government, and an early fruit of this policy was
the National Board for Prices and Incomes whose task would be to
examine price increases and wage demands. In 1966 Labour sought
to strengthen its hand by appealing to the electorate again; it was
rewarded with an overall majority just short of a hundred and
returned to its task with new vigour. However, within two months a
seven-week seaman's strike led to a dramatic collapse in the value of
sterling. Once again a Labour government found itself obliged to
introduce a policy of deflation, including a wage and dividend freeze.
The five-year plan was thus effectively torpedoed and the unity
which had existed for four years was severely shaken. And things got
worse. In June 1967 the balance of payments was adversely
influenced by war in the Middle East; soon began a damaging
national dock strike. In November the pound was devalued and
drastic cuts in public expenditure were to follow, including the
reimposition of NHS prescription charges.[32]

However, the government's strategy was not completely destroyed
by any means. An Industrial Reorganization Corporation was
created in 1966 to encourage and assist the restructuring of industry.
The following year iron and steel were renationalized. Welfare
spending increased substantially in real terms and so did the number
of house completions. The government also began to dismantle the
selective system of secondary education, promoting comprehensive
schools and discriminating positively in favour of inner-city schools.
Moreover, Labour sought to improve the lot of the underprivileged
by a new supplementary benefits scheme, by paying family
allowances directly to mothers, by redundancy payments, rate rebate
schemes and new allowances for the long-term sick and disabled.

If these policies mollified fundamentalists within the party,
Wilson's attempted reform of the trade unions did the opposite. The
proposals were unacceptable not only to the unions but also to much
of the parliamentary party and many within cabinet. Wilson

managed to offend the fundamentalists, who saw the proposals as an assault on the working class, and many social democrats who thought them unwise and unnecessary. Wilson was obliged to give way after six months of struggle which, like Gaitskell's attempt to reform clause four, left a legacy of bitterness. However, the government believed that its performance in office would secure it a victory at the polls and in May 1970 parliament was dissolved.

Labour's unexpected defeat led, as ever, to a period of recrimination. Many within the movement believed that the Labour leaders had abandoned fundamentalist socialism entirely for the pragmatic welfare-labourism of the social democrats. In the words of one backbencher, a middle-class Conservative government had been replaced by a working-class conservative government: nothing more. For the social democrat the inability to prevent damaging strikes and to plan effectively (which for some were two sides of the same coin) was a major indictment. Whatever historians may make of its record, most Labour supporters, inside and outside parliament, thought that the Labour government, with its large majority, had failed.

The four years of opposition were characterized by attempts on the part of fundamentalist activists within the parliamentary party and the movement at large to 'democratize' the party structure. The fundamentalists believed that they could prevent the leadership 'betraying' them – as they had so often before – only by capturing the party organization, so that they might exercise some control over the leadership in matters such as drawing up the manifesto, selecting the cabinet and electing the party leader. When the party came back to office it was divided not only on major issues of policy but on the general direction in which the party appeared to be moving. Moreover, the party came to office in the middle of a state of emergency, with British industry working a three-day week and the population experiencing regular power cuts, both being the consequences of the dispute between the Conservative government and the miners over the former's pay policy. Labour's majority in February 1974 was four.

Labour's main electoral strategy had been to present itself as the only party which could manage a modern economy by 'consultation not confrontation' and it quickly instituted a social contract, that is, an understanding with the TUC not only on policies to be pursued but on ways of collaborating in the future. During the summer of 1974 the government outlined the policies it planned to pursue, including devolution of power to Scotland and Wales, the public ownership of development land and greater government involvement in industrial development; on this platform Labour called for another election in October, which it duly won though with an overall majority of only three. The narrowness of its success did not prevent the Labour government under Wilson and then Callaghan from implementing many of its policies, including the establishment of the Advisory, Conciliation and Arbitration Service (ACAS), the National Enterprise Board (NEB) and the British National Oil Corporation (BNOC). A new earnings-related state pension scheme was introduced, the push towards comprehensive schools was intensified and steps were taken to abolish pay beds in the NHS.

Labour might also lay claim to a major constitutional development which extended democracy: the referendum. Referendums were used to decide whether Britain should continue to belong to the EEC and whether certain executive and legislative powers should be devolved to elected assemblies in Scotland and Wales. Imaginative though these referendums seem, what they really indicate is the extent of Labour's internal division on both issues. The party conference and the TUC were opposed to continued membership of the EEC, and so were many MPs including several within the cabinet. The leadership and a substantial part of the party were in favour but knew they could not hope to carry the whole party. By allowing a national referendum and absolving cabinet members from collective responsibility the government secured two objectives: its own survival and continued membership of the EEC. On devolution, Labour needed the support of the Scottish and Welsh nationalist parties to maintain its majority in the House of Commons, but its conversion to devolution was less than total and not widespread. That both the referendum in Scotland and the one in Wales should fail to produce a sufficient majority in favour (in fact in Wales very few were in favour) of devolution was probably the ideal solution for Labour but by that time (1979) its days anyway were numbered.

Labour had been sustained in office for eighteen months by an agreement with the Liberal party in which the latter was formally to be consulted on government policy. However the Liberals' main demand, a government commitment to elections to the European parliament under a proportional system, was not acceded to. From the government's point of view this period of comparative stability helped them to pursue their anti-inflation policies based upon wage constraint negotiated with the TUC. This wage constraint, which was a crucial example of Labour's ability to control the modern economy with union support, finally broke when the government insisted on a wage-rise norm of 5 per cent – the rate of inflation was then in the order of 8 per cent – and the TUC refused to co-operate. There followed, in the winter of 1978–79, a series of damaging strikes involving, among others, lorry and petrol-tanker drivers and public service manual workers. Ambulancemen struck, with a consequent direct threat to human life. This was the 'winter of discontent'. The social contract had been shattered and in the subsequent general election in the spring of 1979 Labour was decisively defeated. In a sense the 1974–9 government represented the triumph of the social democrats. There was precious little fundamentalist socialism involved in its legislative programme. Its *raison d'être* was social democratic and it failed comprehensively on its own terms. There were extenuating circumstances, but then there always are. No small wonder that the fundamentalists thought that enough was enough.

After the débâcle of 1979 the fundamentalists began to achieve some notable victories in their campaign to 'democratize' the party, and this concerned the social democrats so much that four of the most prominent left the party eventually to found the Social Democratic Party (SDP). We shall be looking at the process of democratization and the rise of the SDP in later chapters, but the immediate consequence of both was that in the general election of 1983 Labour faced serious competition for the non-Conservative vote and competed with the most radical and fundamentalist manifesto ever; the party sustained its most humiliating defeat since 1931. The resignation of party leader Michael Foot, himself a fundamentalist, and the election to the leadership of the 'dream ticket' of Kinnock and Hattersley did much to restore Labour morale but the party failed substantially to improve its position in 1987.

It is not easy finally to come to any judgement on what Labour party socialism is. What can be said unequivocally is that it has been less successful electorally than conservatism, since on only two occasions has the Labour party held a working majority. Yet in the 1940s and again in the 1960s several commentators spoke of Labour as having supplanted the Conservatives as the natural party of government, and of socialism as being the ideology of the day, and the party has consistently managed to legislate on most of its manifesto proposals.[33] It is certainly true that Labour governments have been blown badly off course by economic storms and there has always been disagreement regarding its capacity to keep the ship of state afloat. There has also been disagreement concerning Labour's contribution to the development of socialism: many members of the party believe that socialism has not yet been reached or even approached.[34] Often Labour has been its own sternest critic and the reason is apparent: there has never been agreement as to what actually constitutes socialism. The problem presented by the two strains of fundamentalism and social democracy, as party history so clearly demonstrates, is that they frequently (though not always) pull in opposite directions.

What has cemented the party in the past has been its commitment to the working class. Unlike the Conservatives, the Labour party has usually been unabashed to anounce its allegiance to a class; it would like to see itself as *more* than a class party, or at least the social democrats would, but it has usually acknowledged that it is *at least* a class party. In recent years, though, not only has the traditionaly solid structure of the working class changed significantly but it appears that the party has drifted away from the working class in the sense that it has, rightly or wrongly, pursued policies which working-class people have not seen as being in their interests.

It might be argued that socialism is so riven by ideological contradictions that it could never have established popular support in the way that conservatism has. This is not necessarily the case because tensions can be creative; indeed R. N. Berki feels that socialism is all the richer for its tensions. Yet there are many in the Labour party and a number in the parliamentary party whose objectives are so radical that they could scarcely be brought about by parliamentary means.[35] Marxism infuses much (though by no means all) of British fundamentalist socialism, and its emphasis on the importance of class war helped to give the party a radical edge, capable of bringing parliamentary business to a halt in the 1920s by the singing of the *Red Flag*. Yet this radical image in a society dominated by a most unradicalized proletariat (suffering, perhaps, from false consciousness) can only have been electorally damaging.

What has just about held the party together in the past has been its commitment to the interests of the working class, stronger, no doubt, among the fundamentalists, but present in most party members. Yet, as we have seen, Labour has lost, perhaps temporarily, even that unifying strength, as the traditional working class has contracted and as Labour has found itself pursuing policies inimical to the perceived interests of that class. Even the party's central policy plank of nationalization has been unpopular with the working class for many years.[36]

In contrast with its Conservative opponent, the Labour party has suffered the consequences of always having been an ideological party. Unfortunately it has never been entirely sure either what that ideology was, or how to put it into effect. Divided still, apparently losing touch with the ground of its support, uncertain of the kind of society it wishes to create, the Labour party – for whom effective administration has never been justification enough – seems to have a future every whit as ambiguous as its past.

Notes

1 Dream of John Ball, in A. L. Morton (ed.), *Three Works by William Morris* (London, Lawrence and Wishart, 1973).
2 But encapsulated most nostalgically in Goldsmith's *The Deserted Village.*
3 *Progress and Poverty*, printed in London, Manchester and Glasgow: this very popular 87-page pamphlet did not not make easy reading.
4 For a full acount of the contribution of these groups see P. P. Poirier, *Advent of the Labour Party* (London, Allen and Unwin, 1958).
5 Hyndman wrote an influential marxist text *England for All* (1881). After its publication Marx's door was always closed to Hyndman; he had failed to acknowledge the master.
6 At first serialized in *The Clarion.*
7 See Poirier, *Advent of the Labour Party*, p. 57.
8 Margaret Cole has written a detailed history of the Fabians: *The Story of Fabian Socialism* (London, Heinemann, 1961).
9 See C. F. Brand, *The British Labour Party* (London, Oxford University Press, 1965).
10 In 1892 three socialists were elected to the House: Hardie (South West Ham), Burns (Battersea), and Havelock Wilson (Middlesborough).
11 The LRC had contested the general election of 1900 with funds of only £33!
12 Quoted in J. Saville, 'The ideology of labourism', in R. Benewick et al., *Knowledge and Belief in Politics* (London, Allen and Unwin, 1973), p. 215.
13 D. Coates, *The Labour Party and the Struggle for Socialism* (Cambridge, Cambridge University Press, 1975), p. 9.
14 H. G. Wells, *The New Machiavelli* (Harmondsworth, Penguin, 1970), p. 243.
15 Coates, *The Labour Party*, p. 12.
16 For a full explanation of this phrase see Stephen Ingle, 'Socialist man: William Morris and Bernard Shaw', in B. Parekh (ed.), *Concepts of Socialism* (London, Croom Helm, 1975).
17 R. N. Berki, *Socialism* (London, Dent, 1975), p. 13. The account of marxism which follows is loosely based upon Berki's longer and more detailed analysis.
18 *A Contribution to the Critique of Political Economy* (1859) quoted in Berki, *Socialism*, p. 67.
19 Marx explores this idea in, for example, *German Ideology*, written in 1845.
20 See Gramsci's *Selections from Prison Notebooks* (London, Lawrence and Wishart, 1971).
21 Robert Tressell, *The Ragged Trousered Philanthropists* (St Albans, Panther Books, 1965).
22 Coates, *The Labour Party*, p. 13.

23. See D. Roberts, 'Labour in office: 1924, 1929–31', in C. Cook and I. Taylor (eds), *The Labour Party* (London, Longman, 1980).

24 R. B. Haldane, *An Autobiography* (London, Hodder and Stoughton, 1929), p. 330.

25 R. W. Lyman, *The First Labour Government, 1924* (London, Chapman & Hall, 1957), p. 148.

26 For a brief account of these events see Brand, *The British Labour Party*.

27 C. R. Attlee, *The Labour Party in Perspective* (London, Gollanz, 1937), p. 53.

28 For a full analysis of these developments see H. Berkeley, *The Myth That Will Not Die* (London, Croom Helm, 1978).

29 Anthony Crosland, *The Future of Socialism* (London, Cape, 1956).

30 Richard Crossman, *New Fabian Essay* (London, Turnstile Press, 1953).

31 John Strachey, 'Tasks and achievements of British Labour', in Crossman, *New Fabian Essays*.

32 This was particularly ironic since prime minister Wilson was one of the three ministers to resign from Attlee's cabinet in 1951 over the original imposition of NHS charges.

33 See David Steel, 'Labour in office: the post-war experience', in Cook and Taylor, *The Labour Party*, p. 136. Steel provides a full acount of the achievements and problems of the postwar Labour governments.

34 Not all, though. Christopher Mayhew, on the right of the party, believed that the Attlee government had more or less established socialism and that only minor adjustments were necessary thereafter (see his *Party Games*, London, Hutchinson, 1969). Mayhew defected to the Liberal party in the 1970s.

35 See R. Miliband, *Parliamentary Socialism*, 2nd edn (London, Merlin Press, 1972).

36 For example, a poll conducted in 1959 for the *Daily Telegraph* showed Labour's commitment to nationalization to be a principal reason fo voter defection.

6 Leadership and Organization in the Labour Party

In organizational and leadership terms the Labour party is a quite different animal from the Conservative party and the difference will be reflected in the structure of this chapter. When analysing party leadership, Williams[1] classifies leaders as either pathfinders, problem-solvers, or stabilizers, quoting Gladstone, Lloyd George and Baldwin as the obvious examples of his typology. The pathfinder inspires some of his followers but alarms others; the problem-solver is admired but not trusted inside or outside the party; and the stabilizer generates public support but not much excitement among the party stalwarts. In the Labour party, with its strong attachment to the principles (if not the practice) of solidarity and collegiality, the stabilizer is particularly favoured: an ability to reconcile the varied sects of what is so often referred to as a 'broad church' is a pre-requisite for leadership. Equally the problem-solver is disfavoured: the nature of his/her skills actually works against consistency, under-emphasizing ideology because of its obvious constraint upon choices of action. For his part, the pathfinder – the charismatic, even messianic leader – is appropriate only to certain periods of crisis in Labour's history; in the mundane world of parliamentary politics he may prove more of a liability than an asset, more likely to divide the faithful or to divide the faithful from potential voters. For these reasons the leadership of the Labour party requires the kind of personality least likely, on the face of it, to be either a successful and innovative prime minister or a great champion of socialism.

The party's first leader was James Ramsay MacDonald and he was regarded by his supporters as a charismatic pathfinder. But MacDonald's public persona did not correspond to the man's real character. His political career had consisted chiefly of problem-solving, of 'fixing', the 1906 electoral pact with the Liberals being a good example. Until 1922 the leader of the party was designated as chairman of the parliamentary party, an elected post; thereafter he was referred to as chairman and leader. Since 1906 there had been no fewer than six chairmen and the position commanded little of the loyalty owed naturally to the leaders of the other parties. The prospect of power, though, brought a new emphasis on the independence of the parliamentary party, especially its leader. So when MacDonald became prime minister he formed his own cabinet without official party consultations, thereby rejecting the precedent set by the Australian Labour party and conforming instead to the practice of the other British parties.[1] In 1931, however, MacDonald the problem-solver sold his party out, leaving what Williams refers to as a permanent scar on the party's psyche. The cult of individualism is still an emotive and powerful charge which will be levelled at any party leader who seeks to assert his own authority unduly.

The most successful of Labour's leaders, Clement Attlee, was, in Williams's typology, a stabilizer. Attlee was not dictated to by ideological considerations when building his cabinet; he was more concerned with the personal and administrative qualities of ministers. He clearly saw one of his most important functions as preserving the unity of his government and had no doubts whatever as to the importance of his own role as leader.[3] He tenaciously held on to power amid considerable cabinet intrigue, and thereby managed to hold the party together. Attlee's successor, Hugh Gaitskell, was of quite a different cut. He was a pathfinder, by inclination and by policy, and he believed that Labour's third successive defeat in 1959 established his case for reform so strongly that he was prepared to attack the very ark of the socialist covenant, clause four of the constitution, which guaranteed to all workers the ownership of the means of production. As the ensuing conference debate demonstrated, Gaitskell's pathfinding leadership was deeply offensive to the left and worrying to all those concerned with party unity. Religious terminology shaped the debate, with clause four referred to as 'The Tablets of Stone' and 'The Thirty-Nine Articles', and Gaitskell himself concluded that he 'wished he led a political party and not a religious movement'.[4] Within a few months he had abandoned any attempts to change the party constitution; he had simply found it impossible to lead a united party down the path to modernization and electoral success which he claimed to have found.

Few would accuse Harold Wilson of pathfinding. Elected leader after Gaitskell's death, Wilson, from the first, operated as a master problem-solver. He sought to make socialism synonymous with technological change and its underlying ethos of managerialism, and in wholeheartedly promoting the latter, to appear to be promoting the former. In reality he was attempting to reconcile the fundamentalists and the social democrats within the party. For a while he appeared to succeed but in major policy areas decisions were taken which offended the fundamentalists, for example the attempt to join the EEC, the retention of Polaris submarines and the acceptance of the 1962 Immigration Act. In his second government Wilson single-mindedly addressed himself to what he took to be the major problems facing the country. Against the advice of a Royal Commission he decided to reform the trade unions by law, but when it became clear that he could not persuade the parliamentary party (nor indeed the cabinet) to support him Wilson simply abandoned the proposals. When he returned in 1974 for a third term, Britain had joined the EEC and Labour party policy was to withdraw. Now Wilson and a number of senior figures in the party thought that this step would be economically damaging. What was the prime minister to do? Wilson's solution was masterful in terms of retaining stability and solving the problem. As we have seen, he called for a renegotiation of Britain's terms of entry, held a national referendum on the outcome and allowed all individuals within his divided government to campaign as they saw fit. As a consequence Britain remained within the EEC and the Labour government remained in office. The problem-solver had turned stabilizer with a vengeance.

Wilson left the party in the hands of the solid, experienced James Callaghan. The problems confronting the government were as great as ever and the success of the nationalist parties obliged Callaghan, whose parliamentary majority was slender, to pursue plans to devolve powers to Scotland and Wales, although this was not generally popular with the party. Nor were his government's deflationary economic policies, nor was the attempt to control wages which produced the winter of discontent. Callaghan left the party in considerable disarray. He had attempted to act as a problem-solver but had been unable to prevent the drifting apart of the fundamentalists and the social democrats and had lost much of the support of the unions.

Michael Foot came to the leadership with his earlier reputation as a pathfinder – a Robespierre-like figure in his early days, 'bitter, intolerant and humourless'[5] – counting for less than his potential as a stabilizer. Foot was highly regarded by many within the parliamentary party though his accession to the leadership owed much to the fact that it prevented an open confrontation between the fundamentalists (Benn) and social democrats (Healey); owed much, that is, according to backbencher Austin Mitchell, to his ability 'to obscure issues'.[6] However, Foot was unable to prevent a divisive contest between Healey and Benn for the deputy leadership, which the former won narrowly, nor to prevent Benn distancing himself from the previous Labour government's policies and attacking Foot's leadership. Foot's failure to recreate stability within his party might suggest that the task had become an impossible one. Certainly it appears to have been wishful to think that he was the man for the job. Foot was never fully able to slough off his other-wordly pathfinder zeal. According to Ken Livingstone, 'his basic humanity and compassion played a part in preventing the destruction of the Labour party by our enemies'.[7] It needs only to be added that he was somewhat less successful in defending the party against its friends.

The new Labour leader, Neil Kinnock, was elected according to the procedures established by Labour's special conference in January of 1981. Perhaps Kinnock's greatest advantage on becoming leader was his general popularity – he was the candidate most preferred by Labour supporters (56 per cent); Foot, by contrast, was only fourth choice of Labour supporters when he became leader.[8] Kinnock's position as leader was unquestionably strengthened by having as his deputy the man whom he defeated in the leadership election, Roy Hattersley. There was a happy balance in personality, temperament and ideology between the two men. Different in each aspect they were none the less compatible, complementary even, unlikely to fall out on major issues of policy. By any standards Kinnock's task as leader was enormously difficult. Although he enjoyed the goodwill of most party members he was faced with a disunited, defeated and depressed party. What made matters far worse was the outbreak in spring 1984 of the miners' strike. The strike, led from his Yorkshire stronghold by Arthur Scargill, was unballoted: the miners, in vice president McGahey's words, were not to be 'constitutionalized out of action'. It soom became clear, though, that the miners were divided and that as a consequence the government was able to maintain supplies of coal both to industry and to homes. The strike provided a Morton's fork for the Labour leaders: should they side with Scargill and suffer general popular opprobrium or should they denounce Scargill and be accused as class traitors by their more radical supporters? For Kinnock this was essentially an exercise in damage limitation but his first year as leader came to a close with the party conference giving a far warmer reception to Scargill than to himself. The strike, marked by intolerance, hatred and violence, had, according to most commentators, a damaging effect upon Labour unity.[9]

The Labour movement was increasingly beginning to oppose government policies outside parliament and Kinnock's leadership was accordingly jeopardized. This widening of the struggle continued after the collapse of the miners' strike in 1985 with the refusal of Labour-controlled local councils such as Liverpool's to set a legal rate. Once again Kinnock's position as the leader of the Labour movement came under threat from more radical elements. For a growing minority of party activists within the unions and the constituencies, Kinnock and Hattersley had come to represent the traditional right-wing leadership that always betrays socialism. All the same, Kinnock rode out these storms. In 1986 he began much more successfully to stamp his authority on the Labour movement by, for example, acting decisively to stem the influence of Militant. More positively, he set in train a revamping of traditional Labour policies, for example substituting 'social ownership' for nationalization as a major objective. Other important changes in Labour's policy profile included a moderation of the party's proposals for re-forming the Conservatives' trade union legislation, a muted acceptance of council house sales, no pledge to leave the European Community, and a strong commitment to conventional defence spending. In 1987 the party went into the election campaign more (apparently) united than at any time in the previous twenty years. The 1987 campaign was a personal triumph for Kinnock, though the influence behind the scenes of senior figures in the party bureaucracy was considerable.

It is safe to conclude, however, that the Labour party requires far more of its leader than does the Conservative party. The actual structure of the party, more federal in nature, poses problems for a leader, but there is more to it than structures. Loyalty plays a great part in Labour party politics, but not loyalty to the leader. Loyalty is owed to a concept: the interests of the working class. But no statement exists of what precisely these interests are, and to equate them with socialism is no help; no precise statement exists of what that is either. What results is a permanent and growing tendency to sectarian division, with the leader finding his/her time and energy taken up by the attempt to keep all the faithful within the 'broad church'.

Since the party leader has traditionally been elected by his/her parliamentary colleagues the relationship with the parliamentary party has usually been less than deferential. In ideological terms the leadership has usually found itself challenged by MPs further to the left and this is partly rooted in the nature of MacDonald's 'betrayal'. It is commonly known that MacDonald preferred the company of the well-connected to that of his party comrades after 1924[10] and no doubt the events of 1931 strongly reinforced the natural desire of left-wing MPs to ensure that their leaders would never again attain such personal dominance. Indeed for many left-wing activists the whole parliamentary party was mistrusted, the ILP referring to parliament as 'territory occupied by the enemy'.[11] After 1931 the TUC began to exercise increasing authority over the rump parliamentary party through the monthly meetings of the national joint council, representing both bodies. However, when the TUC satisfied itself that the new leader Attlee was to be trusted, it placed its considerable power at his disposal, to curb the influence of the left both in the PLP and in the party at large.

For all that, the left in parliament consistently sought to pressurize the leadership into adopting more radical policies. In 1950 a number of left-wing MPs formed themselves into a group called Keep Left under the chairmanship of Harold Wilson. By 1958 a larger and better organized group, Victory for Socialism, had been formed which co-ordinated the struggle against Gaitskell's revisionism. Traditionally the largest of the left-wing parliamentary groups has been Tribune, named after the famous house journal (founded in 1937) of the Labour left. The group itself was founded in 1964 and is the oldest surviving 'pressure group' within the parliamentary party. It has steadily grown in numbers over the years and frequently contains frontbench members in its ranks; indeed Michael Foot and Neil Kinnock were members. In the 1979–83 parliament Tribune achieved a membership of seventy-four, though twenty members later left the group, feeling it to be insufficiently radical. Although the group has traditionally enjoyed considerable political visibility its achievement in actually influencing the policies of Labour governments has been modest.

It was not until the 1970s that the left was able to mount a serious challenge for control of the party. Two groups, the Campaign for Labour Party Democracy (CLPD) and later the Labour Co-ordinating Committee (LCC), attempted to gain control of the NEC. In alliance with trade union leaders more radical than their predecessors they managed to do so in 1974 when the party came into office, when only ten of the twenty-nine members of NEC could be counted upon to support government policy. In 1976 the champion of the parliamentary right, Denis Healey, was voted off the NEC. All in all Butler and Kavanagh concluded that the Labour government was 'obviously at odds with the party machine . . . as if there were two Labour parties, one with the voice of the NEC and the conference and the other with that of the parliamentary leadership'.[12] CDLP remains active among the constituency parties as witness the growing number of conference resolutions based upon CDLP's 'models', though its major objectives (such as mandatory reselection) have already been achieved. For its part LCC, launched at the 1978 conference, is more concerned with policy than organization. Although it would be an oversimplification to describe LCC as a Bennite group, many of its members are his supporters. The group produces a regular broadsheet, *Labour Activist*, and encourages debate between party activists inside and outside parliament.

Generally the left made two claims in the late 1970s, both difficult to refute: that the social democrats' version of socialist planning had failed and that the leadership had consistently failed to fulfil party policy as enunciated by conference and the NEC. As a consequence the left sought to democratize decision-making within the party and their strategy was orchestrated by CPLD, more specifically by Tony Benn. When the party went into opposition Benn sustained his campaign against the leadership, refusing to be bound by shadow cabinet collective responsibility. Through the chairmanship of the NEC's home policy sub-committee he had considerable influence upon the contents of Labour's 1983 election manifesto, generally recognized as the most radical since 1945. Benn's campaign was thought to be motivated not simply by a desire to make the leadership more responsive to the membership but also by a perfectly proper ambition to lead the party,[13] an ambition that might have been realized had he not lost his seat in the 1983 general election.

Support for Benn in parliament comes primarily from the new

Campaign Group, founded in 1982 by the first five MPs to leave Tribune. There are currently around thirty members in this group, though it has no officials. It summarizes its aims as follows: 'To campaign against witch-hunts and expulsions in the Labour party and to campaign for Labour party policy centred on peace, jobs and freedom.'[14] Benn himself has not joined the group. Campaign puts up its own slate for elections to the NEC, though with decreasing success. Several MPs left the group in 1985, two complaining of 'vanguardism of quite staggering proportions'.[15] Kinnock has attempted, with some success, to detach the Tribune group from the 'hard left' and build an alliance against them.

Centre-right MPs, for their part, had long before formed the Manifesto Group, following a meeting organized in 1974 by Dr Dickson Mabon who became its first chairman. The group does not reveal its membership which is open only to MPs but not ministers, but it is considered to have some influence despite the fact that its first two chairmen subsequently joined the SDP.

A significant number of Labour MPs are sponsored by trade unions, and the financial arrangements governing such sponsorship are set down in the Hastings Agreement (1933) which allows for up to 80 per cent of election expenses (though usually less is given). Of the 180 or so candidates who are sponsored, around 130 are usually elected, with the transport workers sponsoring over twenty MPs, currently including Kinnock, Shore and Silkin. It would be unconstitutional for unions to exercise direct influence over their sponsored MPs but it would certainly not be well regarded if a sponsored MP acted directly against the declared interest of the sponsoring union or, more generally, of the TUC. Finally, mention must be made of the Co-operative party, which is officially the electoral partner of the Labour party. In the 1980s some 140 co-operative societies subscribed to the Co-operative party. The party sponsors around twenty-five candidates, mostly in safe seats. In 1981 four Co-operative-sponsored MPs left to joint the SDP. Typically, though, the House will contain between fifteen and twenty such MPs and they form a Co-operative parliamentary group with a chairman and vice chairman.

The Labour group in the European parliament has not made a great impact, which is not surprising given the party's official opposition to membership. In the elections of June 1984 thirty-two candidates were successful and their frequently disruptive tactics have led to comparisons with English soccer hooligans.[16] There are over 130 Labour peers in the House of Lords and since they and the nearly 80 Alliance peers, together with crossbenchers, could potentially outvote the Conservative peers, they have become rather more active than formerly, especially since 1983 when numbers of Conservative peers have been prepared to vote against their own government on such matters as the abolition of the metropolitan counties. All the same, the commitment of Labour peers to the House of Lords cannot be great, given their party's intention, restated in the 1983 manifesto, to abolish the House. So much for parliament.

The role of the conference in the politics of the Labour party is a crucial one.[17] Traditionally this has been explained by the fact that the labour movement grew up outside parliament and consequently the role of Labour MPs was somewhat ambiguously balanced between that of representatives and delegates. In fact moves to control the parliamentary party through the annual conference only really gained strength after MacDonald's 'betrayal'. In 1937 party leader Attlee wrote that conference 'lays down the policy of the party and issues instructions which must be carrried out by . . . its representatives in parliament . . . the Labour party conference is in fact a parliament of the movement'.[18] After he became party leader Attlee had a change of heart but the relationship remained ambiguous. Gaitskell's defeat on the policy of unilateral nuclear disarmament at the 1960 conference was reversed in 1961 and this caused *The Times* to conclude that the party leader had 'exploded the theory that the party conference is the policy-making body which issues orders to the MPs and their chosen leader'.[19] But in fact Gaitskell defeated the earlier conference resolution only through another conference resolution the following year.

There are two practical limitations upon the supposed status of conference as a parliament of the party. First is the claim that conference is far less representative of the movement (and thus less of a parliament) than it ought to be, and second is the argument that Gaitskell put before the conference on the nuclear issue. There was no doubt, he declared, that the majority of MPs were opposed to unilateralism. 'So what do you expect them to do? Change their minds overnight? . . . What sort of people do you think we are?'[20] MPs could hardly fulfil their duties at Westminster if they were tied to pursuing a policy with which they were fundamentally at odds. The first point, about the unrepresentative nature of conference decision-making, needs some elaboration.

In 1973 the Labour party decided to abolish its list of prescribed organizations and several groups of activists entered the party. These new 'hard-left' groups began to coalesce around existing left-wing groups. Tony Benn, the acknowledged leader of this alliance, sought to reopen the whole issue of the relationship between the conference and the PLP by attempting to shift the balance of power towards conference and in particular towards the constituency parties by, for example, obliging sitting MPs to seek reselection.[21] The conference of 1978, however, voted against giving constituencies the power to deselect their MPs (though only because the AUEW forgot to cast its vote, which was to have been in favour). Under Labour's constitution this should have been the end of the matter for at least three years. In 1979, however, the three-year rule was changed; mandatory reselection was reconsidered and passed this time, as was a motion calling for NEC control of the manifesto, though a motion to allow the party membership rather than the PLP to elect the party leader was defeated. This last set-back, however, was not to be final. Pressure was put upon the NEC to appoint a commission of enquiry to consider proposals for constitutional reform and one of the results was an electoral college whose function would be to elect the leader and deputy leader.

The leadership hoped that the subsequent conference in 1980 would vote down these proposals, with support from the major union. But union leaders were no longer able to control their delegations and mandatory reselection and some form of collegiate election for the leadership were passed, though the proposal to give the NEC control of the party manifesto was lost. The results of this campaign had been determined by union votes and these became increasingly unknown factors.[22] When a special conference was held in January 1981 to decide on the shape of the college, two plans were considered, both sponsored by major unions. Success went to the USDAW proposal of 30 per cent of the college votes to the constituencies and the PLP and 40 per cent to the unions. The whole procedure, far from being an exercise of democracy in the 'parliament of the party', was exposed as byzantine and divisive. An old Labour party saying seems apposite: 'It's carrying democracy too far if you don't know the result before the vote'.

Subsequent attempts by Kinnock, when he became leader, to persuade conference that decisions to reselect candidates at constituency level should be made by all members of the party and not by the general management committee were defeated, again because of a failure to 'square' the important unions. Again the vote contained some bizarre incongruities and was, moreover, conducted by party chairman Eric Heffer in a disastrously maladroit manner. Though Kinnock lost, the true nature of the struggle was exposed: it was not about democracy versus oligarchy but about whether an 'unrepresentative grassroots elite [could] seize power from the ruling parliamentary elite'.[23] To an increasing extent Labour party conferences have become, like their Conservative counterparts, parodies of the party's values, though as has been pointed out, those who sing 'Rule Britannia' at Conservative rallies and conferences at least know the words. As one speaker at conference said, if most young voters today were asked about clause four, they would assume it was a pop group.

One important function of the Labour conference which has no equivalent in the Conservative party is the electing of the National Executive Committee (NEC). The NEC is described in the party constitution [24] as 'the administrative authority of the party', subject of course to the control and directions of the conference. It would be a mistake, though, to believe that the NEC is concerned solely with administration, for the constitution gives the NEC the duty to confer with representatives of a Labour government 'prior to the formulation of legislative proposals'. In fact the NEC is a crucial body not simply in the advising on the formulation of legislation but in deciding the content of the policy package upon which a Labour government would hope to legislate. It is, moreover, the hub of a network of advisory committees.

'The present structure of the NEC', says Kavanagh,[25] 'defies any coherent theory of representation'. When the constitution was drawn up the NEC comprised sixteen members: eleven trade union representatives, three representatives of socialist societies, one representative of local trades councils (the forerunners of constituency associations) and the treasurer. As women's sections and individual constituency parties developed, so the NEC changed to reflect the new structure. It grew to twenty-three, with thirteen union and socialist society representatives, five constituency party representatives, four women and the treasurer. After 1918, elections to these positions were by the whole conference (effectively, then, by the union block votes) and it was not until 1937 that the constituencies gained the power freely to elect their own representatives undominated by the unions. Nowadays the NEC is said to comprise four divisions. Division one consists of twelve members nominated by the unions from among their delegates and elected by the whole union delegation at the party conference. Division two consists of one member, nominated by the socialist and co-operative societies from among their delegates and elected by their delegations. Division three consists of seven members elected by the constituency delegations from among their number (though constituency parties may also nominate their MP or parliamentary candidate). Division four consists of five women members, nominated by any affiliated organization. Constituency parties may nominate their female MP or parliamentary candidate. This division is elected by conference as a whole. To these members are added the leader and deputy leader of the party sitting ex officio and the prestigious post of party treasurer, elected by the whole conference.

Since 1945 MPs have provided over half of the membership of the NEC and nearly all constituency and women's representatives. Although the constitution sets store by a formal institutional separation of powers this does not imply a separation of personnel: cabinet ministers frequently sit on the NEC and, as Callaghan's open opposition to Wilson's trade union reforms shows, Benn was not the first cabinet member to use the NEC as a forum within which to attack the policies of his own government.

The position of the NEC in policy matters is pivotal – hence the perennial struggle between left and right to secure domination. Its importance in structural terms is also considerable. Until recently it possessed ninety sub-committees overseeing all aspects of party affairs. Kinnock and the new secretary Larry Whitty have managed to reduce this number to fewer than twenty. One such committee, the campaign strategy committee, set up a review committee in 1984 to consider the structure of party organization and its recommendations were acted upon in 1986. This committee was the third official enquiry into party organization. The first, in 1955, and the second, in 1968, had not proved very productive. In 1980 commissions of enquiry were established which produced much discussion and a further study in 1981 targeted on head office. Finally in 1984 two independent reports made some specific proposals for the reform of the party organization and the review committee can be seen as the NEC's response to this debate.

Traditionally the Labour party headquarters has been characterized by ineffective organizational leadership and an amateurish approach to public relations generally. Many of its recent electoral campaigns have been considered failures, none more so than that of 1983, described as 'Disaster Snatched from the Jaws of Defeat'.[26] In 1985, however, the NEC appointed two new key officers, Whitty as general secretary and Mandelson as head of communications and campaigns. These appointments were among the fruits of the 1984 review committee which considered the reform of headquarters. The structure of organization at headquarters was criticized by the committee for not conducing to a strategic approach nor encouraging co-ordination and flexibility. What was needed was to change the profile of headquarters by shifting resources into campaigning, with the general secretary of the party playing a more central role. The party's new general secretary was greatly concerned to change the whole atmosphere of headquarters from neighbourly anarchy to task-oriented professionalism; in appointing Whitty the NEC must have had the same end in mind. Indeed the review committee spoke of the organization as being less efficient, less adventurous and less flexible than that of the Conservatives. Headquarters should give more attention to recruiting and training than to 'serving the constitutional bodies of the party', said the committee.

The committee sugested a strategic management structure which was put into effect in 1986, headed by the general secretary and three directors, meeting regularly to co-ordinate objectives. The three directors head directorates of organization, of policy development and of communications and campaigns, and the various functions administered previously by the ten separate departments were divided between these three on the basis indicated by their titles. Crucially, the general secretary became responsible for the public presentation of the party and for all NEC committees. The resulting structure has proved more efficient if less cosy than its predecessors: the selling of socialism has gone on to a business footing, with power in the party bureaucracy moving away from the amateur (the politician) and towards the professional administrator. As Mandelson has said, the days when a general secretary could declare that Labour would not present politicians 'as if they were a breakfast food or baked beans' are long over.[27] Positive fruit of Labour's new approach have been the touring pop-propaganda show Red Wedge and the much acclaimed campaign in spring 1986 called Freedom and Fairness. In the summer of 1986 the Labour Freedom road show toured nine holiday resorts, giving free (red) balloons to children and Labour sunvisors to parents. A mobile circus with jugglers, tumblers, buskers and magicians – and fire-eaters – spread the message. The new emphasis on packaging and presentation was never more in evidence than in Kinnock's unambiguously presidential style election campaign of 1987. What Keir Hardie would have made of this is not difficult to imagine.

Of groups not formally attached to the party structure mention has already been made of CDLP and the LCC. There also exists the Labour Solidarity Campaign, a centre-right response to these groups (though it also includes some Tribunites). Several key party figures have been prominent in Solidarity, including Roy Hattersley and Peter Shore. Solidarity, like CDLP, circulates its members with model resolutions for the annual conference. There are also smaller left-wing groups such as the Socialist Campaign for a Labour Victory, formed in 1978, to champion left-wing policies. This group was a prime mover in the campaign for the constitutional changes of the late 1970s. Also, a Socialist Environment and Research Association has recently been established with a three-monthly periodical *New Ground*.

The Labour Party Young Socialists, with a representative on the NEC, have traditionally fallen prey to the extreme left. In 1964 the then Young Socialists were reconstituted because they were thought to be controlled by trotskyists; in the 1980s the position is broadly similar, with the LPYS organizer an acknowledged trotskyist and all fourteen members of the national committee believed to be supporters of Militant Tendency.[28] Active membership of LPYS is thought to be around 10,000. Brief mention must also be made of the plethora of socialist intellectual groups, the largest and most formidable of which is the Fabian Society. Founded in 1884 the Fabian has had innumerable illustrious members many of whom have gone on to the highest office. Today the Fabian has an active branch in most cities and publishes a substantial number of books and policy documents. Its influence on Labour policies over the years has been considerable and, the Bow Group notwithstanding, it has no real counterpart in the Conservative party, nor indeed anywhere in the world.

Originally the Labour party was formed by groups outside parliament, especially the unions, trying to secure increased representation for labour in the House. Indeed the Labour party could not be said to have become a national party until 1918 when it became possible under the new constitution to take out direct membership (previously membership had been through the ILP). Ten years later there were 215,000 individual party members, and this figure grew to a peak in 1951 of over 1 million. After 1963, though, constituencies were only allowed to affiliate to the party on achieving a membership of 1,000 and since the great majority declared membership during the 1960s and 1970s of exactly that figure we may assume that the declared membership of over 600,000 was inaccurate. By 1985, when there were no minimum limits to affiliation, membership stood at 323,000, constituting about 6 per cent of its parliamentary vote, far lower than any similar party in Europe.[29] The number of ordinary members paying full subscriptions stood at 166,000 and the number of reduced-rate members (unemployed and otherwise disadvantaged) was 140,000; 16,800 new members had joined the party under a new scheme which made reduced rates available.[30] Over the period, then, membership had fallen substantially though by exactly how much it is impossible to say. A fall in membership is not the only indication of hard times for the party in the country. There has also been a steady decline in the number of paid agents. In the mid-1950s, when Harold Wilson referred to the party organization as a 'penny-farthing machine in a jet age', there were 296 full-time constituency agents. In the 1987 general election there were only sixty, a number of whom worked in two constituencies.

When the Labour party organization was established in 1918 there existed four types of constituency organization: local affiliated parties with individual members paying fees to the local party; trades councils attempting to co-ordinate electoral efforts on behalf of the Labour candidate; local Labour representation committees comprising the representatives of trade unions and socialist societies in the constituency; finally, constituencies in which the ILP acted as local party organization. Party leaders saw it as essential to establish a much more homogeneous party structure which acknowledged the strength within the movement of the unions. So the constitution which they drew up established the constituency party as the basic unit of organization and acknowledged full individual membership through local parties and indirect membership through trade unions and socialist societies.

There are currently two categories of party membership, individual and affiliated. Individual membership is self-explanatory;

affiliated membership comprises trade unionists whose unions are affiliated to the TUC, and members of co-operative and socialist societies not deemed by the NEC to be ineligible for affiliation to the party. Branches are usually based upon local government wards and their tasks are primarily electoral. Trade unions may also affiliate to the constituency party at branch level. The constituency party is in the hands of its elected general (management) committee which represents the branches, runs the party locally, chooses its delegates to the annual conference and elects an executive committee which has the day-to-day running of the constituency party as its responsibility.

The important task of selecting a parliamentary candidate is nominally in the hands of the general management committee but the executive may draw up a short list. All these arrangements should be conducted after consultations with the NEC. The NEC is required formally to endorse candidacy and indeed will have at its disposal two lists, A and B, of potential parliamentary candidates, with candidates on the favoured A list being sponsored by an affiliated union. Successful nomination in the past has almost always depended upon a candidate's being on list 'A' but this has not always restricted the constituency executive; nowadays the constituencies, as the selection of a number of supporters of Militant Tendency in the general election of 1983 and since testify, are more their own masters, though Kinnock and Whitty, through the NEC, were able to overrule local parties regarding the selection of a candidate in the Knowsley North by-election of 1986 and the candidacy of a Black Section champion for Nottingham East in the 1987 general election.

Above the constituencies and similarly organized are the county or district parties (depending upon the local government structure), though, again for local government reasons, London is somewhat different, with a regional council overseeing boroughs. The importance of the district party varies according to the size of the district; larger districts like Liverpool and Manchester have a substantial regional influence, as do the London regional party and the boroughs.

Just as in the Conservative party this structure is replicated for the LPYS. Branches may be formed at constituency or ward level but are integral parts of the constituency party. The LPYS holds regional and national conferences annually and publishes a monthly paper, *Socialist Youth*. The regional conferences elect representatives onto the national committee which has a general co-ordinative function and reports directly to the NEC. Labour party women, apart from being attached to branches in the normal way, may form women's sections at constituency or branch level and elect councils with the general task of targeting constituency work on women. Like the LPYS, women's sections may elect regional and national committees. The latter organizes annual National Labour Women's Conferences and reports directly to the NEC.

At constituency level the party has experienced a clash of competing values over recent years involving traditional Labour supporters and younger radicals. It would be an over simplification to identify the radical forces as Militant Tendency, for many other radical forces have been at work within the constituencies, including the unemployed, tenants, 'gays' and, significantly, Blacks. As we shall see, battles have been and are being fought at constituency level between those who begin to see Labour, not so much as a broad movement on behalf of the underdog but as a conventicle of the dispossessed. There is one ingredient binding these radical forces together: a belief in the efficacy of extra-parliamentary activity, which does not endear them to the party leadership.

Of these groups only the Blacks have made specific constitutional demands upon the party: for independent Black sections. They argue that thrustful independent Black sections would secure wider representation at all levels within the party and be better able to champion specifically Black causes. Black sections have been formed in over thirty constituencies, with 1,500 members[31], and have been given delegates' status on a number of general management committees. Unconstitutional though this is, it may have helped in the selection of a number of Black candidates in 1985, including parliamentary candidates. The leadership views this development as divisive but the Blacks argue that their case is not significantly different from women and youth in the party and, like them, they want reserved places on management and executive committees at the local level and on the NEC at the national level. A second group, Black Activists Campaign, has been established to press for Black candidates in constituencies with a large Black vote. The party cannot afford to lose the contribution of Black communities in a large number of inner cities,[32] neither can it afford to act so as to prevent the integration of Blacks into the framework of constitutional politics. All the same, the prospect of another 'party-within-a-party' will not be welcome to the leadership and already some Blacks refer to 'BS', a unified movement 'with the potentiality of becoming a major political party of black people'.[33]

Another major problem to have bedevilled constituency politics in recent years is mandatory reselection. In principle, continuous accountability seems so democratically sound that we may wonder why it did not occur to the founding fathers. Since it did not we may also wonder why the issue arose when it did. In fact it was part of the fundamentalists' attempt to 'democratize' the party organization. MPs at risk of deselection were generally social democrats, including major figures like ex-chief whip Michael Cox, who was deselected in 1986, and Peter Shore, who was the target of a virulent campaign in his East London constituency. Others at risk included the more elderly; even those on the left could be outflanked by younger, more radical opponents. Thus Ernie Roberts lost his Hackney North constituency to the young Black Diane Abbott, a champion of BS. Young, active social democrats, such as Frank Field and Robert Kilroy-Silk,[34] were under great pressure on Merseyside, both threatening to fight as independent Labour candidates if deselected. In the event Field was reselected and Kilroy-Silk resigned. Also under threat were the representatives of mining constituencies whose support of the 1984 strike was unenthusiastic. 'Reselection', said one MP, 'is far worse than election. In an election you are united and you're fighting it out together but in this you never know who's for you and who's against you. You just can't operate with it hanging over you for long . . .'[35].

A third problem in the constituencies is infiltration from the far left. Although infiltration, or entryism, is a great cause for concern, it is not new . Neither are militant constituency parties; in 1930 Sidney Webb said that 'the constituency parties were frequently unrepresentative groups of non-entities dominated by fanatics and cranks'.[36] Later, Crossman observed that the party constitution was designed to 'maintain their enthusiasm by apparently creating a full party democracy whilst excluding them from effective power'.[37] Clearly by the late 1970s, when their numbers had been swelled by supporters of the Militant Tendency, left-wing activists were prepared to tolerate this state of affairs no longer.

The party had first acknowledged the existence of Militant Tendency in 1975, following a report by the former national agent Lord Underhill, but though the report was highly critical of Militant no action followed, indeed the findings were not made public. After the electoral defeat of 1979 Militant became much more active in the crusade to save the party for socialism and in 1982 the party felt compelled to establish another enquiry under general secretary Hayward. The report recommended the reintroduction of a register of recognized groups allowed to operate within the party, concluding: 'it is our opinion that the Militant Tendency . . . would not be eligible to be included . . .'[38] Significantly, although the NEC endorsed the report it did so only after a seven-hour meeting and only by sixteen votes to ten. Yet in order to expel Militant supporters the leadership needs active assistance from the constituencies and this neither Foot nor Kinnock got. Foot contented himself with the sacrificial offering of the five members of the editorial board of the *Militant* newspaper.

Towards the end of 1985 an enquiry was set up under general secretary Whitty into the activities of the Militant-dominated Liverpool distict party. The report roundly condemned a number of alleged Militant supporter by name, calling for their expulsion. By an overwhelming majority the district party refused to comply. The following year the NEC, against left-wing opposition which obliged it to change its rules of procedure, expelled a number of Liverpool Militants, though again the district party refused to endorse the expulsions. The problem remains a major one for the leadership; which will prove the more damaging, the growth of the influence of Militant or the possibility of a civil war which would tear apart scores of constituency parties and the youth organization? But this masks an even wider problem: constituency activists (not just Militant supporters) in the inner cities are frequently far more radical than either the leadership or the voters, and the relationship between these activists and the leadership is not mitigated by loyalty. The parliamentary party, too, is split on the issue of Militant. In early 1986, for example, the left, 'soft' and 'hard', united in a campaign against expulsions because they feared that expulsions might not stop at Militant.[39] We shall be returning to Militant in the next chapter.

From the party organization we move finally to the trade unions. The unions played a crucial part in the founding of the party, providing both an organizational infrastructure and a social base,[40] but they also had an influence on ideological development, moving Labour decisively away from socialism, making it very much a trade union party and causing MacDonald to refer to the unions as that 'terrible incubus'. What kind of ideology did the unions favour? Flounders describes it as primarily support for the 'voluntary system': that is, an expectation that a Labour government would intervene strongly in all areas of the economy and of society to secure greater equality but would not intervene in industrial relations.[41]

Union influence has frequently been decisive in the party's history. It was primarily the TUC's opposition to cuts in public expenditure which brought down MacDonald's government in 1931 and it was the two union leaders Bevin and Citrine who took control of the Labour rump after the 1935 election, through the joint national council. If the union leaders saw their task as being to re-establish Labour as the major alternative to conservatism, they clearly did not intend to allow left-wing infiltration to radicalize the party. They rejected requests from the Communist party for affiliation; they refused to co-operate with communist-dominated movements, and they refused to join any popular front movement, whether sponsored by the communists, the ILP, or even the party's own left wing. So secure was the union hold that in 1937, as we have seen, they felt able to agree to an increase in constituency representation on the NEC and to allow these representatives to be elected not by the whole of conference (that is, the union block vote) but by the constituency delegates themselves.

The close relationship between union and party leaders, restored by Attlee, was sustained until the 1960s. The Labour leader usually had at his disposal the block vote of the six larger unions who collectively controlled half of the available 6 million conference votes. The 'block vote' originated as a device to thwart the socialists at the TUC conference of 1894 and the practice was carried over into the Labour Representation Committee and hence into the party itself. In 1922 a constituency attempt to abolish the block vote was defeated, the leadership pointing out that it was a small price to pay for the (then) 95 per cent of party funds contributed by the unions. Thereafter the block vote was used to control the constituencies, that is, the more radical section of the party. The block vote helped to defeat Stafford Cripps and the Socialist League in the late 1930s; it defeated Bevan's left-wing challenge in the 1950s. But when the CDLP challenged the leadership in the late 1970s the block was no longer solid. The unions had begun to elect a more left-wing leadership but more important, the Labour government had, since

1966, initiated a series of assaults on the voluntary system, through incomes policies and trade union reform. Wilson's 'social compact', the fruits of the TUC–Labour party liaison committee established two years earlier, appeared to represent a new *modus vivendi* but the compact died in the winter of discontent. After 1979 the unions were neither willing nor able to take on the left at the leader's behest.

The demise of the patently undemocratic solid block vote should not necessarily be considered a triumph for democracy, though, for it was replaced by a series of smaller block votes often used capriciously.[42]

The future of the relationship between the unions and the Labour party is an uncertain one. In 1981 a group of trade union leaders formed the Trade Unions for a Labour Victory (TULV), an attempt by moderate union leaders to revitalize the links with the party leadership. The radical manifesto of 1983 and the subsequent humiliating electoral defeat could hardly have encouraged them. In 1984 TULV commissioned MORI to discover what proportion of unionists wanted to retain their union's links with the Labour party and to pay the associated levy on union funds. In only three affiliated unions did a majority of members wish to do so.[43] Subsequently the Conservative government sought to question the right of affiliated unions to donate funds to the Labour party on their members' behalf. Unions were required to ballot their members on political levies. The results were astonishing: by the end of 1985, 84 per cent of 7,300,000 unionists had voted in favour of retaining the levy. Paradoxically, when the government required certification of the proportion of individual unionists opting out of paying the levy, it discovered something quite different: 40 per cent of mineworkers opted out; 35 per cent of engineers opted out; 48 per cent of steelworkers opted out. Fortunately for Labour only 2 per cent of transport workers opted out. The involvement and support of the unions is crucial to the Labour party at every level, and though the levy issue shows that, at the very least, old loyalties are not dead, considerable anxiety remains among party leaders that powerful unions such as the electricians, the power workers and the engineers are showing an increasing tendency to act independently of the TUC and to show little enthusiasm for Labour politics.

This concludes discussion of the leadership and organization of the Labour party. In 1960 the general secretary of the party identified three centres of decision-making within the movement: the parliamentary party, the NEC and the conference. 'None of these elements can dominate the others', he said. 'Policy cannot be laid down: it must be agreed.'[44] The general election campaign of 1987, generously sponsored by the affiliated unions, indicated that the basis of that agreement still existed. What the effect of another term in opposition will be is difficult to estimate.

Notes

1 See 'Changing Styles of Labour Leadership', in Dennis Kavanagh (ed.), *The Politics of the Labour Party* (London, Allen & Unwin, 1982).

2 See R. T. McKenzie, *British Political Parties* (London, Heinemann, 1955), pp. 426–31.

3 See Francis Williams, *A Prime Minister Remembers* (London, Heinemann, 1961), p. 535.

4 For an account of this debate, see P. M. Williams, *Hugh Gaitskell: A Political Biography* (London, Cape, 1979).

5 Alan Watkins, *Observer*, 16 November 1980.

6 See Austin Mitchell, *Four Years in the Death of the Labour Party* (London, Methuen, 1984), p. 51.

7 *The Guardian*, 4 June 1984.

8 See Ivor Crewe, *The Guardian*, 30 September 1983.

9 Jimmie Reid, *Observer*, 16 September 1984.

10 See Philip Snowden, *An Autobiography* (London, Nicholson & Watson, 1934), pp. 757–61.

11 R. A. Dowse, *Left in the Centre: The ILP 1893–1940* (London, Longman, 1966), p. 93.

12 These developments are detailed in D. Butler and D. Kavanagh, *The British General Election of 1979* (London, Macmillan, 1980).

13 See Terry Coleman, *The Guardian*, 6 October 1983.

14 *Tribune*, 3 December 1982.

15 *The Guardian*, 12 October 1985.

16 During one debate in Brussels, for example, Leslie Huckfield, who had exhausted his time and thus had his microphone cut off, produced a megaphone to continue his speech. (See *The Guardian*, 23 November 1984.)

17 See L. Minkin, *The Labour Party Conference* (London, Allen Lane, 1978).

18 C. R. Attlee, *The Labour Party in Perspective* (London, Odhams Press, 1937), p. 93.

19 See R. T. McKenzie, 'Power in the party: intra party democracy', in Kavanagh, *The Politics of the Labour Party*.

20 See P. M. Williams, *Hugh Gaitskell: A Political Biography*.

21 His reasons for doing so are set out in *Parliament, People and Power: Agenda for a Free Society* (London, Verso, 1982).

22 For example, a member of the Boilermakers delegation, mandated to vote against reselection, chose to be absent when the vote was taken and his union's vote was cast in favour. An AEW delegate changed his mind on the electoral college issue and switched 900,000 votes to the pro-college lobby.

23 Peter Jenkins, *The Guardian*, 22 October 1980.
24 *Labour Party Yearbook 1984–5* (London, Walworth Road, 1985).
25 'Representation in the Labour party', in Kavanagh, *The Politics of the Labour Party*, p. 206.
26 *The Guardian*, 30 June 1983.
27 *The Guardian*, 25 November 1985.
28 See *Campaign Guide* (London, Conservative Research Department, 1983).
29 See Ian Taylor, 'Ideology and policy', in C. Cook and I. Taylor (eds.), *The Labour Party* (London, Longman, 1980), p. 37.
30 *The Guardian*, 12 April 1985.
31 *Sunday Times*, 9 March 1986.
32 Indeed, disillusioned Blacks in Hattersley's Birmingham Sparkbrook constituency left the party in 1986 to form their own Democratic party. The stakes are potentially high. It has been calculated that the Black vote could be crucial to Labour in as many as forty inner city constituencies. (See *The Guardian*, 19 February 1986.)
33 Bennie Bunsee, 'Black section – the future', in *Asian Herald*, 27 January 1986.
34 In Kilroy-Silk's constituency his left-wing opponents formed new unemployed members' branches and thus swelled the size of the management committee from 85 to 142 in a matter of months. Kilroy-Silk called unsuccessfully upon the NEC to reconstitute his management committee by removing entryists. Indeed his original opponent for the seat was expelled from the party in May 1986 though his expulsion was not endorsed by the district party.
35 *The Guardian*, 14 December 1984.
36 Quoted in McKenzie, 'Power in the party'.
37 Ibid.
38 See *The Guardian*, 19 June 1982.
39 Three members of BS were expelled from the Sparkbrook constituency party after a television appearance. (See *The Guardian*, 26 January 1986. See also note 32 above.)
40 See R. McKibbins, *The Evolution of the Labour Party 1916–1924* (London, OUP, 1974), esp. ch. 7.
41 See 'The Tradition of Voluntarism', in *British Journal of Industrial Relations*, 12, no. 3 (November 1974).
42 See Robert Taylor, *The Guardian*, 5 October 1980. See also n. 22 above.
43 *The Guardian*, 2 August 1984.
44 Quoted in *The Guardian*, 22 October 1980.

7 Who Are the Socialists?

When considering the Labour party in parliament it is important to bear in mind that the party was established expressly to represent labour directly in parliament, and so it comes as no surprise to discover that in its early days not many Labour MPs had been to university! Between 1906 and 1918 no fewer than 89 per cent of Labour MPs came from the working class and even after the party assumed government the proportion was 71 per cent.[1] The great majority of Labour MPs were workers representing working-class constituencies. Just as we might expect. But for how long did the working class retain its preponderance?

Perhaps the first distinctive feature that a student of parties would be aware of when looking at the postwar PLP is its age profile: it has tended to be an older party than its rival. For example, nearly two-thirds of Labour MPs elected since the war have been over fifty. Moreover, a typical PLP would comprise more than 20 per cent over sixty. Although the landslide victory of 1966 brought an increase in younger MPs, the safer seats still were held by older members, leading to the conclusion that a safe seat might frequently have been seen as a reward for lengthy service to the movement. And when times were hard electorally these older members, usually working-class, tended to predominate as a matter of course.

In terms of educational background, nearly one-third of the Labour MPs during the period Mellors studied (1945–74) had been to school only for the minimum period prescribed by the state. In the interwar period the proportion was much higher, at around three-quarters. But Mellors's figures for the whole period, if broken down, reveal a rapid transformation that the averages hide: by the mid-1970s the proportion of Labour MPs with a minimal formal education stood at only 16 per cent. There is no doubt in Mellors's mind that this represents an important shift away from the working class. In particular, they have been replaced by the grammar school/university products, who 'form what has been described as the meritocracy'.[2] Mellors's statistics show that whilst the proportion of MPs with minimal formal education had dropped from 43 per cent to 16 per cent of the PLP in the 1945–74 period, that of MPs with a university education had risen from 34 per cent to 56 per cent. In part this process was the result of a conscious effort by the leadership to improve the 'quality' of Labour MPs. As one Fabian put it, 'With all the education there is about these days Labour must show that its candidates are as well qualified as the Tories'.[3]

We have seen that the safer Labour seats tended to be represented by older members. These MPs were invariably sponsored by a union and almost equally invariably had left school at the earliest opportunity. But even they tended, with time, to be replaced by younger, better educated members.

Finally on the subject of formal education, as we might expect, few of Labour's MPs during Mellors's period had been educated at public school. Even so, at around 19 per cent (in comparison with the Conservative party's 80 per cent) the number is higher than might have been expected; indeed, when we consider ministerial appointments in Labour governments we shall see that the proportion is higher. Significantly, a number of Labour's leading figures, including some leading radicals, have been educated at public school.

Consonant with the changing educational background of Labour MPs is the changing occupational background. The expansion of graduates has been matched by the expansion of professionals. By 1966 the number of professionals within the Labour party had outstripped that in the Conservative party. By the mid 1970s more than half of Labour MPs were professionals whereas the proportion of workers in the PLP had been more than halved. Mellors has characterized this process as the 'displacement of workers by teachers',[4] and we shall be considering this trend in greater detail later. Not only are there more professionals in the modern Labour party than in the Conservative party but they tend to be different kinds of professional. For the Conservatives the armed forces and the diplomatic service form the core of professional recruitment; for Labour it is law and medicine and increasingly teaching. Studies of graduate employment have indicated that it is predominantly the graduate children of manual workers who moved into teaching[5] and thus the increase in Labour's professionals is another facet of the march of the meritocrats. The proportions of this relatively short march are significant: teachers and lecturers have more than doubled their representation since the war.

Another important feature of the make-up of the PLP is the number of trade union officials, representing 12 per cent of Labour MPs. This has been a relatively elderly, relatively stable group which does not often achieve office. In many senses it has provided a kind of ballast for the PLP.

We have already noted the growing importance of local government apprenticeship in the Conservative party. For Labour this kind of experience has always been valued; indeed almost half of Labour MPs had held elective office before entering the House. Mellors called Labour 'very much the party of urban government' and this is still largely true. Moreover, the average period of service of Labour MP councillors is just under ten years, time enough for a measure of an individual's abilities to be taken.

The importance of trade union sponsorship to candidates is obvious. The success rate of such candidates since the war has been in the order of 70 per cent, and in the case of the National Union of Mineworkers (NUM) it is substantially higher. On the whole, sponsorship does not represent a status symbol (though it does for some) but an indication of active involvement in the trade union movement. Nevertheless, there is a clear and increasing tendency on the part of unions to opt for younger, better educated candidates to sponsor in their constituencies, though they have not done so as enthusiastically as other constituencies.[6] Indeed sponsorship probably offers the worker his/her best chance of selection these days, and this is particularly true of NUM sponsorship. Parenthetically, it would be odd if this tendency to sponsor candidates whose union links were tenuous did not have long-term consequences for the relationship between the unions and the Labour party.

Since the war, then, the PLP could be said to comprise three principal occupational groups: the professionals, trade union officials and workers. The professionals comprise two sub-groups: the first are in the older-established professions and are usually solidly middle class and liberal in outlook; then come the newer professions, especially teachers, whose numbers have expanded so rapidly. For their part, the trade union officials (and other miscellaneous groups) have remained more or less static in number. And finally the workers, traditionally occupying a key position in the party's development, and who find themselves increasingly replaced by the new professionals. In comparison with its major rival, the Labour party in parliament is far less homogeneous and, over the last thirty years anyway, substantially less stable in background and composition.

In terms of ideology, research suggests that traditionally the older-established professions have been associated with liberal attitudes towards, for example, humanitarian and third world issues, and by their nature have tended to permit MPs to combine their parliamentary and professional careers, perhaps giving a broader perspective to their political attitudes. The new professionals, though, are 'much more strongly associated with the wider issues and principles of socialism'[7] than either the traditional professionals or, and this is more important, the group which they are tending to replace, the workers. Traditionally the workers have been 'strong on the ... bread and butter issues and more moderate on ideological positions'.[8] So the changing structure of the PLP, according to Mellors, was likely to have substantial effects upon the party's ideological stance. We will certainly need to examine this development further but can conclude our discussion on the postwar PLP with Mellors's comment: 'It is a paradox that as Labour increasingly opens its ranks to meritocratic competition, the more exclusive the social composition of the party becomes.'[9]

Burch and Moran, tracing these developments up to 1983, suggest a modification to the dominant trend, but point out that since the numbers of Labour MPs elected in 1979 and 83 were the lowest since 1935, any generalizations must remain hypothetical. In both of these elections, however, there was a clear fall in the proportion of Oxbridge and public school educated members and a comparable rise in the proportion of manual workers. The authors are right to be wary of generalizing not simply because the numbers concerned were small, but also because, to some extent, the conclusions suggested by the data in 1979 and 1983 are contradictory. However, it is worth making the point that there were proportionately fewer of the new professionals amongst the new recruits to the PLP and proportionately more manual workers. In addition, even more had local government experience.[10]

Kavanagh is less convinced by the putative reversal of the trend towards meritocracy. He points out that in 1979 only 15 per cent of the parliamentary party had elementary education compared with 43 per cent in 1945, and that in 1979 – and we can add in 1983 – the decline in the new professionals could chiefly be accounted for by the failure of Labour to win any but its safer seats, many of which are held by sponsored MPs, the least affected by the meritocratic trend. In 1987, however, sixty-nine MPs joined the parliamentary party. Of these around 40 per cent were what Kavanagh defines as 'new-professional meritocrats (teacher, lecturers, political organizers, welfare and social workers). Approximately the same proportion had been to university (three to Oxbridge) though none had been to public school. There were amongst the new intake only a handful of manual workers. Moreover, the image of a Scottish Labour party more truly representative of the workers is demonstrably false.

Kavanagh points out that two aspects of this trend towards a predominantly middle-class, meritocratic PLP reflect similar changes in society as a whole. He is anxious to emphasize, though, that the rates of change are not comparable.[11]

When we move up the PLP hierarchy, to cabinet level, we encounter a problem as far as Labour is concerned: the numbers are small and could not, for obvious reasons, reflect any post-1979 changes. Nevertheless, earlier trends are clear enough. The student of parties will immediately observe that, in Kavanagh's words, 'the higher one ascends the political hierarchy, the more socially and educationally exclusive it becomes'.[12] All the same, Labour cabinets have traditionally comprised nearly 50 per cent of ministers with elementary education; more than half of Labour ministers had not been to university though just over 25 per cent had been to public school. Moreover, 55 per cent were from working-class families. Many of Labour's 'great names' of the past came from this background, including its first prime minister and leading members of Attlee's 1945 administration, such as Ernest Bevin and Aneurin Bevan. More recently that tradition has tended to be eroded, with Harold Wilson's deputy George Brown being the last senior working-class cabinet figure. It was, in fact, during Wilson's period as leader that the trend we have observed in the party as a whole, that of the replacement of workers by meritocrats, gathered momentum. When Wilson left office in 1970 only three cabinet ministers came from the working class. It is true that Callaghan's ministry contained four but none was senior. Burch and Moran, too, write that there has been a 'changing balance in favour of those who have practised a middle-class profession, at the expense of those who were, at some stage of their adult life, manual workers'.[13]

There are other changes: first, a trend towards ministers educated at university. These are the meritocrats, the products of working- and lower-middle-class homes who have had such an impact on the party at large. They are the beneficiaries of the improved state education system, the scholarship generation, and include many senior figures in the modern Labour party, such as Wilson, Kinnock, Hattersley, Shore, Healey, Mrs Castle (and Jenkins and Rodgers of course). It is they who have been running the Labour party for the last quarter of a century.

Second, Burch and Moran point out that the influence of aristocratic and upper-middle-class families, by way of contrast, is in decline from prewar cabinets; moreover, since 1970 Labour cabinets have contained not a single Harrovian or Etonian, not a single aristocrat. Kavanagh, on the other hand, uses the term 'patrician' rather than aristocrat, therby including upper-middle-class professional families, and in this classification he finds a continuing tradition, including such figures as Attlee, Dalton, Cripps and Gaitskell and more recently Crossman, Gordon-Walker, Jay, Benn (and Owen) – and we might add Michael Foot and Shirley Williams. It is hard to refute the argument that these individuals have been disproportionately influential in the development of the party.

Third, our attention is drawn by Burch and Moran to what they take to be 'the most striking long-term alteration at the top of the Labour party': the substantial number of those meritocratic cabinet ministers who were actually born into the working class but who rose, through education, into the middle class – and often, of course, into the new professions. At first sight this category might appear set to play, as Burch and Moran seem to imply, an important part in the party's long-term future. In a sense they might be thought to bring the best of both worlds: to put it crudely, humane, working-class hearts and educated, middle-class heads. This line of reasoning looks less persuasive on closer examination. The left-wing Labour MP Dennis Skinner has written rather scathingly of the 'smooth-tongued, generally tall, dark, handsome men . . . percolating and permeating their way around the slag-heaps . . . and into the miners' welfare to . . . weave a series of ten minute speeches out of a concoction of the 1926 strike; the beauty of pigeon and whippet racing . . . and grandfather's long-cherished pit helmet and safety lamp!'[14] This new phenomenon, the ex-working class meritocrat, is 'of the people' only by ascription; certainly he or she is seldom considered as such by the people themselves. Moreover, as we have seen, they tend to be more ideologically motivated, less concerned than working-class MPs with 'bread and butter' issues. But there is more to be said: their long-term influence, simply by definition, cannot be great. The post-1944 Education Act meritocrat has to be part of a 'one-off' generation. No foreseeable education change is likely to have a similar impact. There are a number of senior figures in both major parties who find that a consoling thought.

When Kavanagh analyses the background of the fifty-eight ministers who have held a post in a Labour cabinet since 1964 he concludes that exactly half may be classified as meritocrats, a quarter as working class and a fifth as patricians. Kavanagh then goes on to ponder the emergence of a definable Labour establishment and concludes that is is possible to discern the emergence of such an establishment 'based on dynastic and kinship ties'. He gives as examples those sons and daughters of former Labour MPs who sat in the 1974 parliament; they numbered nine. 'If we took acount', he concludes, 'of MPs who were the sons and daughters of trade union officials, of Labour councillors, or nephews and nieces of Labour politicians, then membership of a political family would emerge as an important factor . . . '[15] This is no more than an interesting aside. Kavanagh does not suggest, indeed would not find the grounds to suggest, that these families held any disproportionate sway in the councils of the Labour party. Yet it is interesting to recall that three of the contenders for the party leadership in 1980, each of them left-wingers, were the products of political dynastic families.

All in all, there is considerable evidence of Labour's having become far less of a working-class party in terms of parliamentary representation and leadership since the war, and as we have seen the most recent intake of 1987 tends only to confirm this steady transformation.

It is interesting to note the kind of changes in ideology that might be said to have resulted from this transformation, but we would have to start with the obvious caveat that influxes into the parliamentary party in recent years have not been very great. Even the land-slide victory of 1966 brought only sixty-seven new MPs. In 1974 and again in 1979 the party acquired only thirty-nine new recruits and in the calamitous election of 1983 a mere nine. The influx of over seventy new members in 1987, however, is likely to have a substantial ideological impact, greater than any change since 1966, though whether it will be as noticeable with the party being in opposition is another matter.

There can be little doubt that most critics expect a change in the parliamentary party. In fact, Labour's candidates became an issue during the 1987 election campaign when the Alliance leaders referred to the fact that a great number were considered to be hard left. The phrase '101 Damnations' was coined by David Steel and picked up by the Conservative campaign managers. Labour's opponents feared that in the event of Labour's forming a government a very substantial majority of the newly enlarged parliamentary party would be on the left. In the event only about half of the number necessary for Labour to form a government were elected and their influence will be limited in proportion. Let us consider their likely impact.

When Labour's reselection process had been completed, in June 1986 (apart from a handful of constituencies which had been suspended or were the subject of enquiry) only six of the PLP's 210 MPs had suffered the indignity of deselection, though thirty-three had announced their intention of resigning. As we have already observed, the expected purge of the right did not take place, the only prominent right-winger to be deselected having been ex-chief whip Michael Cox. According to some these figures understate the true effect of deselection, which has been to persuade many Labour MPs in their early or mid-sixties to retire of their own accord. Among the declared retirements are at least four who 'announced their decision not to stand for reselection when it was already clear that they had very little chance of winning'.[16] Apart from these measurable consequences of deselection the effect on the party's morale generally can only be guessed at, and we made our guesses in the last chapter.

In the 1983–87 parliament, Labour's 210 MPs comprised approximately 115 who would generally have been described as centre-right and 95 who would normally have been considered soft or hard left.[17] Of those on the left 63 were in the Tribune group and 34 in the hard-left Campaign group (with some members in both). Of sitting members who did not contest the 1987 election, 32 were of the centre-right and only a handful of the left. Amongst new candidates in 1987 the Campaign group recruited particularly well; in fact, their

candidates had secured a far greater proportion of safe than marginal
seats. Tribune, conversely, did somewhat less well; again, because
fewer of their candidates had secured safe seats and many more the
kind of seats that Labour hoped to win but in the event did not win.
The centre-right group Solidarity claimed that it too would secure 'a
substantial number of moderates in the new intake'.[18] In truth it is
possible that Solidarity will be replaced by Tribune as the largest
single group; indeed Tribune may even have to change from its
traditional room in order to accommodate the influx of new
members.

What will these new MPs look like and how will they act? They
will, we are told, be 'hungry for change'. A liaison committee
was established among predominantly left-wing MPs and
candidates whose vice chairman Peter Hain said that the task
of new MPs would be to 'rejuvenate and radicalize' the PLP.
One veteran Tribunite has said, 'an awful lot of young, new and
leftish people, many of them from Scottish LLC [the liaison
committee] . . . will be the flavour of the PLP after the next
election'.[19]

A senior backbencher Jack Ashton argues that there is little cause
for concern among moderates. 'The House of Commons has been
taking in rebels for centuries and most of them turn out just to be
rascals. Some will get bought off, some will be sold off, some will end
up in the bar, and others will get their heads down and become good
constituency MPs.'[20] Kinnock would have to build up support across
the ideological spectrum, but the soft left will play a crucial role.
Already it has aligned itself behind Kinnock to an extent that would
have been considered unlikely at the time of the miners' strike, and
this has altered the balance of power in the parliamentary party,
perhaps crucially. The clarion cry of nationalization has been
replaced by a more sophisticated call for 'social ownership' and the
party leadership, with general though by no means universal
support, has endeavoured to press the point, without success, that its
non-nuclear policy does not make it 'soft' on defence.

These are real advances for Kinnock and for mixed economy
socialism, though to what extent they will be reflected in the parliamentary party in the 1987 parliament remains a matter for debate. In terms
of the perennial debate between social democracy and fundamentalism
these advances appear to suggest that the social democrats are once
again beginning to gain the upper hand. In replacing nationalization

by social ownership (without a whisper of clause four) Kinnock appears to have succeeded where Gaitskell utterly failed. All the same, doubts persist as to how substantive and permanent the victory is; it clearly rests on compromise though, as the commitment to unilateral disarmament, somewhat unconvincingly endorsed by the centre-right, demonstrates.

Kinnock will find among his new left-wingers some uncompromising characters and Lord Wilson has expressed considerable anxiety about Kinnock's ability to cope with the challenges.[22] Ignoring the enigmatic Ken Livingstone (now MP for Brent East), ex-leader of the Greater London Council, who has already begun to build up a personal following in the London area, a number of new MPs have stated their radical views categorically. The member for Bow and Poplar is alleged to have described her party leader as 'an obstruction to socialism' who 'must be removed' and is considered by the trotskyite *Socialist Organiser* as a 'life long class fighter against capitalism and against the reformist Labour leadership'; in his victory speech the new member for Brent South declared that his constituents could not be free until the people of Soweto were free, and the candidate for Bradford North wants to 'abolish the monarchy, the House of Lords, the sacking of the generals, the admirals, the air marshals, the senior civil servants, the police chiefs and, in practice, the judges, and people of that character'. The predominantly left-wing target Labour government group has declared: 'We are not interested in reforming the prevailing institutions . . . through which the ruling class keep us "in our place". We are about dismantling them and replacing them with our own machinery of class rule.'[22]

What Kinnock will hope, and with some justification, is that this group will form only a small minority in the parliamentary party and that its militancy, together with what he will regard as the electorate's unambiguously anti-extremist preference as manifested in the 1987 general election, will drive the soft left even more firmly into his camp. His personal ascendancy in that campaign and its apparent success will make a good starting point.

It is worth reflecting, though, on what a Labour government would have looked like in 1987 because that gives a clear indication of what a future Labour government might look like, unless Kinnock manages to transform the constituency parties (as there is every indication that he wishes to). A survey of 121 of the 130 marginal seats in 1987 (23) revealed that the candidates were very preponder-antly middle class; only three had a background of manual work. More than half of the group were in their thirties (whereas the average age of the 1983–1987 PLP is fifty-four). The largest single occupational category will come as no surprise: teachers and lecturers comprised 34 per cent of the total, with 'researchers' and local government officers providing the next largest category. More than one-sixth of the group were local councillors and approximately 70 per cent belonged to the Campaign for Nuclear Disarmament. A Labour government, then, would almost certainly be younger, more middle class, better educated and, probably, more radical than any of its predecessors. Kinnock's ability to control such a government would depend upon a number of factors. Apart from his own stature in the party in the country there would be the matter of reselection. Some left-wingers have argued that reselection, if its method of operation is not changed, will only become a sharp weapon when Labour is in power. Constituencies could threaten to deselect MPs who had collaborated in the postponement of manifesto commitments. No doubt it is for reasons like this that Kinnock will attempt as soon as possible to involve all local party members, and not just activists, in the deselection procedure. Equally important will be the extent to which the hard left is able to organize its forces. Peter Hain of the left liaison committee (with which Livingstone is associated) feels that the 'new radicals' are too well practised in the 'art of political manipulation' to be blown off course. 'The failure of a Labour government to deliver on issues dear to the left wing and the Labour conference would result in an explosion of dissent. . .'[24] All the same, the problems which Kinnock would face if he were heading a Labour government must remain speculative for the time being.

The important consideration in assessing both of these factors is constituency feeling. If the hard-left can mobilize constituency opinion behind it then not only might deselection become a sharp and discriminating weapon but collectively at conference the constituencies might have a larger say in the policies adopted by a Labour government than they have hitherto. It is appropriate, now, to turn our attention to the constituencies.

In a detailed study of Labour constituency parties Janosik[25] analysed the background of local leadership in the 1960s and, in many respects, although it was not his intention, he explains the genesis of the problems which came to beset many constituencies in the following two decades. It will be helpful to look at his findings in some detail. First he examines the age structure of local activists and the local leadership (defined as MPs and candidates, chairmen, secretary-agents and annual conference delegates) according to Labour's strength in the constituency. Thus 40 per cent of activists in what he calls 'strong' constituencies had first become involved before the General Strike of 1926, whereas only 9 per cent of activists in marginals had been involved for this length of time. As for local leaders 47 per cent had been active since before Attlee's government took office. In terms of age, 46 per cent of leaders in 'strong' constituencies were over fifty-six years old and only 6 per cent were under thirty-five, whereas in the marginals only 11 per cent were over fifty-six and 17 per cent under thirty-five. As for occupational background, 31 per cent of leaders in the 'strong' constituencies were from a professional or business background, with an almost identical figure for the marginals, whereas although 32 per cent of 'strong' constituency leaders were from a skilled or semi-skilled working background only about half as many helped to lead marginal constituency parties. Moreover, over 80 per cent of party members in 'strong' constituencies were trade union members and 19 per cent of the leaders were trade union officials; the comparable figures for the marginals were, respectvely, 64 per cent and 21 per cent. In educational terms 69 per cent of 'strong' constituency leaders had elementary education compared to 49 per cent in the marginals, whereas only 17 per cent of the first group had any post-secondary education in comparison with 23 per cent in the marginals. When these figures are further broken down they disclose wider variations between MPs and candidates on the one hand and their officials on the other: 57 per cent of MPs and candidates had received some form of post-secondary education compared with 11 per cent of officials.

All in all these figures give a good idea of what the constituency parties looked like for much of the postwar period. The 'strong' parties tended to be controlled by older men whose political inspiration came from a different period. In terms of occupational background, unlike the Conservative party, there was not an overwhelming preponderance of businessmen and professionals, but much more of a balanced mixture, in both 'strong' and marginal constituencies, with a powerful trade union presence which has no equivalent in the Conservative party. In educational terms, though, the general pattern was not so dissimilar: the more important the position, the more likely it was to be held by somebody with post-secondary education. In the Labour constituency parties, though, this apparently meritocratic tradition was leavened by a substantial component of manual labourers with a basic state education, and this was particularly true of the 'strong' constituencies. We find, then, the typically 'strong' party to have been led, probably, by older men, possibly somewhat out of touch, many of whom were workers without much formal education. As the 1960s turned into the 1970s, many more of these constituencies were to provide easier pickings for determined groups of young well-educated activists than did the marginals.

Clearly the role of the trade unions in the constituency parties is a crucial one, especially in a typical safe seat. However, one aspect of trade union dominance which probably has as much importance as any is frequently overlooked: the unions put up the money. This means that in many a safe seat the constituency party does not engage in fund-raising activities. We have already seen how important this activity is for the Conservative constituency parties, for it binds the membership together in a continuous non-ideological activity. This is also true for the Alliance parties and indeed for many Labour parties in marginal constituencies. Fund-raising tends to bring people together, not divide them; it produces camaraderie and, equally important, a formal and an informal infrastructure. It is possible that the absence of this kind of continuous communal activity, with specified and attainable goals set periodically, has been one of the reasons why Janosik's 'strong' parties did not compare in membership or enthusiasm with many of the marginals.

Janosik went on to consider the political attitudes of his constituency activists and discovered that, on the whole, they were by no means as extreme as was generally supposed. Indeed Martin Harrison had earlier drawn attention to the exaggerated contrast between extremist constituency associations and moderate trade unions, pointing to the considerable extent of overlappping membership between the two groups,[26] though he, like Janosik, also acknowledged the unpredictable and often divided nature of constituency parties. When asked to assess the party's policies, more than half of local leaders in both 'strong' and marginal constituencies were supportive though around 40 per cent in both were in favour of moving 'slightly to the left'. Moreover, 11 per cent in the marginals favoured a move 'sharply left' as compared with only 2 per cent in

the 'strong' constituencies. Needless to say, all who favoured moves
to the left thought this would prove electorally advantageous and
bring greater unity to the party.

In a final chapter on factionalism, Janosik considers these attitudes
in greater detail. His findings lend support to Miliband's earlier
analysis of the divisions between the 'revisionist' (i.e. social
democrat) right and the 'fundamentalist' left in which he had argued
that 'genuine compromise between revisionism on the one hand and
socialist purpose on the other, is impossible; and . . . any verbal
compromise which may be reached on the basis of ingenious
formulas . . . ensures, in practice, the predominance of policies
favoured by a revisionist leadership'.[27] We have seen that this
conflict became central to the development of British socialist
ideology; we have seen it in the parliamentary party, so it comes as
no surprise to find the conflict between fundamentalists and social
democrats at constituency level. Janosik tells us that he found no
genuine consensus at constituency level; what he found was more of
an armed truce.

Janosik took trouble to emphasize that despite his generalizations
there were considerable differences between constituency parties
which went far beyond his categorization. This point emerges even
more clearly from a detailed study of three London constituencies
undertaken by Turner[28] He emphasizes the imprint of the socio-
economic character of the constituency on the values of local parties.
Safe Labour seats are almost invariably in stable working-class
communities and activists tend to remain associated with the party
over a long period of time. 'As veterans in a party that is never
threatened by the opposition, they develop routinized ways of dealing
wih problems . . . [and] the party's goals remain unchanged',[29]
leading to traditional socialist policies with a strong 'bread and
butter' focus being favoured. Marginal constituencies, on the other
hand, usually have to contend with a higher rate of mobility and thus
a more rapid turnover of personnel with a consequent continuous
influx of 'new ideas'. These constituency parties, he says, 'can hardly
escape the intellectual jousting and sharp clash of ideas, with the
likelihood that ideological splits will be interwoven with personal
rivalries'.[30]

It is ironic that one of the constituencies which Turner studied was
the 'safe' seat of Bermondsey where 'the crisis threats of an
opposition were but memories'. Five years later, though, Bermondsey

fell to the Liberals at a by-election and as we consider Turner's analysis of an ageing leadership rooted in 'bread and butter' issues, and bear in mind the overall picture that Janosik built up of such constituencies, we begin to understand how a determined minority of able, better educated young activists, whose political vocabulary and imagery were more global and more ideological than that of the old guard, could take control of such a seat. After all, the old guard presided over a closed and largely non-participatory system; any change of leadership would represent not a social but a palace revolution. In Bermondsey, though, the old guard hit back and it was chiefly the consequent split which allowed the Liberals to win the seat.

What was true of Bermondsey was true of a considerable number of inner city seats in London, Liverpool, Manchester and other large cities. An elderly, often out-of-touch, well-entrenched leadership did little to encourage new members who wished to participate in the constituency's affairs and so when the palace revolutions came, the old guard had little support. Many marginal constituencies, by contrast, made a virtue of necessity and possessed organizational structures which were far more open and more receptive to new activists and new ideas. They, too, were influenced by the move towards greater militancy but were not such easy prey for take-overs. The consequences of these differences have now become apparent in, for example, the kinds of candidates adopted by the Labour party for the last two general elections and indeed for the next one. As we have seen, the hard left has won strong representation in many of the safer seats, but in many of the marginals it is soft-left or indeed centre-right candidates who have tended to be selected. Collectively these new constituency activists have had a much more profound impact upon the party than did their predecessors, especially in securing the constitutional changes which, they would claim, have democratized the party.

These changes took place at a time when, as Paul Whiteley shows[31], Labour party membership was falling substantially. Whiteley argues that the failure of the Labour governments of the 1960s to solve the various 'bread and butter' problems which affected many traditional supporters had a disproportionate effect upon working-class activists. These men and women had been motivated to join the party by what Whiteley calls instrumental reasons (he uses the word in much the same way as we used it when discussing the working-class Conservative vote): for example, to provide ordinary people with better social services. The predominantly better-off and better-educated, by contrast, had been motivated by more 'diffused and generalized' considerations when becoming active: for example to build social justice. The instrumentally motivated would clearly be more likely to become disenchanted by what they considered to be the failure of their party in government, whereas the more generally motivated would be likely to take a longer perspective and probably be more concerned with the next and not the last Labour government. The difference is really between those who think concretely and those who think in an abstract or ideological way. In Orwell's *Animal Farm*, when Squealer, the ideologist, announces the figures for the farm's record harvests, the animals declare that they would prefer less statistics and more food. Like the farm animals, numbers of working-class activists decided that the party in power had failed them and they left it.

Equally important, says Whiteley, the working-class activists, for reasons we have already discussed, began to find themselves at odds with a party that was becoming increasingly middle class and ideological. He concludes: 'Thus a small articulate group of middle-class activists may paradoxically drive out working-class activists.'[32] It is not at all clear why Whiteley considers this a paradox.

It was not until the late 1970s that the general shift towards the left produced fruits and we have already looked at most of these. As far as the constituencies were concerned, mandatory reselection of MPs was clearly the most important. In January 1981 the Campaign for Labour Party Democracy produced a booklet entitled *How to Select and Reselect Your MP*. This booklet contained an analysis of how every Labour MP had voted in eleven divisions which were considered to judge their socialist commitment and also listed the MPs who had signed the statement organized by the centre-right opposing the outcome of the Wembley conference of January 1981. Only eight MPs were deselected in this first round, though it is possible, to say the least, that a number of those who joined the SDP were, in fact, 'jumping before they were pushed'. Criddle gives brief accounts of the deselection of the eight[33] which tell much the same story; that of a 'take-over' by groups of left-wing ideologists – 'public sector middle-class activists – caricatured as "the polyocracy" '. One deselected MP in East London was specific, blaming his defeat on 'the bed-sit Trotskyists from the North East London Polytechnic, the usual lefties, community relations officers, people who have only been in the party a few years'.[34] Denis Healey was prompted to declare his opposition to the replacement of MPs by 'professional idealogues'.

It would be inappropriate to imagine that every teacher or polytechnic student is a trotskyist. Certainly David Coates has written a rosy picture of the new radicals who, in alliance with the traditional 'sources of resistance and radicalism', will, he hopes, become an important force in British politics. Whether Mr Kinnock would be quite as enthusiastic must be open to doubt, but what is not is that this new class comprises less, maybe appreciably less, than 15 per cent of Labour's vote.

Of the various groups of ideologists who have helped to 'radicalize' the Labour party in recent years, driving out working-class activists as it did so, none has received more attention than the Militant Tendency. We have already considered the impact of Militant upon the party organization; its effects, real and symbolic, upon the constituency parties, have been equally profound. The Militant Tendency is nationally organized, with a ruling central committee (six of whom are still members of the Labour party), with some 300 full-time workers, so it has been claimed (compared to Labour's 200),[35] with a regional and district structure, and which publishes not only *The Militant* but also a number of papers aimed at specific groups of workers, such as *Militant Miner*. One of its principal objectives has been to infiltrate the Labour party and the trade union movement. It has enjoyed a considerable measure of success particularly in the north-west, more specifically in the Liverpool district party. As we have seen, the Labour party was sufficiently concerned to establish three major enquiries into the activities of Militant and as a result of the third, to take action to expel·Militant supporters from the party. The principal charges against Militant supporters were that they were in breach of the constitution in belonging to a party-within-a-party and that in achieving their influence, for example in Liverpool, they acted in a grossly irregular manner, by the 'swamping of delegate meetings by unelected members, selective notification of meetings, false accounting of membership and, most serious of all, intimidation of ordinary members' so that 'the Liverpool district party, run in this way, has hi-jacked control over the party's other processes'.[36] As a consequence of Militant's success the Labour-controlled Liverpool city council became embroiled in a bitter rates controversy with the

Conservative government in the mid-1980s in which the city was the loser.

Although many of those who have become active in the Labour party in recent years have been middle class, rank-and-file Militant supporters are usually aggressively proletarian. Not for them the 'middle-class fads like gay lib, student protest or radical feminism. What matters is the struggle of the working class . . . '[37]

Labour supporters might urge that it is unfair to include Militant activists when seeking to answer the question 'who are the socialists?' and they clearly have a point. The fact remains, though, that, no doubt for all the reasons we have been discussing, the Labour party of the 1970s became increasingly open to take-over in the constituencies from extremist groups of whom Militant is only one (though the most important). If we were to turn our attention not to Liverpool but to Manchester we would find a district party which had also been taken over by extremists, though not Militant supporters. Here hard-left activists had taken control from an ageing, moderate leadership through tactics so dubious as to prompt NEC adjudication on no fewer than five occasions. The difference between the 'old-school' Manchester activists and the new has been analysed as follows: 'The moderates were mostly Manchester born and bred, usually skilled workers or small businessmen, working-class and not university educated. The left had been involved in student politics and came from middle-class homes in the South of England.'[38] Here again the pattern of a changing, radicalized party in the large cities is seen to emerge.

The Labour leadership has not found it easy to expel Militant supporters from the party and its attempts to do so have hardly ruffled the surface, though the cases of Mulhearn and Hatton could be viewed as symbolically very important. The extent to which individual constituencies have the capacity or indeed the desire to act against Militant supporters will differ widely. However, as the case of the Manchester district party illustrates, there are many in the constituencies whose party bona fides are less easily challenged but who would nevertheless be considered extremists by ordinary Labour supporters. These will help to shape the Labour party of the future.

It is important not to get these changes completely out of proportion; similar things have happened in the Labour party before. On the other hand, it is equally important to state what appears to be an unequivocal fact that at the local level as at every other level the Labour party appears to have become more middle class and more ideological over recent years. It remains now to assess the extent to which Labour voters have followed a similar path.

Karl Marx was absolutely convinced of the ultimate political triumph of the working class, given universal suffrage, and he was equally convinced that the triumph of the working class would be synonymous with the triumph of socialism. Other commentators have expressed a similar view more prosaically, pointing out that Labour had only to mobilize its natural class support to win every general election. It is not certain whether this is true any longer; what is certain is that Labour has seldom managed to do so in the past. We have already discussed some of the more important reasons for this failure in a previous chapter but a more general point needs to be made. It is abundantly clear from the history of the Labour party, going back over a hundred years, that the great mass of Labour support, unionized labour, was not strictly socialist. Hardie's description of their ideology was 'labourism'. Until the Labour governments of the 1960s a clear identity of interest frequently existed between socialism, labourism and the interests of the working class in general. Policies designed to promote greater equality, for example, would have been supported by each camp. This was partly because a very substantial section of the population considered itself underprivileged; indeed, enough to vote in a Labour government. But to the extent that a Labour government actually succeeded in pursuing policies leading to less inequality, so the underprivileged naturally became fewer in number and the interests of the recently elevated no longer necessarily coincided with those who remained underprivileged. The interests of a generally well-paid work-force (or one that believes it is well paid) are not the same as those of the unemployed. A Labour government committed to egalitarian policies will therefore not necessarily be representing the interests of the majority of workers. In other words, to the extent that Labour governments pursue policies leading to greater equality they become, at least in the short term, victims of their own achievements, increasing the number of instrumental voters.

In chapter 4, we spoke about other factors which may have tended to loosen Labour's hold on the working-class vote: 'populist-authoritarian issues' which, research tells us, are considered important by the majority of ordinary people. On each issue it is the policies of the Conservative party which come closest to representing the beliefs of the working-class voter. Labour's policies on these issues are not shaped by the perceived interests of the working class but by socialist ideology. All parties will feel obliged to pursue policies which they consider to be 'right' even when the electoral consequences are damaging. But if they are wise they will ensure that the damage is limited by the fullest explanation of what they are doing; if they are wise they will listen to what those whom they claim to represent have to say. This debate is reminiscent of that early in the party's history: should the Labour party give the people what they want or what it thinks they ought to want? Those who answer that, of course, it must be a mixture of the two, must remember the importance of dialogue. A party which purports to speak for the mass of ordinary people must, when it is departing from their perceived interests, take care fully to explain why it is doing so.

The Labour party, in the last twenty years, has moved increasingly away from its traditional voter. In his report to the annual conference in 1982 general secretary Mortimer said: 'It is not the party's policy, but public opinion which needs to be changed. No socialist worthy of the traditions of the Labour movement should refuse, on occasions, to go against a strong current of public opinion if . . . he believes that such a course is necessary for the purpose of social progress.'[39] There can be little doubt that the election manifesto of 1983 represented a position further from that of public opinion than any of its postwar predecessors and many in the party were unhappy about what the head of the research department called the 'failure to prepare a manifesto, and a policy programme which accurately reflects the concerns and needs of ordinary voters'.[40] Denis Healey wrote after the election that the battle had been lost not in the campaign itself but in the preceeding three years when the party acquired a 'highly unfavourable public image'. It is an open question whether it was the actual policies or the terms in which they were expressed which caused the damage, but Healey points unequivocally to the lack of dialogue between the party and its supporters. The same was said about the 1987 campaign, which was far more professional in every respect, but which was also preceded by years of unfavourable publicity.

Butler and Kavanagh conclude their study of the 1983 general election by observing that the election had witnessed a 'spectacular retreat' from Labour amongst working-class voters. Labour became the party of a 'section of the working-class, only 38 per cent of manual workers and 39 per cent of trade unionists voted Labour, while 32 per cent of trade unionists voted Conservative. Members of the relatively affluent working class . . . clearly preferred the Conservative party.' Moreover, Kellner demonstrated that many who actually voted Labour did so in spite of its policies and not because of them.[41]

Whiteley, it will be remembered, argued that the fall in active support for the Labour party was tied, amongst other things, to the party's performance when in office. Performance was measured in terms of 'bread and butter' policies relating to unemployment and the retail price index. He used the same model to test the effect of 'poor performance' on Labour voting with much the same consequences, indicating the growing importance of instrumental voting. 'There is also', he added, 'survey evidence to suggest that the fragmentation of the working class brought about by changes in the occupational structure is a significant factor' in explaining the decline of the Labour vote.[42]

Accounts of the death of the Labour party have been much exaggerated. The party's heartland, though not as solid as it once was, showed its residual strength in 1987. All the same, having considered the geo-political map, we recognize that the preponderance of British people live in 'Tory Britain' and that Labour must do much more than hold on to its heartland if it is to win power again. This will not be easy as long as the Alliance parties remain vigorous especially in southern Britain. There is little doubt that Labour will remain a major force for the foreseeable future; there is little doubt that since 1983 the party has taken important, possibly decisive, steps to improve its central organization and especially its public relations machine, as 1987 amply demonstrated; there is no doubt whatever that much more needs to be done if Labour is once again to become anything more than the party of a section of the working class.

Notes

1 See Dennis Kavanagh, 'Still the workers' party? Changing social trends in elite recruitment and electoral support', in his edited *The Politics of the Labour Party* (London, Allen & Unwin, 1982).
2 Colin Mellors, *The British M.P.* (Farnborough, Saxon House, 1978), p. 50.
3 Quoted ibid., p. 51.
4 Ibid., p. 74.
5 R. K. Kelsall et al., *Times Higher Educational Supplement*, 25 February 1972.
6 See W. D. Muller, *The Kept Men* (Hassocks, Harvester, 1977).
7 See S. E. Finer, H. B. Berrington and D. J. Bartholemew, *Backbench Opinion in the House of Commons 1955–59* (London, Pergamon, 1961), pp. 104–14, and H. B. Berrington, *Backbench Opinion in the House of Commons 1945–55* (London, Pergamon, 1963), pp. 183–84.
8 Mellors, *The British M.P.*, p. 120.
9 Ibid., p. 125.
10 Martin Burch and Michael Moran, 'The changing British political elite', *Parliamentary Affairs*, 38, no. 1 (Winter 1985), pp. 7–8.
11 Kavanagh, *The Politics of the Labour Party*, p. 100.
12 Ibid.
13 Burch and Moran, 'The changing British political elite', p. 10.
14 Quoted in Mellors, *The British M.P.*, p. 78.
15 Kavanagh, *The Politics of the Labour Party*, p. 103.
16 *The Guardian*, 10 June 1986.
17 Figures taken from *The Guardian*, 6 July 1986.
18 Ibid.
19 Ibid.
20 *Sunday Telegraph*, 20 July 1986.
21 Ibid.
22 Ibid.
23 *The Times*, 30 July 1986.
24 Ibid.
25 E. G. Janosik, *Constituency Labour Parties in Britain* (London, Pall Mall Press for The Foreign Policy Research Institute, 1968).
26 Martin Harrison, *Trade Unions and the Labour Party since 1945* (London, Allen and Unwin, 1960), pp. 238–9.
27 R. Miliband, *Parliamentary Socialism* (London, Allen & Unwin, 1961), pp. 344–45.
28 J. E. Turner, *Labour's Doorstep Politics in London* (London, Macmillan, 1978).
29 Ibid, p. 313.
30 Ibid, p. 314.

31 See Paul Whiteley, 'Declining local membership and electoral support' in Kavanagh, *The Politics of the Labour Party*, pp. 111–34. See also his *The Labour Party in Crisis* (London, Methuen, 1983), esp. chap. 3.

32 'Declining Membership and Support', p. 123.

33 Byron Criddle, 'The election locally', in D. Butler and D. Kavanagh, *The British General Election of 1983* (London, Macmillan, 1984).

34 Ibid.; p. 223.

35 See Michael Crick, *The Militant Tendency* (London, Faber, 1986).

36 Peter Shipley, *The Militant Tendency* (London, Foreign Affairs Publishing Company, 1983), p. 72.

37 *The Guardian*, 27 February 1986.

38 *Sunday Times*, 1 Decemeber 1985.

39 K. Roberts, F. Cook and E. Semeonoff, *The Fragmenting Class Structure* (London, Heinemann, 1977), esp. chap. 9.

40 Quoted Butler and Kavanagh, *The British General Election of 1983*, p. 278.

41 Ibid. The original is in italics.

42 Peter Kellner, *New Statesman*, 23 June 1983.

8　The Parties of the Alliance

We have spent three chapters on each of the major parties and yet will be dealing in this single chapter with two parties, the Liberals and the Social Democrats. This apparent lack of proportion is entirely due to the obvious fact that, whatever part these parties may play in the future of Britain, they have played very little part in its immediate past; Lloyd George was the last Liberal prime minister almost seventy years ago. On the other hand, since the 1960s the Liberals have enjoyed a revival, or series of revivals, which have made them once more a force to be reckoned with, especially in local government. Moreover, their alliance with the Social Democratic Party (SDP) in 1981 was potentially the most important development in British politics since the advent of the Labour party.

If we wish to recount the story of the Alliance we had better start where all good stories are supposed to start: at the beginning. The difficulty in this case is that there is no certainty when the Alliance 'began'. Some would suggest that the Alliance began when the so-called gang of four left the Labour party and issued the Limehouse Declaration (25 January 1981) which led to the establishment of the SDP. Others would want to go back to the Orpington by-election of 1982 when, as we have seen, the Liberals overturned a very substantial Conservative majority and showed that the hitherto unshakeable hold of the two major parties could actually be broken on occasions. Both possibilities assume a reflexive role for 'the Alliance': in 1981 the SDP emerged as a response to Labour 'extremism'; in 1962 the Liberals had popped up simply as a kind of reflex to the increasing unpopularity of the Conservative government.

There is another possibility. Suppose these vehicles of modern voters' discontent represented something more than a fairly recent electoral reflex; suppose they also represented a distinctive view on politics which was in fact independent of fluctuating electoral support and much older. Where might we look for the origins of such an ideology? Why not amongst the confusing cross currents of political doctrines caused by the sudden re-emergence of socialism and trade unionism in the 1880s and 1890s where, after all, the major parties took on their present forms?

The politics of this late Victorian period included three distinct but generic political traditions on the left – the radical liberal, the social democratic and the fundamentalist socialist, distinct but not separate because of overlapping support. There was clearly a great deal of fluidity regarding political allegiances at the time with new groups forming and reforming almost continuously, and what they stood for and how they related to other groups continues to be a subject for debate.[1] There were, for example, the 'new liberals' who claimed to speak in the interests not of the traditional nonconformist middle class but of the industrial working class. They argued strongly that the state ought to be prepared to intervene in the economy in the interests of the individual liberties of all citizens. About the same time as the new liberals were changing the contours of liberalism the 'new socialism' was beginning to establish itself. There was much in common between the movements, not least the friendship between the leading members. Indeed several leading Fabians attempted to form a common group with leading 'new liberals' in 1891, though without success. All the same, collaborative undertakings of an intellectual nature did occur, such as the Rainbow Circle,[2] including Hobson and Herbert Samuel for the liberals and Ramsay MacDonald and Sidney Olivier for the socialists. This group claimed to espouse a gospel called amongst other things new radicalism and collectivism. The liberal magazine *The Nation*, declaring the left-wing liberalism merged imperceptibly into socialism, believed that the way ahead would be charted by adherents to a broad progressive platform that it presciently called social democracy.[3]

As time passed clear differences of approach appeared amongst these various progressive forces but the most serious separated not socialists from liberals but fundamentalist socialists (of both moralistic but especially scientific varieties) from social democrats and liberals. The scientific fundamentalists, in contrast to the social democrats (and liberals), had great faith in bureaucratic expertise: it was Beatrice Webb who said that socialism ought to be bureaucratic, bourgeois and benevolent. Symptomatic of the divergence of views was the reaction accorded to the Webbs' plan for the break-up of the Poor Law which involved compulsory retraining for the able-bodied unemployed and the provision of detention colonies for malingerers. Both liberals and social democrats rejected the scheme as inhumane. In fact Hobson, a radical liberal, condemned all socialism that did not represent an expression of popular will, whereas the (especially scientific) fundamentalists were ready to define socialism as what the people *needed* not what they *wanted*; they operated what Peter Clarke perceptively called an 'ascribed class consciousness'. The real cleavage was essentially over the proper relationship between political elites and public opinion, and the social democrats were on the side of the liberals and not that of the fundamentalist socialists. 'It is better to give [the people] what it wants than something "technically better" which it does not want.'[4]

We know of course that within a comparatively short time the Liberal party was to cease to be a major force and that the social democrats, and indeed many former Liberals, were to join the ranks of the Labour party. But hindsight lends an inevitability to this development which it scarcely merits. Moreover, unless we are careful it lulls us into forgetting that the two traditions of fundamentalist socialism and social democracy (with Liberal elements) did not merge, though with the domination of the Labour party by Fabians and ex-Fabians, faith in the state bureaucracy became well established. We find G. D. H. Cole writing in the 1950s that Labour's task should be to try to stimulate democratic activism among the masses yet this was what the bureaucratic mind was indisposed to do. R. H. S. Crossman wrote later of a tendency among Labour party leaders towards a 'profound distrust' of active democracy. He believed that socialism could develop either towards some 'veiled form of totalitarianism' or towards 'increasing, even at the cost of "efficiency", the citizen's right to participate in the control of government and industry'.[5]

It has been suggested by fundamentalist critics that the social democrats within the Labour party were quite content with this superficial unity as long as they dominated the party leadership. The evidence for this allegation may be circumstantial but it is pretty overwhelming. On the other hand, the social democrats have not been strong enough always to pursue the kind of policies they would themselves favour, though they could usually hope if not to dominate then at least to exercise considerable influence upon the policies and indeed the destiny of the Labour party. Their ability to do so, reinforced ideologically by the two celebrated 'revisionist' tracts which came out in the 1950s, Crossman's *New Fabian Essays* and Crosland's *Future of Socialism*, reinforced in policy terms by the defeat of unilateralism (the left's *cause célèbre*), reinforced institutionally by Gaitskell's leadership, was shown to be tenuous. Two blows fell, the first painful, the second almost fatal: Gaitskell's decision to oppose entry into the European Community and Wilson's accession to leadership following Gaitskell's untimely death. The first divided the social democrats, the second broke their hold on policy-making machinery; as the decade wore on so their struggle with the fundamentalists became more bitter, intensified rather than abated by two periods in government.

Until quite recently reasons abounded for the social democrats to remain within the party and to continue the struggle for control of the party policy-making machine. Writing before the end of the last Labour government, Peter Jenkins[6] drew attention to the divisions between the right whom he saw as the inheritors of 'Croslandite Socialism' (and whom he, too, referred to as social democrats) and the left, and he argued that these social democrats wished to lead their party down the same road as the West German SPD. Jenkins suggested that their success would depend upon Dennis Healey's becoming the new party leader after Callaghan, a development he thought likely at the time. He assumed, that is to say, that the struggle would take place, as it always had, *within* the Labour party.

Indeed it is clear that even after the 1980 conference and the election to the party leadership of Michael Foot, leading social democrats shrank from a break with the party. Peter Jenkins echoed their own thoughts when he wrote: 'The Labour Party has a strong residual base, the Liberals would be uncertain allies, and the electoral system is powerfully hostile to third parties.'[7] All the same, it is apparent that Owens, Rodgers and Mrs Williams had concluded that the Wembley Conference on 24 January was to be symbolically decisive. If that conference were to accept the suggested 30–30–40 collegiate structure for leadership elections they would announce their intention to leave the party. It did so and on 25 January, together with Roy Jenkins, the three made their Limehouse declaration, establishing the Council for Social Democracy and promising to set up a new party before Easter 1981.

Having withdrawn from the protective shell of the Labour party it became necessary for the Social Democrats to make some ideological justification of their position and it fell to their most experienced politicians to do so. Roy Jenkins in fact had already done just that in 1979 in the Dimbleby Lecture in which he appealed to all non-fundamentalist socialists and progressive to recognize certain realities of modern politics. He took as his starting-point the ossification of the British party system and the deleterious effects, especially on the economy, of adversarian politics. He argued that the two great parties were coalitions but that no real community of interests existed within the parties any longer. All that remained was the original structure locked, as it were, in ice. He argued for the building up, through a proportional electoral system, of 'living' coalitions. He dismissed the counter arguments that such coalitions could not provide the effective and coherent government which the first-past-the-post system (however unfairly) tended to produce: 'Do we really believe that we have been more effectively and coherently governed over the past two decades than have the Germans . . . ?' He spoke of the disproportionate power of Labour's left wing within present systems, referring to them as a small group of activists with the power of political life or death over an MP elected by 20,000 to 30,000 voters. Jenkins argued that Britain suffered from an inability to adapt consistently, together with too great a capacity to change inconsistently. 'The paradox is that we need more change accompanied by more stability of direction.' To this end it was necessary to harness the 'innovating stimulus' of the free market and yet avoid the brutality of 'untrammeled distribution of rewards' or indeed indifference to unemployment. Jenkins clearly saw a role for state intervention but his social democratic state was to be important, not omnipotent – it 'must know its place'. Market forces, too, would be used but were clearly insufficient left to themselves.

It was important, wherever possible, to devolve decision-making, giving parents a voice in the school system, patients a voice in the health system, residents a voice in neighbourhood councils, and so on. Social Democrats would be unequivocally committed to end the class system but had no wish to replace it with a brash meritocracy. Above all Jenkins believed it to be necessary somehow to involve in politics at a variety of levels the considerable and growing nmber of people presently alienated from the business of government, for he feared that if the centre could not 'hold' then the extremists on both sides would compete for power.

The three ex-Labour ministers wrote at length along similar lines to Jenkins. A principal theme of David Owen's *Face the Future*[8], William Rogers's *The Politics of Change*[9] and Shirley Williams's *Politics is for People*[10] is the rejection of rigid central control of political and economic life. Owen's concern is to re-establish a sense of community involvement in politics. He quotes appreciatively from William Morris (Morris's avowed marxism notwithstanding) whose socialist watchword was 'fellowship' and who argued consistently for small units of production – though scarcely along the kind of lines the SDP would care to follow. Owen shows himself to be 'anti-corporation' (and anti-nationalization) but, he argued then, not anti-socialist. He discussed with approval many diverse forms of social ownership and industrial democracy, all within the decentralist tradition. All the same, Owen clearly saw himself as the champion of a tradition which he describes as radical, libertarian and decentralist, a tradition which, so he claims, seeks to revive the concept of 'fellowship and community within a participatory democratic society'.[11] Socialism, he says, has become fixated with equality and yet 'the record of state controlled societies in overcoming inequality is not such as to make any thinking democrat change his or her predisposition for liberty'.[12] 'A true democracy', he claims, 'will mean a progressive shift of power from Westminster out to the regions, to the county and town halls, to communities, neighbourhoods, patients, tenants and parents.'[13]

Mrs Williams, in a more closely argued work, writes that the social democratic consensus was based above all upon constant economic growth but these days are gone because the basis for Britain's steady if unspectacular growth was cheap raw materials and cheap food. Without growth, redistributive politics become much more painful and welfare expenditure, tending always to grow to meet growing demand, cannot be so readily increased. Like Owen, Mrs Williams finds the British economy dominated by over-large corporations. In fact she goes much further. In every sphere of state activity the units have become too large, impersonal, bureaucratized and unresponsive. This is true of large business corporations, large trade unions, the National Health Service, the education system and even 'local' government. Wherever possible Mrs Williams argues for 'the need to strengthen the structure of self government at lower levels'.[14] Power, she says, must be diffused through society. Industry must be democratized and a whole range of administrative bodies, such as school governors, hospital managements, housing estate managements, and so on would be opened to wider democratic participation. The social services, too, could be 'given to the people', says Mrs Williams, 'through mutual help, family grouping and the use of volunteers . . . . If the welfare state is for people, then people must not be reduced to being seen as claimants or clients.'[15] The operating principle in every case 'is what will benefit our citizens, rather than our corporate organisations'. Most of the nation's problems, writes Mrs Williams, are better tackled by involving 'the community'.

The phrase 'community politics'[16] provides a convenient and obvious signal for a change of course. It is appropriate at this point to consider how closely SDP ideology resembles that of its Liberal ally, to whom we shall now turn. It follows from what has gone before that what the parties have in common originated not just in the hastily contrived alliance of the 1980s but also in the shifting alliances of the 1890s; common ground was discovered following the adaptation of the *laissez-faire* liberalism of the nineteenth century to encompass state intervention in the interests of social justice, and Liberals had always been aware of the common ground. Lloyd George, frequently argued strongly for a Liberal–social democratic alliance because he believed that a class-based socialist party would frighten the middle class into reaction. Since the Liberal revival party leaders (none more so than Grimond) have sought consistently to establish a realignment of the left, excluding the fundamentalists. The Social Democrats were soon to realize that they had much in common with the Liberals besides electoral necessity. The Liberals believe in a society in which the individual is able to *participate* to a greater extent than at present in the decisions which shape his or her own life; the attempt to build such a society is an essentially radical exercise.[17] But it is more than radical, it represents one of the basic tenets of traditional liberal faith: man's rationality. Jo Grimond argued that men are bound by a common rationality; for him it takes the form almost of natural law: 'If you believe that people might freely choose such things as the legalization of indiscriminate murder of one's children, then there really is no basis for Liberalism at all.'[18] 'What is destructive', Grimond goes on, 'is the untimely submission of our will simply to what we are ordered, without any consideration of whether it is right or wrong.' The objective of liberalism for the modern Liberal, then, is the creation of opportunities for men and women to become self-directing, responsible persons. 'Certainly it is impossible to *make* men self-directing responsible citizens', says another Liberal writer. 'They must do this for themselves. But society can create opportunities for them to become so, and encourage them to take them.'[19]

To return to the radical nature of the task of creating a Liberal society: Liberals have never been happy with the label of 'centrists', or middle-of-the-roaders. 'By any strict language Liberals are the true Left, the real progressives', said Elliot Dodds.[20] Moreover, Donald Wade rejects the whole idea of a left–right spectrum based merely on attitudes to public ownership; for Liberals it is more important to measure from libertarian values to totalitarian ones and in terms of this classification the extremes of left and right (in standard terminology) fuse into each other. There are only two senses in which the Liberals (and their SDP allies) may be said to be unequivocably centrist: first, their attitude to 'public' versus 'private' debate is entirely pragmatic, and second, they enjoy substantial support from the middle classes. Liberals supported the nationalization of coal and opposed that of steel, they supported the sale of council houses in some areas and oppose it in others. As for middle-class support, it is after all chiefly though by no means entirely this sector which currently seeks to participate, that is, to shape the decisions affecting society. All the same, the involvement of many more citizens in the shaping of decisions, the extension downwards and outwards of decision-making machinery along the lines and of the reasons advocated by J. S. Mill, are hardly middle-of-the-road policies.

Participation, then, is the keyword of modern Liberal policies and it stands in contradistinction to what it considers to be the bureaucratic elitism of fundamentalist socialism and the social elitism of the major strands of conservatism. But equally important to the understanding of modern liberalism is the context of participation. At the grass roots the context is provided by the *community*. Community is defined as 'a group of individuals with something in common: nationality, neighbourhood, religion, work, workplace, victimisation', and so on. In the pamphlet *The Theory and Practice of Community Politics*[21] the authors claim: 'People establish identities in relation to the communities to which they feel they belong. Within them they establish a sort of role or status, a level of expectation of behaviour in their own and other people's eyes which they use as a measure of their own success and worth.' Moreover, membership of a community implies some responsibility for other members, and thus communities possess a capacity for mutual care and support. But community does not necessarily imply neighbourhood or geographical proximity; it might be based upon membership of some voluntary organization, for example, though it usually presupposes a local or regional setting.

Community politics for the Liberals is both a means and an end. It is a means of creating a less unequal society superior to the state socialist's public ownership and it is an end in so far as giving as many citizens as possible a say in the decisions affecting their lives is a goal of traditional liberalism. Liberals reject the notion of class politics, claiming that the working class is not everywhere oppressed, exploited, or indeed opposed to capitalism and is certainly not always sympathetic to those who are oppressed and exploited, Moreover, the political 'mouthpiece' of the working class, the trade union movement, is regarded by many Liberals as an increasingly unrepresentative vested interest which stands in the way of local industrial democracy. In a liberal society party politics (and thus class politics) would cease to dominate, giving way to group politics and community politics.

The implications of participation are by no means limited to the context of community politics, however. Participation is a basic ingredient of the policy of decentralizing government, of giving more not fewer powers to democratically elected local authorities, of inserting a regional tier into the British system of government which would require devolving executive powers to assemblies in Scotland and Wales. Again these are hardly middle-of-the-road policies; they would radically shift the balance of power in Britain away from London.

More important to Alliance strategy, though, is the parliamentary and electoral context of participation politics for, as is well known, both parties are firmly committed to electoral reform. The constitutional impact of electoral reform, certainly in the long term anyway, could be considerable. Not only would it be likely to produce coalition or minority government but as a direct concomitant it would weaken party influence, with voting in the House less easily controlled by the whips and with backbenchers consequently seeing their parliamentary careers more in terms of active membership of committees than of party loyalty. Parliament, as a consequence, would become a much more important body and its select committee system far more competent, in terms of scrutinizing government policy and eventually perhaps of actually helping to shape policy.

With a weakened party system and a strengthened committee system the pressure for more open government would be much more difficult to resist and a change in the nature of the relationship between backbenchers and the civil service might well ensue, thus affording better protection for the individual citizen (another traditional liberal aim). In short, given time, a proportionately representative House of Commons could revolutionize British parliamentary practice. This prospect may be considered as enticing or terrifying but it may not, surely, be considered middle-of-the-road.

Paradoxically the Alliance parties would hope that the policies emanating from such a parliament would be, if not middle-of-the-road, at least consensual, enjoying the support of the majority of the population.[22] Critics have argued that there is nothing new in this aspiration, indeed that it has long been realized within the British political system. Successive governments since Macmillan's have followed 'me too-ist' policies enjoying support of the majority of the population, with singularly unsuccessful results. Indeed, say these critics, the architects of postwar society were consensus liberals – Keynes and Beveridge. Jack Straw MP suggests that the major parties have become more polarized recently precisely because of the manifest failure of the kind of consensus politics that Liberals and Social Democrats are promoting. 'If the centrist policies . . . had worked, there would be no Margaret Thatcher and no Arthur Scargill.'[23] However, it can be countered that no government of either party pursued consensual policies with conviction and none had the institutional backing to implement them successfully. Labour's support for the mixed economy, to give one example, has never been more than equivocal. Besides, Straw's only alternative to consensual politics is surely polarized politics; he does not *end* with Thatcher and Scargill (and a moan of despair), he actually *begins* with them. The anomaly of Straw's position, from an Alliance perspective, is that he is obliged not simply to argue that socialism is better than consensualism but that socialism plus conservatism is better, because in a two-party democracy government by one party today implies government by the other tomorrow (or next week!). What the Alliance argues is that adversarian politics are *ipso facto* inappropriate for the solution of modern industrial social and economic problems.

There are two lines of criticism of the Alliance, though, which may be considered more substantive than Straw's. The first is that the

Alliance has failed so far to establish any readily identifiable national policies, except on constitutional reform. The second is that where such policies can be identified, they do not fit easily into the participatory pattern. Statutory control of incomes is a good example. The Alliance would seek to answer these criticisms by arguing that a reformed parliament, free of the self-destructive tendencies of adversarianism, would provide a framework within which policies would emerge as pragmatic responses to problems. (Hence, presumably, Owen's advice to a constitutent to go to the other parties if he wanted a manifesto.) In reality, at the national level (though not at the local one), the Alliance could be said to be offering little more than its services as honest broker to the major parties.

It is ironical that in both parties of the Alliance, with their emphasis on participation, cries should frequently be heard from the rank and file of over-domineering leadership. In 1985, for example, the SDP leadership was accused of reversing policy passed at its council (against the advice of the platform) calling for a ban on the use of plastic bullets in Northern Ireland. One ex-Labour MP declared: 'There's a lot of outrage at the way in which council decisions are being ignored. It's very near a resigning matter.' There can be no doubt that since the founding of the SDP David Owen has dominated party affairs to the extent that in many people's minds he has come to personify the party and its aspirations. Owen's often-quoted reluctance at the idea of the two parties merging,[24] for example, has been a decisive influence. Most commentators refer to Owen's single-mindedness, some to his 'unwavering sense of self-righteousness',[25] a leader who believes 'not in policy but in himself', compared by one commentator to General de Gaulle or even Joan of Arc.[26] Whatever the constitution of the party, there can be no doubting Owen's dominance in terms not only of presentation but of policy itself. Owen himself acknowledges his pre-eminence, declaring: 'As leader, of course, I'm seen to be out in front on quite a lot of thinking and policy-making.' It has been suggested that Owen views the SDP as being united principally in support of himself, rather like a US political party. Yet the dominance of minority party leaders is nothing new: Grimond, Thorpe and Steel were each criticized for being domineering and certainly Grimond's influence on Liberal policy, way-marked by his writing and TV appearances, was profound. Owen's influence over his party is likely to take a form not readily defined in standard left/right terms, though generally his commitment to equality, as indicated by his writing, seems less than robust.[27]

Owen's position as party leader is not very different from Steel's in the Liberal party, though Steel's party critics are more vociferous. When he appointed Alan Beith as his deputy in 1985 (a post which party activists had tried unsuccessfully to create two years previously) there was considerable and well-publicized resentment inside and outside parliament, with the radical MP Michael Meadowcroft taking a leading role. In 1986 Meadowcraft renewed his attack upon Steel's style of leadership in the party newsletter, *Liberator*. The most stinging criticism of Steel's dominance, though, was made as a consequence of his almost single-handed building of the understanding which sustained Mr Callaghan's government in office in 1977 and 1978. It was Steel's uncompromising belief in the necessity of showing that Liberals could and should share power (however disproportionately) that carried the day, not any democratic decision. However, plans have been laid to reduce the leaders' powers by the possible creation of a new post of chairman of the parliamentary party and by the election (not selection by leader) of the chief whip.

With two such dominant leaders the question of who could lead an Alliance government or Alliance party (if as is possible a decision to merge were taken over the next election) becomes acute. Liberal leaders were sufficiently concerned about this issue to exclude its being debated at the party's assembly in 1985. There is an understanding that the leader of the larger party (almost certainly the Liberals) would assume leadership, though this could prove to be only a temporary measure. Owen's reluctance to see the parties of the Alliance merge owes something to a fear of his party's and his own ambition being submerged. Hence he and his henchman Thomas (chairman of the SDP's powerful organization sub-committee) have dampened local enthusiasm for joint candidate selection even in areas, like South Cambridgeshire, where the local feeling was strongly in favour. Owen and Thomas are arguing strongly for a rough parity of winnable seats for obvious reasons, though it has to be said that the bulk of the seats have been settled.[28] In the longer term, the leadership issue is likely to be resolved by the respective popularity of the two leaders and it is clear that, possibly because Steel decided to take a 'sabbatical year' out of politics, he was less popular in 1985 than Owen, especially among the better-off and in the south. Both Owen and Steel have taken a calculated risk in purveying quite different public personas: Owen as a Thatcheresque conviction politician, Steel as a persuasive healer. Yet Steel's toughness should not be underestimated; he has been described as arrogant, manipulative and 'prepared to give the nod to a dirty trick or two'.[29] Much will depend upon which has judged the public mood more correctly.

Although some SDP leaders might find the idea of a merger between the two parties distasteful, many rank-and-file members do not share their inhibitions. Constitutionally the two parties cannot operate jointly but, according to the Liberals' secretary-general, 'there are certainly quite a few places where it is mysteriously the case that the meetings of both parties happen to be in the same place, in the same room, at the same time'.

It is appropriate at this point to say something about the organization of the two parties, though for obvious reasons not appropriate to say a great deal. To begin with the Liberals, the pattern of organization is similar to that of the major parties. Liberal membership, though impossible to measure accurately, is said to be around 185,000. At the grass roots are the constituency (and ward) associations, whose functions are electoral and include candidate selection, but also political, in the direct sense, through community politics. Active constituency associations produce broadsheets concentrating on local issues including 'grumble sheets' to be sent to local activists who will take up issues with the local authority. There are twelve regional associations for England, and associations for Ulster, Wales and Scotland. The annual assembly of the party consists of representatives from the constituencies and from the 'recognized bodies', that is, the National League of Young Liberals, the Women's Liberal Federation, the Union of Liberal Students, the Liberal Candidates Association and finally the important ginger group, the Association of Liberal Councillors, together with agents and organizers from headquarters and MPs. Apart from debating policy the assembly elects the party president and officers of the party in England and Wales and the members of the Liberal Council. The council meets quarterly and pronounces on policy matters, organizes fund-raising, maintains the party headquarters and formally adopts candidates.

In fact the party is run, for the most part, by a series of small committees, chief of which are the finance and administration board, the national executive committee and the standing committee. The finance and administration board, broadly speaking, runs party headquarters. On it sits the secretary-general, who heads the whole organization, and the treasurer. Both positions are appointed by the board. The national executive committee, appointed by council, is responsible for the day-to-day running of the party; it elects the finance and administration board which is responsible to it. For its part the standing committee, elected in the main by council, adopted candidates and MPs (and always chaired by an MP), co-ordinates the parliamentary and extra-parliamentary activities of the party. It is also responsible for long-term policy development as well as responding to urgent issues. Together with the national executive committee it is responsible for campaign and strategy.

In 1983 the party undertook a major exercise in devolution (true to party principles). Staff at party headquarters were cut from thirty-six to twenty-eight and 30 per cent of the annual budget of around £400,000 went to fund new regional appointments. Elections to the leadership have, since 1976, been by secret ballot in each constituency. Constituencies are then allocated electoral votes according to the number of votes the candidate received at the previous election and the length of the affiliation to the party. When members have voted, the votes allocated to the constituency are recorded proportionately. David Steel was the first leader to be elected by a method whose convolutions seem specially designed to appeal to Liberals.

Tensions within the Liberal organization have traditionally been felt between the leadership and the Young Liberals, who have a reputation for radicalism (not, like YS, of the trotskyite kind but of a more anarchistic nature)[30] and, since the founding of the Alliance, between the leadership and the Association of Liberal Councillors (ALC). This important group, pioneers of community politics, has its own headquarters at Hebden Bridge in Yorkshire and has an annual budget of £80,000, six full-time staff and considerable information resources. It produces three regular publications and numerous occasional booklets. The tension between ALC and the leadership stems from the former's belief that Liberal policies were being diluted to suit the SDP. Generally speaking, though, the ALC is more concerned with organizational and local political issues than with national policies, and it has come increasingly to accept the Alliance as inevitable. After the 1983 election the YLS attempted without success to weaken the leader's control of the manifesto but the leadership took pains to drw the ALC more into the party's policy-making machinery.

For its part the SDP, with a membership of 50,000 (from a peak in 1981 of 78,205), is organized not into constituencies but into area parties, with a minimum membership of around 200. The areas are responsible for selecting parliamentary candidates and electing a representative to the Council for Social Democracy. The council consists of 400 members and meets three or four times per year with the party president in the chair. According to the constitution the council is responsible for policy but in fact it does not make policy but simply accepts or refers back policy proposals emanating from the key policy committee. The policy committee oversees the membership, organization and terms of reference of some twenty-five policy groups, which publish their proposals as green papers. After consideration by area groups and other interested groups they then become white papers, which are presented to the council.

The constitution provides for the election of a leader of the parliamentary committee (i.e. the SDP leader) and a president, both to be elected by a postal ballot of the whole membership. Roy Jenkins became the first leader, defeating David Owen by 26,300 votes to 20,900 (though Jenkins resigned after the 1983 general election and Owen took over unopposed); Shirley Williams was elected the party's first president. The party organization, much smaller of course than that of the other parties, is under the control of the national committee, representative of all sections of the party, and chaired by the president. There is no corporate or group membership of the SDP and no serious internal disputes have become public, though the position of president is powerful enough to present a threat to the party leader at some future time.

It is well known that despite the parties' common approach to politics there have been important differences of emphasis on educational policy and major differences on defence. Machinery exists in the form of joint commissions to resolve these differences provided the will exists. Already on the major disagreement on defence Liberal defence spokesman James Wallace has presided over the dropping of the party's commitment to the unconditional and immediate removal of Cruise missiles at the 1985 conference. (In the same year, though, Scottish Liberals at their conference voted for the removal of all US bases from Scotland.) In 1986 a joint commission attempted to strike a compromise between the Liberals, who still wanted to remove all Cruise missiles from Britain eventually (and who have a strong unilateralist wing), and the essentially pro-Cruise and pro-nuclear deterrent SDP. Polaris would be retained for ten years, said the commission, thus delaying any decision about its replacement. Their efforts were sabotaged by Owen who refused to 'fudge' the issue (to be fair a majority of SDP candidates supported his position). At their assembly in 1986 the Liberals voted narrowly to retain their unilateralist stance. The defence issue still divides the parties, and indeed causes divisions within them. But in any case it is rather whimsical to believe that joint commissions will automatically settle differences through compromise formulas. The 1986 report of the commission on Northern Ireland, for example, was more radical than either Owen or Steel considered acceptable. Generally speaking the Liberal party is more radical than its SDP partner and the rank and file of both parties are more radical than the leadership. All the same, major problems have been resolved; the selection of parliamentary candidates for two elections has been surprisingly successful. Moreover, the process by which joint policies are discussed and formulated has usually worked well, though it will have difficult issues to handle in the future apart from defence.[31]

It is also true that differences exist at personal level not just between the Liberals and the SDP but among the SDP leaders themselves. Several of the younger leading figures see themselves as representing the (predominantly northern) working-class Labour tradition. For them the SDP was the Labour party reborn. They would have regarded themselves as anti-consensus and certainly anti-Liberal, and though they may be less vocal than they were, they are little more enthusiastic about the Alliance. In addition to this group are the Jenkinsites – pro-Liberal, middle-class and intellectual. Finally comes David Owen and his supporters. Owen may be classified more in terms of his psychological orientation than his political one; he is 'tough-minded' and has taken stands on issues such as the 1984 miners' strike very much further to the right than any of his Liberal partners. In short, anybody who believed that by leaving the strife-torn Labour party the Social Democrats would achieve ideological unity amongst themselves, leave alone with the Liberals, would have to be blind and deaf to be happy.

For all this, the Liberals and Social Democrats share a commitment to a new kind of politics the most immediate, tangible and symbolically important ingredient of which is proportional representation. This new kind of politics would seek radically to change the nature of local and regional government, the relationship between the executive and the legislature and that between the citizen and the official. A tall order indeed, necessitating what Mrs Williams called a 'quantum jump' in the thinking of politicians, and yet in so far as it seeks to redress the balance between the individual citizen and those who make decisions on his or her behalf, perhaps it is an objective which captures the spirit of the age.

Part of this 'new politics' is the attempt to abandon the traditional left versus right classification. Owen has made it a virtue openly to support the Thatcher government on occasions. SDP leaders have spoken of four polarities, measuring collectivism versus enterprise and liberalism versus authoritarianism. The intention is to identify the Alliance support as liberal/enterprising, an identity which, as Hugo Young points out, 'owes nothing to the language of the other two parties'.[32] It is obvious, too, from what has been said, that both parties of the Alliance concentrate not so much on substantive policies as on approaches to policy. Owen's *A United Kingdom* (1986), for example, suggests that 'we are badly governed, not because of the malice or lack of forethought of our leaders, but because the structure of our government and our society is fundamentally flawed'.[33] Steel, too, when listing his priorities for an Alliance government, speaks of constitutional reform – a Bill of Rights, repeal of the Official Secrets Act, the introduction of a Freedom of Information Act, the reform of parliament and of local government, devolution to Scotland and Wales and decentralization to the English regions all incorporating electoral reform. In 1986 a joint campaign was launched, entitled *People in Power*, pledging an Alliance government to these aims. The Alliance seems to argue, then, that governments have failed basically because they were unrepresentative and unresponsive; by implication, when they become representative and responsive they will not fail. Logically this does not follow but then, logic rarely plays a large part in politics.

Before moving on to consider the Alliance's electoral performance it is necessary to say just a word about the Alliance's record in parliament. How well do the parties hold together? Figures for the last parliament show that of 283 important divisions in the House of Commons between 1981 and 1983, all Liberal and SDP members voted the same way in 227. On no occasion did the parties oppose each other. The Alliance has a higher parliamentary profile in the present parliament, especially since 1985 when the leader of the Liberal party, by formal arrangement, was given the right to choose the topic for debate in three of the twenty 'Opposition Days'. Representation in the House's select committees is very thin, though they are represented on the committee of selection. The Liberals also have the right to raise their own amendments to the Queen's speech at the opening of each parliamentary session. There are around fifty Alliance peers, most being hereditary Liberals; the number of regular attenders is much smaller, however, but they do have the support of an administrative secretary and a research assistant.[34]

Over the past quarter of a century British politics has been invigorated by periodic eruptions of support for parties other than the major two. This support has usually gone to the Liberals but Plaid Cymru and the Scottish Nationalist party have also been recipients. On no occasion has such an eruption proved to be permanent, though the Liberals have been able to sustain small advances throughout the period. Since their first major postwar electoral triumph at Torrington in 1958, the Liberals secured an average of 19 per cent of the votes in all contested by-elections. There is, however, a significant variation in the Liberals' performance relating to which party is in office. In by-elections under Conservative governments the Liberals have averaged 23.3 per cent whereas under Labour the average by-electoral vote for the party is only 14.6. Studlar[35] has compared the Liberal performance over the whole of this pre-Alliance period with that of the Alliance itself and notes that, in their three periods of 'revival', which he dates at 1958–9, 1961–3 and 1972–4, the Liberals received an average vote at by-elections of 27.1 per cent, 29.4 per cent and 31.3 per cent respectively. In the period 1981–3 the Alliance scored an average vote of 31.2 per cent, a performance apparently similar to that of the Liberals, though not directly comparable because, as Studlar suggests, the Liberals were far more selective about which by-elections they contested.

The first by-election to be contested by the 'Alliance' was at Warrington in July 1981. Officially Warrington was fought by the SDP, though by the time the by-election took place an informal alliance had been made with the Liberals, and Roy Jenkins, the SDP candidate, enjoyed the considerable support of the Liberal by-election machine. By and large Labour was totally confident of holding its working-class citadels, of which Warrington was one of the strongest, against the new party. Warrington, everybody agreed, was going to prove a comfortable Labour victory.[36] In the event Jenkins secured 42.4 per cent of the vote and Labour's Douglas Hoyle 48.4 per cent. The Conservative candidate polled 7 per cent and lost his deposit. The next by-election test for the Alliance was at Croydon North West in October. The seat was marginal, with a Conservative majority of 3,769 in 1979, but the Alliance candidate was an unknown, the Liberal William Pitt. Pitt was successful, taking 40 per cent of the vote, with the Conservative at 31 per cent in second place. The Liberal party in Croydon North West had a membership of only thirty-two when the vacancy was declared. The Labour candidate predicted: 'It would be an election result the like of which we have not had since 1832 for Pitt to win here. When did a candidate who lost his deposit in one election win the seat in the next one?' Other notable triumphs followed for the Alliance. In November Mrs Williams scaled the heights of Crosby with its Conservative majority of 19,272 and in March 1982 Roy Jenkins won a narrow but notable victory from the Conservatives in Glasgow Hillhead. Thereafter support for the Alliance peaked, and with the dramatic impact upon domestic politics of the Falklands War soon to be felt, there was little but cold comfort for the Alliance. In only one of the post-Falklands by-elections did the Alliance win, and that victory was in the Labour bastion of Bermondsey where, as we have seen, special factors applied.

One of the dominant characteristics of these by-elections seems to give the lie to an important claim made by Alliance leaders: that they would inject a new vitality into the moribund electoral processes, that they would bring more people back to the polling stations. The increase in non-voting, especially after the Falklands War, was substantial. It is simply not true to say that Alliance intervention has dramatically altered the public's appraisal of by-elections. If we consider the 1983 election, the Alliance's best results, turn-out at 72.7 per cent, was down from 1979 by 3.3 per cent. Although this difference can be explained by the age of the electoral register, it was nevertheless one of the lowest of the century and shows that so far, at least, the Alliance has not enticed missing voters back to the booths.

Support for the Alliance in the general election of 1983 was remarkably consistent across the social spectrum, being lowest amongst the office and clerical category (C1) at 24 per cent, highest amongst semi-skilled and unskilled workers (D) at 28 per cent.[37] Similarly, support amongst the age groups and between the sexes was consistent. Moreover, unlike that of its major opponents, the Alliance role is not geographically polarized either north/south or urban/rural. 'Anyone seeking to find a reliable predictor of Alliance voting', says Norton, 'would be hard pressed to find one.'[38]

The 1983 general election was, predictably, both a triumph and a disaster for the Alliance: a triumph becuase of the 7.8 million votes gained (compared with 4.3 for the Liberals in 1979), because in more than half the seats contested the Alliance candidate came in second (only 11 deposits lost compared to Labour's 119); a disaster because the Alliance won only twenty-three seats, because of the twenty-six SDP members who stood after defecting from Labour (and in one case from the Conservatives) only four survived. In general terms the Alliance suffered from what is referred to as the 'plateau effect'; its share of the vote increased least where it was already strong, probably because the Labour vote had already been squeezed dry. It is almost certainly for this reason that so few of the so-called 'golden' seats, about fighting which Liberals and Social Democrats had been in considerable dispute, actually fell to the Alliance.[39] Of the 397 elected Conservative MPs no fewer than 273 faced Alliance candidates as their main opponent. It is ironic, as Butler and Waller point out,[40] that whilst the Conservatives spent their time fighting a Labour opposition in the House of Commons, two-thirds of them had to contend with the Alliance opposition in their constituencies.

Why did not the Alliance fare better? It is worth pointing out that 26 per cent of the popular vote constituted a better result than any Liberal campaign since 1923, and if twenty-three seats seemed (indeed were) poor reward for nearly 8 million votes they were still more than the Liberals had managed to muster since 1931. But had the Alliance scored 6 per cent more of the popular vote (thus becoming the second best supported party) it is quite conceivable that they would still have gained only seven more seats.[41] In other words, in terms of seats won, the Alliance simply could not realistically have done much better.

If the 1983 election left a bad taste in the mouths of the Alliance leaders it was soon to be replaced by the sweet taste of by-election and local government successes. On the by-election front there were four notable successes of which the most crucial was Greenwich, where the Alliance defeated a left-wing Labour candidate in a seat which Labour felt confident of holding. The local government elections in 1985, 1986 and 1987 showed substantial gains for the Alliance. Yet as commentators pointed out the Alliance did not manage to cut significantly into the Labour vote; in 1986 and 1987, for example, although gaining over 600 seats overall, the Alliance actually lost ground in the inner cities to Labour. Indeed, since the formation of the Alliance it has never managed to detach more than 3.5 per cent of the Labour vote. During this period the Alliance tended to do best when it distanced itself clearly from Labour policies, thereby winning over disaffected Conservative voters.[42]

All in all, there can be little doubt that by 1987 the Alliance had made a major impact upon local and national politics and that this impact was recognized and resented by the major parties.

Buoyed up by its excellent results in the Greenwich and Truro by-elections, the Alliance came to the 1987 general election with great hopes: in the event the result was a more bitter disappointment than even 1983. The Alliance's manifesto *The Time Has Come*, based upon the catch-phrase, was generally considered to have been a failure: 'Although it contains numerous good and sensible ideas, they are presented abysmally. The overall impression is one of timidity and incoherence.'[43] As the election campaign unfolded it became apparent that the manifesto had captured its flavour faithfully; it was lacklustre and diffuse. One of the most persistent complaints concerned the two-headed leadership, more especially the input into that leadership of David Owen. He was accused of aiming to win over Conservative dissenters at the expense of positively projecting the Alliance as a centre-left group. Owen it was who gave such prominence to defence; who pursued the idea of holding the balance of power instead of maximizing Alliance support; who emphasized a preference for a deal with the Tories and not Labour. This is not to imply that Owen was necessarily tactically wrong but in doing these things he was at odds with his Alliance partners, especially David Steel. Soon after the start of the campaign Alliance tacticians knew that they were likely to be facing a major set-back; to the end Alliance leaders clung publicly to the hope of a late surge in support, such as they had often got in by-elections. In every sense this was an admission of defeat.

Let us put 1987 in perspective. The Alliance secured over 7,300,000 votes – nearly one in four voters supported them. True, they were restricted to 23 seats (exactly the same as 1983) but as we have seen, the British electoral system always penalizes broadly-based third parties. True, Steel said during the campaign that anything less than thirty seats – and that was a 'rock-bottom figure' – would signal the failure of the campaign, but a failure is not a disaster. The potential disaster for the Alliance resided in their response to the defeat. Almost immediately Steel urged that the parties merge and Owen and his close supporters let it be known that they had no intention of merging. Others in the SDP argued that if Owen succeeded in blocking a merger the party would disintegrate. It was inconceivable, they thought, that Jenkins, Williams and Rodgers would stay in an SDP which stood alone.[44]

A number of possibilities confronted the Alliance after 1987: disintegration, with Owen and his diminished party slipping towards the Conservatives and the Liberals returning to the margins of politics; merger, with Steel and Owen contesting the leadership and the party's role in the political system depending on which won (no foregone conclusion despite the preponderant size of the Liberal party); an enlarged Liberal party, with a new name, with Steel as its leader, which would then set about arriving at an understanding with the Labour party which might transform the British electoral scene.

This broad canvas of possibilities ought not to distract the eye of the Liberal leadership from a detail with the widest ramifications. The defence dispute with the SDP exposed organizational deficiencies, especially relating to the role of the conference. Owen felt that ineffectual leadership made the Liberals unreliable allies, and cited policy on defence, terrorism and the miners' strike as examples.

Despite its problems, the Alliance remains the major opposition to Conservatism in the south of Britain. Its future does not lie entirely with the decisions of its leaders but also with the thousands of activists and millions of voters to whom it offers the only viable alternative to Thatcherite conservatism.

Notes

1 I am indebted to Peter Clarke's *Liberals and Social Democrats* (Cambridge, Cambridge University Press, 1978) for much of the factual basis of what follows. However, as the date of his book indicates, he was not concerned to make connections or draw conclusions with the Alliance in mind and so the interpretations are my own.

2 It is interesting to note that a half-hearted attempt was made in 1984 to resurrect the Rainbow Circle by right-wing Labour MPs like Frank Field. This was part of a general debate on the desirability of arriving at some electoral arrangement between Labour and the Alliance with a view to forming an anti-Conservative coalition government.

3 Clarke sets out the principles of social democracy in a chapter entitled 'Liberals and Social Democrats in historical perspective', in Vernon Bogdanor's edited collection *Liberal Party Politics* (Oxford, Clarendon Press, 1983).

4 See *Liberals and Social Democrats*, ch. 4.

5 'Towards a philosophy of socialism', in *New Fabian Essays* (London, Turnstile Press, 1952), p. 29.

6 *The Guardian*, 23 February 1979.

7 *The Guardian*, 3 December 1980.

8 David Owen, *Face the Future* (London, Cape, 1981).

9 William Rogers, *The Politics of Change* (London, Secker & Warburg, 1981).

10 Shirley Williams, *Politics is for People* (Harmondsworth, Penguin, 1981).

11 *Face the Future*.

12 Ibid., p. 9.

13 Ibid., p. 14.

14 *Politics is for People*, p. 205.

15 Ibid.

16 Community politics is dealt with in Bogdanor, *Liberal Party Politics*, in terms of its electoral appeal (Michael Steed: 'Electoral strategy of the Liberal party') and in terms of its guiding principles (Stuart Mole: 'The Liberal party and community politics').

17 Michael Meadowcroft, *Liberal Values for a New Decade* (Manchester, North West Community Newspapers, 1981), p. 6.

18 Jo Grimond, *The Liberal Future* (London, Faber 1959), p. 15.

19 Elliot Dodds, 'Liberty and welfare', in *The Unservile State* (London, Allen & Unwin, 1957), p. 33.

20 Ibid., p. 25.

21 Published by the Association of Liberal Councillors, at Hebden Bridge, 1981.

22 See Alan Beith, *The Case for the Liberal Party and the Alliance* (London, Longman, 1983), esp. chs 4 and 5.

23 *The Guardian*, 30 March 1981.

24 See for example an interview in *Observer*, 20 January 1985.

25 *The Guardian*, 20 May 1985.

26 *The Guardian*, 23 September 1985.

27 *The Guardian*, 25 March 1986.

28 *The Guardian*, 28 December 1984.

29 Susan Crosland in *The Times*, 7 July 1985.

30 Their 1979 manifesto *Fighting for Tomorrow*, for example, recommended direct action including, if necessary, breaking the law.

31 John Pardoe, for example, who contested the Liberal leadership with Steel, and who has a key function in aligning the policies of the two partners before the next election, has declared himself to be in favour of a voucher system for secondary education (*The Guardian*, 28 October 1985). This stance, if supported, could provoke considerable disagreement.

32 *The Guardian*, 10 September 1985.

33 David Owen, *A United Kingdom* (Harmondsworth, Penguin, 1986), esp. ch. 2.

34 See Nicholas Baldwin, 'The House of Lords: behavioural changes', in P. Norton (ed.), *Parliament in the 1980s* (Oxford, Blackwell, 1985).

35 See D. T. Studlar, 'By elections and the Liberal–SDP Alliance', *Teaching Politics*, 13, no. 1 (January 1984), pp. 85–95.

36 It was described in the *Observer* (19 July 1981) as 'an apparently impregnable Labour majority of rock-hard working-class voters in the unpropitious North country'.

37 *The Guardian*, 13 June 1981.

38 Philip Norton, *The British Polity* (New York, Longman, 1984), p. 85.

39 There were thirty-one seats in which the Liberals had come a 'good second' in 1979. In the allocation of seats between the Alliance parties only three were fought by the SDP in 1983.

40 See D. Butler and R. Waller, 'Survey of the voting', in *The Times Guide to the House of Commons: June 1983* (London, Times Books, 1983).

41 Martin Harrop, 'The Alliance and the general election of 1983', in L. Robins (ed.), *Updating British Politics* (London, Politics Association, 1984), pp. 104–15.

42 *The Guardian*, 6 May 1985.

43 *The Independent*, 25 May 1987.

44 *Sunday Times*. 21 June 1987.

9 Parties and the Business of Government

So far we have considered political parties in their own right; we have examined their histories, their ideologies and the nature of their support. We shall now be considering their function within the context of the governance of the modern state. It is appropriate to begin by exposing an ill-considered but none the less popular misconception concerning the role of parties: that they were created to serve a purpose in the democratic polity, were designed to act as channels of communication between governors and governed, shaped so as to provide the voters with a viable series of choices. Now if this were the case it would give rise to a set of unchanging expectations concerning how the system should operate and what kind of goods it should deliver. The truth of the matter, however, is quite different. Political parties existed in Britain in a clearly recognizable form long before the advent of mass democracy and hence they could not have been *designed* to serve any democractic purpose whatsoever. The truth of the matter is that parties have continually adapted to meet the changing needs of the polity. The truth of the matter is that parties changed so as to fulfil the needs of a developing democracy. Indeed, the only unchanging expectation which we may reasonably hold concerning the British party system is precisely this capacity to change.

The major parties have come to occupy a pivotal position between governors and governed. They are generally held to represent the interests of the great social classes and to articulate those interests in the form of competing ideologies which spawn competing policies. The sanctioning, by means of a general electoral victory, of one or other ideology provides a mandate for the party concerned to legislate on the basis of its policies. The policies themselves will present a consistent and reasonably comprehensive framework within which the executive will operate. This two-party model is not to be understood as representing a version of what A. H. Birch called the 'liberal model' of the constitution, a largely romanticized view beside which he juxtaposes the more realistic 'Whitehall model' in which the civil service is seen to be responsible for much of a government's legislative programme.[1] What the two-party model presumes is that modern party politics provides a *framework* for policy, a framework within which the civil service, too, will tend to operate. That framework will, for both major parties, represent the fruits of a complex interaction between party leaders, 'experts', activists and supporters, set within the context of the party's ideology. For the victorious party that framework will enclose a viable programme for government for the following five years. For the party defeated at the election a similar framework will exist from within which it will criticize the government's policies, thus providing accountability and choice.

The preceding chapters have cast considerable doubt upon the nature of this 'complex interaction' between leaders, experts, activists and supporters, and they have impugned the integrity of the ideological context within which these interactions are said to take place. All the same, the realist will want to argue that the two-party model works, despite its imperfections, so long as it continues to provide effective government and continues to provide what the voters consider to be genuine choices.

In this chapter we shall consider the sharp end of party politics: the business of government. We shall consider in turn some of the main arguments concerning the impact of party politics upon government policy-making. It would be inappropriate to deal with this topic without leaning upon the work of Richard Rose, whose *Do Parties Make a Difference?*[2] has been the major contribution in the field. Rose addresses precisely the problem which we have chosen to confront: he considers the extent to which party policies, which present the voters with an apparent choice, actually do provide the framework for the legislative programme of parties when they come to power. We shall be turning to his arguments shortly but there is a prior problem. Jack Hayward suggests that Britain's economic policies, and there is surely no area of policy more important, are determined by forces others than those commanded by parties in government. Leaving aside the cultural and international constraints, over which governments clearly have little direct influence, Hayward argues that 'the major source of Britain's difficulties is to be located among the non-state actors and . . . the efficacy of a subsidiary state intervention cannot be great when industrial firms, banks, and trade unions – who are directly involved in economic activity and *decide* in a more direct sense than do British governments – are unable to invest, produce, and sell efficiently . . . Politicians in power prate and posture, taking the credit and the blame for the diverse fortunes that ensue from the interplay of international market and institutional forces, without . . . usually being genuinely responsible for either the good or the bad results.'[3] Hayward is not suggesting that the party system is a sham, rather that it simply is not the prime actor in economic policy, and surely, for similar reasons, in any major area of policy. Changes in the party complexion of government and changes in the party system, then, are simply not particularly important as far as Hayward is concerned.

This line of argument it is not new. It was expressed many years ago by Bernard Shaw, whose industrialist Andrew Undershaft berates his politician son in the strongest terms:

Do you suppose that you and half a dozen amateurs like you, sitting in a row in that foolish gabble shop, can govern Undershaft and Lazarus? No, my friend: you will do what pays us. You will make war when it suits us, and keep peace when it doesn't. You will find out that trade requires certain measures when we have decided on those measures. When I want to keep my dividends up, you will discover that my want is a national need. When other people want something to keep my dividends down, you will call out the police and military. And in return you shall have the support and applause of my newspapers, and the delight of imagining that you are a great statesman. Government of your country! Be off with you, my boy, and play with your caucuses and leading articles and historic parties and great leaders and burning questions and the rest of your toys. I am going back to my counting house to pay the piper and call the tune.[4]

Shaw may be taking a typically robust position on the ineffectuality of party government but, like Hayward, he makes a point that requires the most careful attention. Let us consider, then, the extreme position, that parties play the tune called by the major industrial and commercial interests. A similar view was expressed by the radical Liberal Hobson[5] in the early years of the century when writing about the likelihood of Britain's creating an imperial federation with common defence and trade policies. He outlined the difficulties of such an enterprise but concluded that the economic advantages to British industry and capital were such that an imperial federation would certainly be established. His arguments were accepted and suitably embellished by Lenin who, like Hobson and Shaw, believed that British governments played the tunes called by their paymasters. In fact no imperial federation was created and one of the major reasons was the replacement of a quasi-protectionist Conservative administration in Westminster by a free-trade Liberal administration. It would be a strange society in which powerful economic forces exercised no political influence but theirs is not the only power and need not always be decisive. So much for Shaw's extreme position. We will have ample opportunity to consider Hayward's less extreme position as the argument develops, but there need be no initial disagreement about the fact that party governments are not free agents: the extent to which they are prisoners of events over which they have no control whatever is what we shall be considering. Now we can return to Rose.

Rose seeks to examine in detail the validity of the claim that 'adversarian' politics (two parties with opposed ideologies competing for and alternately winning power and tending to reverse each other's policies) produces policy inconsistencies of such a magnitude as to make medium- and long-term planning impossible.[6] Rose attempts to show that this charge is unfounded, suggesting that party politics do not seriously impact upon government policy in any obviously adversarian way because policies are shaped by a range of prior considerations; in short, according to Rose we do not need to worry about adversarian politics because they do not work. 'What parties say', says Rose, 'is not what parties do.' The adversarian argument has it that the old consensus-based politics up to the 1950s gave way by the 1970s to ideology-based politics; up to the 1950s values were shared and parties competed more in terms of the personality of the leader and a 'generalized image of competence' but by the late 1970s party competition became dominated by ideologies: socialist planning versus market forces, public versus private ownership, high public spending versus low direct taxation, and so on. Rose is not disposed to dispute the reassertion of ideology but simply believes it to have been largely rhetorical. Nothing is new, he tells us. 'The frustrations of the left with the 1964 and 1974 Labour governments are part of a recurring historical pattern. Labour and Conservative governments have been complementary parts of a moving consensus; in office in the past, they have not acted upon mutually exclusive ideological principles.'[7] In other words, if we look at history we will see that in opposition parties tend to move towards their ideological extreme but when in government they move towards consensus politics; explicitly Rose believes that, despite its apparent move to the left after 1979, a future Labour government would be likely to assume a far less radical posture. So too with the Conservatives; even the supposedly ideological government of Mrs Thatcher has, according to Rose, been predominantly consensual. 'While the proportion of consensus Acts of Parliament [those, that is, which did not divide the House on principle] was lower than at any time in the 1970s, nonetheless 63 per cent of all Acts in the first session of the 1979 parliament were consensus Acts.'[8]

In crucial areas such as the economy Rose, echoing Hayward, urges that major developments were simply not much influenced by changes of government: whether one examined economic inputs (matters within the government's own hands, such as setting the minimum lending rate, the level of public sector borrowing and public expenditure) or economic outcomes that are only partially influenced by government (such as inflation, unemployment and economic growth), the conclusions were much the same: 'the direction of the British economy is primarily influenced by long-term secular trends independent of party and not the movement of parties in and out of office'.[9] What is true for the economy is true for all areas of government activity. Rhetoric does not transform reality, or as Healey explained to the 1982 Labour party conference à propos economic policy, general elections do not change the laws of arithmetic.

Other writers have attacked the adversarian thesis on different grounds, suggesting that such major policy changes as take place tend to occur not so much between governments as within them. Lord McCarthy, for example, counted four changes in policy during the Labour government of 1964–70, four changes of policy during the 1970–74 Conservative government and five changes of policy during the 1974–79 Labour government in the field of incomes policy alone.[10]

There seem to be solid prima facie grounds, then, for rejecting the adversarian thesis, and Rose presses home his case for the prosecution by means of a detailed analysis of the policies of successive governments. We shall follow his case in some detail.

First Rose takes the adversarians to task for their insistence upon the importance of the party manifesto. For him a party manifesto is 'immediately important as an exercise in party management',[11] its function being primarily integrative and co-ordinative, a search for consensus within the party, for some common ground upon which to fight the election. This is particularly important for opposition parties, especially for Labour when in opposition. For the Conservatives the process of drawing up the manifesto is directed 'from the top'. The committees established for the task seek to represent the aspirations of 'those below' but they are not directly involved in the process and indeed on some occasions Conservative leaders have assumed personal responsibility for the manifesto. The Labour party, by contrast, is fully involved in the process 'from below', formally at least. Party policy emerges from resolutions at the annual conference which command a two-thirds majority, and those aspects of party policy which appear in the manifesto are selected by the NEC working in conjunction with the parliamentary leadership. Traditionally the party leadership has had the last word in what amounted to a compromise, though in 1979 the division between the two sides was all but unbridgeable and the leadership insisted upon getting its way. Conversely in 1983 party leader Michael Foot gave final responsibility to the NEC, much to the annoyance of his parliamentary colleagues. The resulting manifesto, Labour's most radical for many years, was later described by Peter Shore as the longest suicide note in history.

But do manifestos serve no purpose beyond the immediate one of integration? Not much, according to Anthony King, who regards them as having a 'virtually random' relationship to what the parties do when in office.[12] Rose, though, is of another opinion. 'Both the Conservative and Labour governments', he declares, 'act consistently with the manifesto model of government; in office they do the majority of things to which they pledge themselves in their opposition manifesto'.[13] At first sight this appears to run counter to Rose's substantive thesis, but not so: manifestos are predominantly non-adversarian. What they represent is not so much parties contradicting each other as parties 'talking past' each other. He explains. 'A systematic analysis of the 1970 and 1974 manifestos shows that slightly more than half (57 per cent) of all manifesto pledges are nonpartisan.'[14]

Moreover, Rose tells us that manifesto-driven legislation forms only a small part of a government's programme (8 per cent of that of the Conservative government of 1970–74 and 13 per cent of that of the Labour government of 1974–79).[15] He then categorizes legislation into policy and administration bills, by which he means bills that involve substantial changes in public policy and those which do not:[16] policy bills amount to not much more than 50 per cent of the total in the governments of the 1970s. More significant, of all policy bills only about 20 per cent were subject to major division. Rose concludes that even the relatively contentious parliaments of that decade were characterized more by consensus than by adversary politics. Indeed the sternest opponents of both government and opposition policies, as Norton has shown, came from within the party's own ranks.[17]

For all these reasons Rose feels able to conclude that far from being an adversarial system Britain's is predominaly consensual because governments 'owe their position to popular election, and the British electorate tends towards agreement rather than disagreement on major issues'.[18] More than this, according to Rose, once in office a party will not push its own wishes too far because of a recognition that this will encourage its opponents to act similarly when they gain office. Prudent self-interest, he claims, limits controversial changes in the rules of the game. Finally, if these reasons were not sufficient to dispose parties towards consensual politics, the awesome responsibilities of running the state with the assistance of a permanent non-political civil service, together with the general constraints upon its freedom of manoeuvre, would certainly toll the knell for any government seeking to act in a consistently adversarian manner. New ministers will face old problems, and with the same advice as their unsuccessful predecessors. As the *Economist* said in respect of economic problems, 'Like tricoteuses, Treasury-watchers sit around a new government waiting for the slaughter of proudly proclaimed economic policies . . . '[19] According to Rose, the evidence is conclusive: with each new government the thud of the guillotine of exigency is certain and continuous.

Rose's book first appeared in 1980 and the publishers must have felt that the turn of events thereafter might be thought to have cast some doubts upon Rose's thesis; a new edition came out in 1984 with its author quite unrepentant. Labour's catastrophic defeat in 1983, he wrote, was a result of its breaking the consensus rule: it addressed its manifesto to a 'well-defined but small audience, namely committed socialists'.[20] Stray outside the consensus compound and destruction is certain. Game, set and match, surely, for consensus politics . . .

Perhaps. But before considering some of the supportive arguments a little more closely it is worth pointing out that Rose does not take issue with the claim that adversarian politics are harmful. In point of fact he clearly believes that they are[21] but insists that consensus politics and not adversarian politics are practised in Britain. Turning to Rose's substantive thesis, we find it buttressed with an impressive sweep of architectural statistics not all of which are entirely convincing. He tells us, for example, that 63 per cent of all government legislation in the 1970s can be defined as consensual rather than adversarian. Leaving aside the problem of classification (not to oppose legislation formally should not be taken as indicating that the opposition is necessarily in favour), we are still left with the possibility that over one-third of a government's programme might be not merely adversarian but fiercely so. Moreover, it is surely naïve not to distinguish between the relative importance of legislation. If only one bill of the 1970–74 government (in fact there were certainly more!), that on industrial relations, could be classified as adversarian, its symbolic importance and practical effects were such as to make the label 'consensual' for the Heath government palpably inappropriate. Moreover, that Act was removed from the statute-book in a flurry of pro-trade union legislation by the next Labour government which turned the relationship between the unions and the state upon its head, only for the same relationship once more to be reversed by the Thatcher government. Rose's statistical analysis simply does not buttress his argument effectively here; it leans unsupported.

Much the same criticism may be levelled at Rose's analysis of manifestos. It may be true that the majority of manifesto commitments are not overtly adversarian but it is straining credulity beyond reasonable limits to insist that major manifesto commitments during the 1970s could be considered consensual. Even on Rose's statistics adversarian commitments provide 43 per cent of all commitments; it is possible that they provide nearly 100 per cent of major commitments. Rose cannot be allowed to ascribe Labour's 1983 defeat to an adversarian manifesto; he himself readily acknowledges that manifestos never decide the outcome of a general election.

Rose, like Hayward, attaches much importance to the restraints which inhibit incoming governments, domestically what he calls 'long-term secular trends'and internationally the state of the world economy and the global political situation. There is clearly much in this argument but if taken to extreme it produces an unhealthy and unrealistic fatalism. Though these restraints are certainly important, to consider them necessarily paralysing is to ignore those occasions when nations have reversed 'long-term secular trends', with considerable repercussions for their economic and political world roles. Thus we speak of the German or the French or the Italian 'economic miracle'. There is, then, no inevitability about Britain's decline into genteel poverty. Government policies may be not as decisive as some politicians would have us believe but it is equally unrealistic to believe that they have no impact whatever.

With regard to the role of the civil service, obviously vital and obviously beyond the direct control of adversarian politics, two factors need to be borne in mind. First is the ability of a party in government to generate a different atmosphere within the service by influencing key promotions, for example, or by bringing leading figures into the service from outside or by making use of expert advice from outside the service, all of which the present government has done. Indeed, according to Peter Hennessy[22], many permanent secretaries have been selected personally by the prime minister. 'They have been promoted for qualities of style and commitment', says Hugo Young. 'During the tenure of one prime minister, a top echelon of officials has been created which, thanks to her scorn for neutralism, is no longer seen to embody neutrality.'[23] Another commentator wrote: 'It is one thing to promote efficiency and bypass the traditional buggins turn; it is quite another to tempt civil servants to endorse enthusiastically and overtly the policies of the government.'[24]

The second is that civil servants regard it as their duty to try to act and to advise within the framework of known governmental dispositions. For example, civil service advice on taxation systems differed in the late 1960s and early 1970s according to the attitudes of successive governments towards joining the EEC. Labour was advised of the disadvantages of VAT, the Conservatives of the disadvantages of purchase tax and SET: each was told what it wanted to hear. It is well known that departments of state prepare themselves for the implications of electoral victory for each of the major parties. Of course they will attempt to dissuade politicians from adopting policies they believe to be unworkable, as the advice from senior officials in the Department of Education and Science to

Sir Keith Joseph regarding the introduction into secondary education of a voucher system clearly indicates. Nevertheless, they will generally give loyal support to a Minister's policies, as Sir Keith's period of office amply demonstrates. In short, important though these restrictions upon adversarian government are, they do not render it totally inoperative[25].

Finally we come to Rose's most deep-rooted general objection to the adversarian thesis: that it confuses rhetoric with reality. It fails to distinguish, he writes, between what parties say and what they do. Here Rose may be said to be offering a view of reality which is somewhat fey; he asks us to believe that what people say is not part of reality. Now this makes sense only if it is always and everywhere true that people do not mean what they say. Otherwise how can we be sure? If a man says, 'One day I shall kill you', then our 'reality' would certainly be transformed even if he did not actually do so. Our 'reality' would only be quite unaffected if we were certain beyond a doubt either that he did not mean it or that he was incapable of carrying out his threat. If the Labour party announces in its manifesto that when it gets into power it will abolish the House of Lords, or public schools, may we assume that these bodies will take no cognizance whatever of the commitment? Are we to assume that it is taken for granted that the Labour party either has no intention whatever to honour its promise to take British Telecom and British Gas back into public ownership or that it simply would not be able to do so for managerial reasons? In fact 66 per cent of the general public believes that Labour will renationalize these companies.[26] But the substantive point goes beyond that; it is that rhetoric is very much part of reality. In S. H. Beer's words, party stances establish 'the framework of public thinking about policy'.[27] Labour party rhetoric, especially, is real in another sense too. Although Labour governments have not transformed the mixed economy, party rhetoric often threatens to do so in particular policy areas. This is frequently to persuade loyalists of the party's good intentions, but it often has a profound effect upon other actors, especially overseas, who may be somewhat ingenuous and unfamiliar with the practices of British party politics.

All in all, although Rose's work will lead us to appreciate the limitations within which parties have to work and to recognize how considerable is the common ground between them, we have to conclude that even on his evidence parties do make a difference and that if we take any note of the influence of what Rose dismisses as rhetoric then they make a very substantial difference. To quote Beer again, 'parties themselves, backed by research staffs, equipped with nationwide organizations, and enjoying the continuous attention of the mass media, have themselves in great part framed and elicited the very demands to which they then respond'.[28]

A number of other studies have been concerned with the effect upon specific areas of policy of party competition and some reach conclusions very different from Rose's. David Coombes, for example, examines economic and more particularly industrial policy[29] and adduces four consequences of adversary politics which have characterized relations between government and industry over the years: an increasing tendency towards major changes in government policy, the manipulation of economic policy for short-term electoral advantage, the premature abandonment of policies that require a long-term non-adversarian approach and a reluctance by particular economic groups to accept sacrifices seen by government to be in the long-term national interest, presumably in the expectation that an election will bring in a government more favourably disposed to the group's interests. The electoral cycle itself, according to Aubrey Jones, ex-Conservative cabinet minister, ex-chairman of the Prices and Incomes Board, most recently unsuccessful Alliance parliamentary candidate (1983), is a major factor in causing some of Rose's long-term secular trends which confound incoming governments. 'A government with a life expectancy of four years', he says, 'spends the first two . . . seeking to master the inflation generated by its predecessor and the next two . . . in generating its own. The political cycle dominates and causes the economic.'[30] Changes of policy which Rose and McCarthy may justly claim occur in the lifetime of one parliament and not as a result of changes of government are none the less caused by the constraints of the adversarian system, if Jones is right. Policy changes emanating from changes of government, though, are even more likely, as the Hansard Society reported:

The election manifesto, conceived in an aggresively partisan spirit has come to be seen as committing parties more and more to legislation early in a term of office almost regardless of the possibility that views might be changed by contact with the reality of administration and the experience of civil servants. The tendency to legislate in a hurry . . . all too often produces laws which, because they are evidently in need of amendment, readily fall victims to the root and branch repealing instinct of a triumphant opposition: and so the cycle is perpetuated, to the detriment of long-term thinking and planning.'[31]

Coombes believes that the idea that democracy requires parties to draw up and if elected implement distinctive programmes actually encourages parties to proffer short-term and simplistic solutions to long-term and very complex problems. 'In no other European country could political, let alone economic issues be reduced to such simple terms as to expect party to play such a role effectively.'[32]

Coombes, too, has exposed the interface between reality and rhetoric. Parties arrive with their simplistic promises only to encounter a reality not at all conducive to the implementation of their intentions, and thus politicians 'begin to suspect some sinister conspiracy against themselves', however much civil servants refute such allegations. Yet here too the reality which confronts party rhetoric is itself partly the creation of past rhetoric which has inhibited long-term planning. Party rhetoric has shaped the reality which it is incapable of managing because it has sought to foster 'illusions about the significance of the electoral process and its capacity for endowing governments with the authority or the aptitude to manage the economy'.[33]

Coombes is not the only recent writer to turn his attention to the relationship between economic policy and adversarian politics. Gamble and Walkland's book[34] is a useful if unusual exploration of the relationship; unusual because in agreeing to differ about their conclusions the authors give the benefits of two books for the price of one. They begin by elucidating three varieties of the adversary politics thesis. The first suggests that the workings of the two-party system have caused significant and frequent reversals in policy as a result of competing for office. (This is the thesis we have explored with Rose.) The second variety of the thesis suggests that it is not so much competing idelogies which produce policy reversals as the need to 'pursue policies and adopt programmes that maximize votes'.[35] This competition generates excessive expectations, quite unrelated to costs, amongst not only the general public but amongst friendly pressure groups. These two varieties might, surely, be considered as two sides of the same coin. The third, however, is quite distinct. It suggests that the superficial nature of adversary politics concentrates debate and competition upon only a few major issues, while policy in other areas is neglected. It suggests that adversary politics requires a major stage on which to act out its plays; it requires, that is to say, a strongly centralized state apparatus. This variety of adversary politics is thus the enemy of decentralized, and indeed more open, government.

Having clarified the terminology, Gamble considers what he calls (economic) stablization policy and concludes that in the postwar period neither of the first two varieties of the adversary thesis may be said to have operated, at least until the 1980s. The major change in stabilization policy, he argues, was the substitution of monetary for Keynesian orthodoxy, but this was the consequence of the world recession, not of a change in government. As to the third variety, Gamble finds it both appropriate and interesting as an explanation of continuity. 'The surprising thing about adversary politics is not that it destroys continuity of policy in some areas, but that it protects a narrow and unreflecting consensus on some of the most important determinants shaping economic policy.'[36] Suddenly adversary politics is exposed as a conspiracy theory, and Gamble is not the only writer to say so. Ashford, too, argues that, superficial adversary politics notwithstanding, in times of stress an 'elite consensus' emerges which concentrates decision-making within cabinet and the higher levels of the civil service, and this consensus acts independently of party ideology or indeed parliamentary influence.'[37]

Gamble develops his theory further. Political stability demands continuity of policy so the electorate 'can be offered an effective choice between teams of leaders but not between policies'.[38] If these leaders were ever actually to operate an adversarian system then a 'real rather than a symbolic polarization' would take place. In fact, says Gamble, adversary politics are not taken seriously and anyway, the first two varieties of the thesis simply exaggerate the role that parties play in policy formulation and implementation. Adversary politics of these varieties is a sham. 'If the two parties ever became genuine adversaries the system would cease to be workable.'[39]

Unlike Walkland, who is much more convinced of the deleterious consequences of the two other varieties of adversarian politics, Gamble remains convinced that adversary politics, like Bernard Shaw's democracy, is only a game to catch the attention whilst someone is picking your pocket. It would have been easy to accept such an argument during the 1950s and early 1960s; it is not so easy in the 1980s. Gamble's contention that the shift from Keynesian to monetarist economic policies is not an indication of adversarian discontinuity but simply a product of world recession is disingenuous to say the least; it leaves us unable to distinguish between the kinds of economic policy that Labour pursued after 1975 and those of the Conservatives after 1979. In brief, even if we are all monetarists now, we are emphatically not the same kind of monetarists. Moreover, Gamble's assertion that 'genuine' adversary politics cannot exist because they are unworkable is similarly unhelpful. It is universally accepted that part of the function of political parties in a constitutional democracy is to contain conflict: after all, 'genuine' adversaries beat each other over the head. Whether it makes sense to call a system adversarian is thus a far more sophisticated judgement than Gamble will allow.

We have seen the wide element of disagreement that exists between observers as to the kind of influence that party politics have upon the business of government. Most of the debate centres directly on the impact, or lack of impact, of changes of government upon policy, especially economic policy. We can think of this direct influence debate as referring to the legislative dimension of adversarian politics. Here the influence of parties is measured against that of, for example, civil servants and pressure groups. From the perspective of the late 1980s, the balance of argument may be judged to weigh in favour of the adversarians: parties do make a difference even in the legislative dimension and it is hard to imagine many working in the areas of, for example, health or education let alone key economic areas such as regional policy and taxation, who would dispute this claim. We have only to consider the Thatcher government's policy of privatization, constituting what Andrew Cox has called 'a fundamental reappraisal of the state's role in the British economy'.[40] Cox lists five major planks of this policy, each of might easily be reversed by a future Labour government. They are: denationalization and the sale of public assets; 'liberalization' to engender greater competition in the public and private sectors; contracting out of public services in central and local government and the NHS; reduction of the public role in regional, industrial and inner city development; finally, reappraisal of and increased charges for certain key welfare services. Cox concludes that these policies are ideologically based, manifesto-led and would probably be reversed.

There is, moreover, another dimension to the relationship between party and policy, which might be referred to as contextual. Here the influence of adversarian politics is far more profound, for it shapes the expectations of all the actors in the drama of government and minutely directs the whole production. As was stated earlier, adversarian politics help to shape the reality which parties confront when they come to power. Senior civil servants and pressure group leaders clearly have their expectations shaped by the complexion of the government and the likely complexion of future governments. We have only to consider movements on the stock exchange following unexpected by-election results towards the end of a government to understand this, or to recall comments made by, to take one example, the Police Federation at its annual conferences in 1985 and 1986 regarding possible problems in working with a future Labour government. There is strong evidence, then, that adversarian politics influence this contextual dimension too. If Rose were willing to amend his question to 'does the two-party system make a difference?' the answer would have to be a resounding 'yes', in both the legislative and the contextual dimension.

Discussion so far has been of a general and sometimes theoretical nature. It would be wise, before we leave this debate, to consider the issues raised in a specific policy context. In *Parliament and Health Policy*[41] the authors consider in detail the influence of parliament in the creation and scrutiny of health policy in the period 1970–75. Every major aspect of health policy in that period was considered and although this had not been the purpose of the study, some clear indications of the influence of adversarian politics emerged.

The study began by analysing the kind of contributions which backbench MPs might make to policy formulation and scrutiny and this was done simply by asking a number of backbenchers what they considered to be their most important function. On the basis of their answers their functions were categorized as follows. First there was a deputational function through which the MP is deputed to protect and further the interests of his or her constituents. The emphasis in this function is on looking after 'my constituents', 'the ordinary man and woman', and so on. Second was the partisan-ideological, or what we would call the adversarian, that of offering support to party leaders so long as they pursue the objectives of party policy. 'Our task as a government is to pursue the policies on which we were elected . . . you can't have any issue which isn't partisan.' Third was the advocative function, where the emphasis is on representing certain interests. It was this function which prompted Chancellor of the Exchequer James Callaghan to say in 1965, 'I look at them and say "investments trusts", "capital speculators" . . . I have almost forgotten their constituencies but I shall never forget their interests.'[42] Finally came the custodial function, where the emphasis is on protecting the constitution, preserving the proper and traditional way of doing things. This function is non-partisan and uses vocabulary in which words like 'commonsense' and 'reasonable' tend to dominate. The purpose of these categories was not to label MPs but to attempt to categorize their contributions to debate on the floor of the House and in committee in order to get the measure of the way parliament actually operates.

During the period under scrutiny one major piece of legislation passed through parliament, the reform of the administrative structure of the National Health Servive (NHS), the first major overhaul in nearly thirty years. Now, the purpose of reforming the NHS was not at issue, neither was any major reallocation of resources, neither was any major political principle. Yet a tabulation of major contributions to the second reading debate on the Reorganization Bill, measured in column inches of Hansard, shows that partisan-ideological inputs comprised 36 per cent, by far the largest category. In comparison the deputational input was 23 per cent, the advocative 20 per cent and the custodial 21 per cent. The authors conclude: 'for parliament to spend over a third of its time on partisan point-making, with the full knowledge that it would have no effect on the shape of the policy before it, is an over indulgence'.[43]

What was true of the major debate on the floor of the House was true also of contributions in committee. In fact the most successful influence – and it was successful only in details – upon the government was the House of Lords (where, incidentally, similar categorization indicated that partisan-ideological inputs accounted for only 4 per cent of all contributions). Now, there were major issues at stake in the proposed legislation concerning, especially, accountability in the new structure, and backbenchers on both sides of the House raised them, but they were never given adequate consideration and every issue was decided as a matter of party loyalty. Party loyalty 'was the only significant factor in the debate on managerialism and local democracy'.[44] Parliamentary influence upon this piece of major legislation was minimal and partisan-ideology (or adversarianism) was the principal explanation. What may not be entirely unrelated to this lack of parliamentary influence was the fact that within five years NHS reorganization was back on the political agenda: the 1974 reforms were almost universally considered to have been failures.

Perhaps even more damaging as a measure of the domination of partisan-ideology is the issue of free and comprehensive birth control. The House of Lords, where the bill had begun its parliamentary journey, had called for a free and comprehensive scheme of birth control under the NHS. A Commons early day motion (no. 177) in support of this call was signed by seventy-three MPs, sixty-four of whom were Conservatives. The Conservative government would offer only a prescription-based service and when the issue was voted in the Commons the government whips were put on, though the opposition allowed a free vote. The amendment was lost only to be reinstated when the bill went back to the Lords. When it came back to the Commons both parties instituted a three-line whip and the amendment was lost by 247 votes to 220. Only £5 million of public money were at stake here, and no issue of party principle. Nevertheless, the government was quite prepared to insist upon the support of its own backbenchers 'when it had certain knowledge that they did not wish to give it . . . '[45] As goes almost without saying the next (Labour) government reversed this policy.

There is much more in the study to tell a similar story. The House seems only able to perform effectively in the area of detailed scrutiny and only then when, as with the creation of the NHS Commissioner (Ombudsman) and his committee, detailed and often technical knowledge precludes partisan–ideology and emphasizes deputational, advocative and custodial inputs. The authors conclude their study by suggesting: 'This double failure, lack of parliamentary influence and unsuccessful government policies, are not unconnected . . . . If health is any guide, the nature of policy making is becoming increasingly technical and as a result less amenable to partisan–ideological presentation. The British model of parliamentary government requires partisan policy inputs, requires that policies be presented as simple alternatives forthe public choice. Yet in an increasingly complex age, policies are far less amenable to presentation as simple partisan choices, and policy inputs come increasingly not from parties but from experts within the executive. The precedures for assessing these policies, however, continues to operate as if they *were* partisan-ideological and so remain basically adversarian.'[46]

However, adversarian politics have by no means given up the

ghost. The Thatcher government has been accused on several occasions of misinformation for self-protection. In 1986, for example, a statement emanating from the Foreign Office regarding sanctions against South Africa was contradicted by one from Downing Street. *The Scotsman* commented: 'The Foreign Office and No. 10 cannot both be right and it is a matter of regret that most will conclude, simply from previous experience, that No. 10 is the guilty party.' The Thatcher government's cavalier attitude to statistical information is also open to question. Since 1979 the way in which unemployment statistics are presented has changed on sixteen occasions.[47] The government's attitude, according to Robert Taylor, is 'bringing into question the reliability of official statistics . . . this is one of the ways in which tyrannies behave'.

Barbara Castle once said of her work at the European parliament, 'You don't have to make laws in order to make a noise', and health politics in the period studied seem to suggest that making a noise to which few listened was all that parliament was able to do. If Mrs Castle thought this good enough, many did not. The experiences of a 'hung' parliament in the late 1970s gave backbenchers a taste for more influence and gave them, also, a more perceptive appreciation of the possibilities of opposing their own government without bringing it down. Recent reforms of parliament have been consciously aimed at making the relationship between parliament and government less adversarian and to the extent that they have been successful the nature of that relationship has changed and will continue to change. Perhaps members of parliament have got things wrong but the majority clearly believe that good government is best served by weakening adversarianism.

The first and most significant of these reforms was the appointment of select committees associated with the 'expenditure, administration and policy of the principal government departments'.[48] Although there were some parliamentarians, including senior figures in both major parties, who were opposed to this development, twelve such committees were established in 1979 by a majority of 248 to 12.[49] Later committees for Scottish and Welsh affairs were added to the number. In all, these committees produced 193 reports during the 1979–83 parliament and they have been at least equally productive since. It is not so easy to assess how effective the committees have been. Norton has this to say: 'Clearly, by being able to summon ministers and to submit them to hour-long questioning on a specific topic, the committees perform an important role of scrutiny. Their access to specialist advisers has enabled them to focus their questioning, providing them with an alternative source of guidance and information . . . Thus . . . the committees . . . help keep Ministers and officials on their toes.' The question is, though, what notice does the government take of the work and recommendations of these committees? It has to be said that there is in fact no constitutional requirement on the government's part even to debate the committee reports, though nowadays some of the Estimates Days are used for that purpose. Even if debated a report may not be accepted by the House, and certainly there is no constitutional obligation on the part of the relevant government department to take any action whatsoever in respect of a committee report. As Norton remarks, 'On occasion, they have even treated reports with undisguised contempt.'[50]

On the other hand, every time a committee institutes an enquiry some aspect of public concern not selected by the government is brought under scrutiny, a department of state is obliged to defend its actions in public, and opposition members gain access to information which formerly would have been denied them. A good example of what these committees can and cannot achieve is given by the defence committee's enquiry into the Westlands helicopter affair, which prompted the resignation of two members of Mrs Thatcher's cabinet. The committee concentrated the minds of the public not so much on government decisions as upon the manner in which government business was being conducted with a focus hitherto unattainable. This critical focus was not adversarial and therefore the government could not take refuge behind its own adversarial procedures, nor dismiss the accusations levelled against it as simply being part of the old game of parliamentary rough-and-tumble. In the event, though, the government would not have been displeased by the fact that the committee's report[51] did not appear until the last week of the 1985–6 session, when the public's attention was more taken up with a royal wedding. The report criticized as 'disreputable' the leaking to the press of parts of a letter from the Solicitor-General, and as 'flimsy to say the least' the reasons given by the prime minister for releasing the information. The report went on to list without comment evasive answers given to the Commons by the prime minister and generally painted a picture of 'buck-passing, shabby conduct, leaking and counter-leaking, and muddle in

Whitehall, including Mrs Thatcher's own office'.[52] But the committee's sharpest criticism was saved for the head of the home civil service who had prevented the committee from taking evidence from the senior civil servants directly involved, which the committee found simply 'extraordinary'. It needs only to be added that the chairman of the defence committee, and thus its major public spokesman, was a Conservative.

Other reforms of a non-adversarian nature have also been implemented in recent years. The provision of three Estimates Days each session on which the House might debate estimates which had been the subject of a select committee report hardly constitutes a revolution but it has at least given the House an ability to discuss specific estimates more or less of its own choosing (in fact of the liaison committee's choosing). Again, this reform seems designed to improve the House's capacity to scrutinize the government but not in an adversarian manner. In the same area, following a successful private member's bill (that itself is significant) a National Audit Office was established to replace the old Exchequer and Audit Department generally considered to be too much under Treasury influence. The estimates of the Office are examined by another creation of the new Act, the Public Accounts Commission, with some degree of independence from government. The Commission comprises nine MPs, including the chairman of the public accounts committee and the leader of the House. Again, this move strengthens the House's capacity for scrutiny in a non-adversarian manner.

Another recent innovation has been the reform of standing committees, and yet again the intent has been to weaken adversarian procedures. The old standing committees were, according to the study of parliament group, liable simply to provide a ground for the continuation of adversarian battles joined during the second reading debate and as such were unpopular with government backbenchers, who were only attending to outvote their opponents, and with opposition backbenchers who knew that their efforts would prove in vain. 'If at the end of the day', the select committee on procedure was to say later, 'the committee has actually improved (made "more generally acceptable") the contents of a Bill – as opposed to approve the amendments introduced by the Minister in charge of the Bill – it is . . . an unusual and unexpected benefit.'[53] In 1980, by way of experiment, three special standing committees (SSCs) were established, which would meet prior to the normal standing committee stage. Three Bills went through such a stage, with considerable success, during that session, but although the procedure was continued it was applied to only one other bill. Yet the procedure was highly regarded by backbenchers[54] and critics alike.

Finally we need to look at the reform of the old Supply Days system. In the postwar period these twenty-nine days officially allowed for the scrutiny of estimates were firmly regarded as opportunities for the opposition to chose any topic for debate. By the 1970s, however, the position had become somewhat muddied by changes which weakened still further the House's ability to scrutiny estimates and by the fact that certain debates were becoming almost ritual, for example the armed forces, Scottish affairs and the EEC,[55] and ought arguably be held in government time. As a consequence in 1982, following a recommendation from the select comittee on procedure, the twenty-nine Supply Days were replaced by nineteen Opposition Days, in which the topic for debate would be selected by the leader of the opposition. In what sense can this be said to be a reform which weakens adversarianism? The new system was modified in 1985 by the addition of a twentieth day and by the provision that three of the Opposition Days would be 'given' to the second largest party of opposition, currently the Liberal party. Previously the Liberal leader had been extended the courtesy by the Labour leader of initiating the debate on one Supply or Opposition Day; he now has the right to do so on three days. Simply because adversarianism becomes much more difficult to sustain between three or more parties this modification will effect a change towards a more non-adversarian form of scrutiny.

These changes are not accidental. They are some of the products of a general mood in which government backbenchers have shown an increasing willingness to challenge their own government. Norton argues that such dissent was first generated by personal hostility to the premiership of Edward Heath but as we have seen Labour governments have traditionally lacked the sense of unity which has marked their opponents and this lack was very conspicuous in the 1966–70 Labour government of Harold Wilson. In any event, during the 1970s cross-voting amongst backbenchers increased. 'Gradually, their old deferential attitude was replaced by a participatory one. Members wanted to be more involved in the scrutiny of government', says Norton,[56] and they recognized the importance of institutional change to enable them to do so effectively. Hence the changes we have noted.

It is not difficult to discern a drift in these changes. They are clearly designed to increase the power of parliament at the expense of the executive. How far such changes might extend in the present party system is impossible to say but it is appropriate to make certain observations relating to their relationship to the role of political parties. We have seen on all sides a decline n the strength of parties. By-electoral results such as that at Crosby in 1981, Bermondsey in 1982 and Ryedale in 1986 have badly mauled the concept of the 'safe seat'. Mandatory reselection in the Labour party has profoundly affected the relationship between centre and periphery in that party, and local pressures are becoming increasingly important for Conservative MPs too. Ideological differences between parties are nowadays openly matched by such differences within each of the major parties at both extra- and intra-parliamentary levels. Inside parliament the idea of two monolithic structures confronting each other across the floor of the Chamber no longer corresponds to reality. What these developments add up to is a decline of the party system that dominated in Britain from 1950 to the mid-1970s. The changes in parliamentary procedures we have been speaking of, then, appear to be part of a broader development.

Supporters of the Alliance parties have argued that it is they who have 'broken the mould' of British party politics; others might see first the growing influence of the Liberals and then the emergence of the SDP more as products than causes of a breaking mould. This is an important distinction to draw because we should not believe that future developments in the party system depend upon initiatives from the Alliance parties, still less upon the implementation of their most radical policy, electoral reform. All the same, a stronger Alliance presence in the next House of Commons and the possible implementation of proportional representation would add a far greater urgency to the changes that seem likely to happen anyway. What are these changes? Voting in the House of Commons seems likely to become far less easily controlled in the future than it has been in the past, with backbenchers increasingly seeing their parliamentary careers more in terms of active membership of committees than simply loyalty to the party leaders in order to achieve promotion. Parliament, as a consequence, could become a much more important body and its select committees far more influential in terms of scrutiny and eventually actually of the shaping of policy. With a weakened party system and a strengthened committee system the pressure for more open government, of which there have been many portents recently, none more significant than the judgment in the Ponting trial, would become difficult to resist. A change in the nature of the relationship between parliament and the civil service might result, thus affording better protection for the individual citizen.

Policies emanating from a transformed House ought, paradoxically, to be more consensual and moderate. If the Alliance were to gain in strength and certainly if the electoral system were reformed, formal and informal coalition governments or minority governments would be likely, and this would severely restrict the adversarian input into government and opposition. Greater continuity of policy might be expected to result, after initial teething problems, and planning for the longer term might be more feasible than it appears to be at present. The impact upon the legislative dimension of policy-making would be immediate but more important, these changes would begin to impact upon the contextual dimension of policy-making and that might have profound consequences. None of these changes depends solely upon Alliance pressure, or indeed upon electoral reform; as we have seen, they are already beginning to happen. But each could be constrained, even reversed, by a strong adversarian government. None of these changes would lessen the international economic pressures which restrict the freedom of manoeuvre of successive governments, neither would they limit the impact of the various sectional domestic pressures which, as Hayward has pointed out, have greatly influenced decision-making over the years. What they might do, though, is to provide a context for decision-making which is less obviously partisan and short term, more open and, dare we say it, rational. None of these changes would necessarily make the business of government more efficient; what they might do is change both the context and procedures within and through which that business is conducted.

Notes

1 A. H. Birch, *The British System of Government*, 4th edn (London, Allen & Unwin, 1980).
2 Richard Rose, *Do Parties Make a Difference?* 2nd edn (London, Macmillan, 1984).
3 A. M. Gamble and S. A. Walkland, *The British Party System and Economic Policy 1945–83* (Oxford, Oxford University Press, 1984).
4 Bernard Shaw, *Major Barbara* (Harmondsworth, Penguin 1960), p. 124. (The play was first performed in 1905.)
5 J. A. Hobson, *The Crisis of Liberalism: New Issues of Democracy* (London, King, 1909).
6 For example, S. E. Finer, *Adversary Politics and Electoral Reform* (London, Wigram, 1975).
7 Rose, *Do Parties Make a Difference?*, p. xxviii.
8 Ibid., p. xxvii.
9 Ibid., p. xxix.
10 See Lord McCarthy's 'The politics of income policy', in D. Butler and A. H. Halsey (eds), *Party Politics: Essays in Honour of Norman Chester* (London, Macmillan, 1978).
11 Rose, *Do Parties Make a Difference?*, p. 56.
12 See Anthony King, 'Death of the manifesto', *The Observer*, 17 February 1974.
13 Rose, *Do Parties Make a Difference?*, p. 65.
14 Ibid., p. 69.
15 Ibid., p. 72.
16 These categories are taken from Ivor Burton and Gavin Drewry, 'Public legislation, a survey of the session 1968–69', in *Parliamentary Affairs*, 23, no. 2 (1970), p. 161ff.
17 Philip Norton, Dissension in the House of Commons 1945–74 (London, Macmillan, 1975) and *Dissension in the House of Commons 1974–79* (Oxford, Oxford University Press, 1980).
18 Rose, *Do Parties Make a Difference?*, p. 143.
19 *The Economist*, 15 December 1979, quoted in Rose, *Do Parties Make a Difference?*, p. 159.
20 Ibid. p. 169.
21. See ibid., pp. 156–7.
22 Peter Hennessy, *Cabinet* (Oxford, Blackwells, 1986).
23 Richard Norton-Taylor, 'When consensus politics becomes a dirty word', *The Guardian*, 27 November 1984.
24 Hugo Young, 'The strong-arm tactics that politicised Whitehall', *The Guardian*, 17 July 1986.
25 Sir Leo Pliatsky, 'Ministers and officials', *London Review of Books*, vol. 10 (July 1980).

26 S. H. Beer, *Modern British Politics* (London, Faber, 1965), p. 347.

27 Gallup poll published in *Daily Telegraph*, 21 July 1986.

28 Beer, *Modern British Politics*, p. 347.

29 David Coombes, *Representative Government and Economic Power* (London, Heinemann (Policy Studies Institute), 1982), p. 116.

30 Aubrey Jones, *The New Inflation* (Harmondsworth, Penguin, 1973), p. 120.

31 Hansard Society for Parliamentary Government, *Policy and Industry – the Great Mismatch*, quoted Coombes, *Repesentative Government and Economic Power*, p. 116.

32 Ibid., p. 119.

33 Ibid., p. 118.

34 A. M. Gamble and S. A. Walkland, *The British party System and Economic Policy*.

35 Ibid., p. 25.

36 Ibid., p. 91.

37 Douglas Ashford, *Politics and Policy in Britain: The Limits of Consensus* (Oxford, Blackwell, 1981).

38 Gamble and Walkland, *The British Party System and Economic Policy*, p. 171.

39 Ibid., p. 184.

40 See Andrew Cox, 'Privatization and public enterprise in Britain 1979–85', *Teaching Politics*, 15, no. 1 (January 1986).

41 Stephen Ingle and Philip Tether, *Parliament and Health Policy, The Role of MPs 1970–75* (Farnborough, Gower Press, 1981).

42 Quoted in R. Butt, *The Power of Parliament* (London, Constable, 1967), pp. 432–33.

43 Ingle and Tether, *Parliament and Health Policy*, p. 143.

44 Ibid., p. 147.

45 Ibid.

46 Ibid., p. 155.

47 Robert Taylor, *The Guardian*, 3 August 1986.

48 *House of Commons Debates*, vol. 969, cols 247–50.

49 See Philip Norton, 'Independence, scrutiny and rationalization: a decade of changes in the House of Commons', *Teaching Politics*, 15, no. 1 (January 1986), pp. 69–97.

50 Ibid., p. 80.

51 *Westland plc: The Government's Decision-Making*, 4th Report for the Defence Committee (London, HMSO, 1986). 52 *The Guardian*, 25 July 1986.

53 Select Committee on Procedure, 1984–85, Minutes of Evidence: 18 December 1984.

54 A survey by the all-party Commons reform group found that 79 per cent of repondents judged SSCs to have been a success (see Norton, 'Independence, scrutiny and rationalization', p. 89.

55 Norton, 'Independence, scrutiny and rationalization', p. 89.

56 Philip Norton, 'Britain's reform Parliament', *The Parliamentarian*, 76, no. 2 (April 1986), pp. 59–65.

10 Today, Yesterday and Tomorrow

'Do you mean to say that the story has a moral?' said the Water Rat.
'Certainly', said the Linnet.
'Well, really', exclaimed the Water Rat in a very cross manner. 'I think
you should have told me that before you began. If you had done so I should
certainly have not listened to you. In fact, I should have said – "Pooh!" '
Oscar Wilde, *The Devoted Friend*

Perhaps the Water Rat is wise to disdain stories with a moral; the
trouble is that sometimes morals creep up unnoticed, in the shape of
implications. We cannot avoid the fact that this account of political
parties in Britain has its share of implications, and we shall be
turning to these before long. Our first task, though, is to complete the
account of parties by considering one last question. To what extent
do parties represent the electorate and offer the voters a realistic and
manageable choice today?

In their recent book *Voters Begin to Choose*, Rose and McAllister[1]
distinguish between what they call 'closed-class systems' and 'open-
competition systems' and consider that Britain, traditionally one of
the former, has recently developed into one of the latter. In the
closed-class system the Conservatives were seen to represent the
interests of the middle class and the principles of capitalism, and the
Labour party the interests of the working class and the principles of
socialism. The system was never so closed that capitalists might
consider throwing themselves off Westminster Bridge if Labour came
into power, or that groups of workers might arm themselves against
the possibility of a Conservative electoral victory. Indeed this takes
us back to Tweedledum and Tweedledee and the proper limits of
conflict. All the same, there have traditionally been clear if not
always substantive differences between the parties for much of the

time, and these were well perceived by the voters. In the closed-class system the supporters of the major parties viewed the state and the opposing party from a class perspective. Agreement between the supporters of one party, say Rose and McAllister, would be complemented and enhanced by hostility towards the views of their opponents. The closed-class system of voting behaviour suggests that voting for one party rather than another implies the endorsement of party policies on a whole series of issues and this, in turn, implies that traditional political attitudes have, in large measure, been related to class. Hence their consistency.

We have seen that the history of the British party system since the advent of the Labour party at least has followed this pattern fairly closely. We have already seen that support for each of the major parties is in fact generated more by hostility to the other side than by any positive enthusiasm for the policies of one's own side. Indeed in 1983 Gallup asked respondents to say which was the stronger, their like of the party for which they were voting or their dislike of the opposition; 52 per cent said they disliked the opposition whereas only 35 per cent claimed any positive preference for their own party.[2] The closed-class system feeds upon this kind of mutual antagonism, which is bolstered by ignorance of, and lack of contact with, 'the other side'. Ignorance and isolation, in turn, are features of a static social system with very little mobility, either geographical, social or cultural. Traditionally in Britain two class-bound cultures existed which hardly ever intersected. Disraeli wrote about precisely this division; George Gissing, in *Demos: A Story of English Socialism*, wrote on the same subject nearly half a century later and the differences were still equally marked. More systematically than either, George Orwell wrote about the life-styles of the two great classes in *The Road to Wigan Pier*. In terms of housing, dress, education, health care, entertainments, music, even sport, the British were indeed two nations who knew little and cared not much more about each other. Emblematic of the political consequences of this social antagomism, which continued into the 1950s, is the following verse, sung in the general election campaigns of 1950 and 1951, by East London schoolchildren, to whose parents Winston Churchill was not only a great wartime leader but also a class enemy from an earlier period. Somewhat modified, the song ran:

> Vote, vote, vote for Mr Attlee,
> Punch old Churchill on the jaw.
> If it wasn't for the King,
> We would do the blighter in.
> Then he wouldn't go a-voting anymore.

This rhyme did not represent any degree of political knowledge or indeed any great interest on the part of the children: but it showed that they knew which side they were on.

Times have changed. Social mobility, different levels and patterns of consumption, a more open education system, somewhat better health facilities, better housing for many (and the consequent destruction of working-class communities) have tended to erode working-class solidarity. The extent and importance of each of these developments can easily be overstated; their cumulative effect is impossible to ignore. But by the same token, middle-class solidarity has also been eroded. Jimmy Porter, the middle-class anti-hero of Osborne's *Look Back in Anger* was a spokesman for the values not of his own class but of the working class. He set a trend. The working-class heroes of the social commentary films of the 1960s, such as *The Loneliness of the Long Distance Runner* and *Saturday Night and Sunday Morning*, were symbols of middle-class romanticizing about working-class values. Not long after, television series, such as the long-running *Coronation Street*, paraded working-class life-styles and values before a captive all-class audience. At the same time the huge growth of the popular music industry gave prominence not to middle-class adults with middle-class values but to young working-class men with working-class values and accents. Their impact, like that of the whole 'kitchen-sink' drama movement, was cross-class. In the face of this cultural onslaught the middle class lost its way. The media, especially television, forsook any obligation to preserve middle-class cultural values; 'Auntie Beeb' was an image the BBC sought to jettison, not to cherish. Nowadays many of television's cult figures, often from the world of sport, are overtly working-class. The jump from C. B. Fry to Ian Botham, for example, is more than one of time. What all this amounts to is that, for the first time since the industrial revolution, perhaps since the medieval period, most young people in Britain share a common culture which is not bound by class.

These changes are not complete and they are not universal. There are significant pockets in Britain's cities where little has changed, but they form a minority. Most citizens have succumbed to the blandishments of the mass culture which has accompanied the embourgeoisement of the working class and the proletarianization of the middle class. It is doubtful whether the virtues of Mr Kinnock are extolled in song by many primary schoolchildren today, as were Mr Attlee's thirty or so years ago.

All this suggests that the conditions for the closed-class system no longer exist in Britain, and what no longer exists cannot be expressed in political terms. Indeed Rose and McAllister's analysis shows precisely this point. A factor analysis of Conservative, Labour and Alliance voters shows a substantial measure of agreement in the three key principles of welfare, traditional morality and racialism. Indeed, out of forty-five issues Conservative voters were in substantial agreement with both Labour and Alliance voters on thirty. The authors conclude: 'Only one principle, socialism, discriminates to some extent between partisans, dividing Liberal and Labour voters, whilst uniting anti-socialist Conservatives.'[3] On the basis of this analysis Rose and McAllister feel able to make two general statements which indicate the extent of break-up of the closed-class system: the most common form of disagreement is within parties rather than between them; how a person votes is a poor guide to what a person thinks about most issues today.[4] To take the first, Labour voters disagree on twenty-six out of forty-five issues, Alliance voters on twenty-five, Conservatives on nineteen. To take the second, the substantial Conservative majorities in 1979 and 1983 did not represent a groundswell of support for Thatcherism, and in any case the Conservative vote actually fell in 1983. Moreover, Mrs Thatcher's appeal, though limited, is not limited to Conservatives. The proportion of Labour voters who admire her pugnacious style is actually higher than the proportion of admiring Conservatives.[5]

In earlier chapters we established that the relationship between class and voting was never more than around 70 per cent (at least since these relationships have been measured). Rose and McAllister show that since 1959, when Labour first became publicly concerned about its long-term future, only an average of 46 per cent of electors eligible to vote in successive elections have actually reported voting for the same party in both. Together these figures add weight to the theme sketched above; no party can win an election through reliance on a stable base of support. This amounts to what Rose and McAllister call an open competition where, to be successful, parties have to secure the support of 'intermediate strata' in a class structure that is becoming diamond-shaped.

When we couple these findings with the authors' previous generalizations – that voting was not much related to opinions on issues, that disagreements were within rather than between parties, and that more people voted against than for a party – it becomes clear that electoral success goes to the party that offends least those intermediate strata, or to be more accurate, which offends *the least number* amongst those strata. This is an important distinction to draw because the unreliability of class-based support applies to this growing middle class too. After all, this is the class which provides many of the new younger activists and indeed MPs and candidates in all three major parties.

To see what impact this changing social structure has upon party support we need look no further than the 1987 election results. Not for the first time, commentators began to ask whether the Labour party could ever hope to win power again. John Curtice questioned whether 'the process of electoral change [has] so undermined Labour's electoral base that the Conservative party can look forward to being in government for the rest of this century'.[6] A similar question arose in deceptively similar circumstances in 1959 when Labour suffered a third successive electoral defeat and its long-term future seemed to be in serious doubt. Five years later though Labour began a period of six years in government when the question then being considered by commentators was whether Labour had replaced the Conservatives as the natural party of government. All the same, there are important differences between 1987 and 1959 and none of them seems to be favourable to Mr Kinnock. The first is that the Conservative leader Macmillan was a genuinely popular prime minister; the second is that unemployment was negligible; the third is that Labour secured only 5 per cent fewer votes than the Conservatives. In 1987 by contrast an unpopular prime minister presided over a government whose record on welfare was regarded as poor and on employment as almost indefensible, yet the Conservatives secured eleven per cent more votes than Labour. Moreover, if Labour's performance were compared not with 1959 but with 1983, we find more cause for concern. In 1987 there was 'no "winter of discontent", no split on defence policy, but rather what was universally recognized as one of the slickest election campaigns ever'.[7]

Curtice rejects the argument that the greater affluence which the majority of the electorate has enjoyed has eaten away Labour's base permanently. Like Whitely he urges a variation of what we have referred to as instrumental voting on the part of an increasing number of people – the middle of the social diamond – suggesting that 'economic optimism is a short-term influence on behaviour which affects the electorate as a whole and its continued benefit to the Conservatives is dependent upon the continued good management of the economy'.[8] However, he does concede that geographical polarization, with Conservative support tending to concentrate in the south and in rural England, and Labour support in the north, Scotland and Wales, and in the inner cities, has led to a halving of the number of seats susceptible to a small national swing. Moreover, the effect of this geographical polarization, as we have seen, has had a major effect upon the structure of the parliamentary parties: 'each is more than ever concentrated in its heartlands.'[9]

Curtice concludes that the numerical decline in the working class and the apparently ever-growing geographical divide make it increasingly difficult for Labour to win a substantial parliamentary majority. It does not follow, though, that Conservative government will become a permanent feature of the political landscape: 'hung parliaments are still on the agenda of British politics. The mould of British politics may not have been broken, but its shape has changed dramatically'.[10]

These apparently conclusive arguments are deceptive. If we agree that the fat middle of the diamond-shaped electorate votes instrumentally, we must also accept that it votes rhapsodically – everybody agrees about increased volatility. The consequence is that our definitions of safe seats and likely swings is outmoded. Curtice fails to take into account the fact that voters generally vote against and not for parties. To ask, as he properly does, what Labour needs to do to win middle class votes is important; even more important is to consider what the Conservatives might do to lose them. They have wide enough scope to do so. The Conservative party finds itself in a familiar position: in power with a good majority. On this occasion it is confronted across the floor of the House by a weak and divided opposition. This is not such good news for the Conservatives as it might appear. A two-party system, after all, needs two parties; it needs to be sustained by the cut and thrust of adversarian debate, the dividing of the world into 'them' and 'us', the Buffs and the Blues. If the official opposition fails to fulfil its part of the bargain, then the Conservative backbenches will provide the opposition to their own government. If the achievements of Mrs Thatcher's first two governments prove transitory during her third, the unity of the party might suffer dramatically. There are other, more immediate problems for the Conservative government, principally the disaffection of the Scots. In 1987 the Conservatives were humiliated in Scotland, losing eleven of the party's twenty-one MPs, including two Scottish Office Ministers. Labour in Scotland, and of course the SNP, will argue that Mrs Thatcher has no mandate for her policies in Scotland. Dubious though this may be as a purely constitutional argument, it will present very real political problems for the government, which might be well advised not to turn its back upon further devolution as a policy option.[11] It is quite inappropriate to put the north/south divide in the same category. In the north of England the Conservatives polled more votes (37 per cent) than Labour managed over the country as a whole; indeed they polled only five per cent fewer than did Labour in the north. All the same, Mrs Thatcher was wise to declare as an immediate government priority the tackling of the problems of inner-city decay. To conclude, the news, it seems, is not particularly good for anybody.

Nowadays the politician's lot is not a happy one. MPs today are less respected than ever. A recent poll amongst electors too young to vote when Mrs Thatcher came to power[10] indicated that 3 per cent of the sample, when asked to list respected professions, had most respect for MPs. By comparison 76 per cent had most respect for doctors. Only journalists ranked lower than politicians. Moreover, these young voters were preponderantly of the view that 'most politicians don't care what people like me think' (53 per cent agreed; 29 per cent disagreed), and substantially of the view (61 per cent) that ordinary people are 'powerless to change things'. Yet this is the generation which, through its support for Live Aid, Band Aid and Sport Aid, has tried to change the world. Two very small steps were taken in the 1987 election to make the House of Commons marginally more representative of today's Britain: there are now four blacks (the first since 1929) and forty-one women (the most ever) in the new intake. These changes will scarcely transform the House in the eyes of a jaundiced young electorate, but they constitute a beginning.

Our review of political parties is now complete; it hardly amounts to a eulogy. We have seen that, under the guise of a two-party system, Britain has been administered chiefly by Conservative governments over the last century. For more than half a century voters have had a choice between a class party (Labour) dedicated to an ideology concerning which it was deeply divided and for which there was little public support and a party (Conservative) which could not agree as to whether it had an ideology at all. To all intents and purposes, though, the two major parties represented class interests; without that interest their ideologies appear inconsistent in the light of their historical development. Those class interests and those ideologies are, according to the evidence we have considered, simply inappropriate to modern British society. They do not represent the bulk of voters any more who, as we have seen, vote against rather than for party policies. This, in turn, casts doubt upon the nature of the electoral exercise. Manifestos are drawn up and put to the electorate; the victorious party, nearly always representing a minority, then proceeds to attempt to conduct its business, to some extent at least, in the light of its manifesto commitments. Yet each electoral study tells us that only a minority of that minority which supported the victors actually read their manifesto and most of those disagreed with much of it anyway. And this system, since the first world war at least, has produced predominantly Conservative governments.

This is a phenomenon not unique to Britain, for it has marked other Westminster-type systems with class-based socialist parties, such as New Zealand and Australia. A possible explanation of the Conservative dominance was suggested many years ago by Lloyd George. In a speech already referred to, in Cardiff in 1910, he contrasted the Liberal party with the new Labour party in terms of their ability to win office. Liberalism, he said, brings to the working man's assistance the support of the middle class. 'No party could ever hope for success in this country which does not win the support of a large portion of this class . . . and I would strongly urge the importance of this consideration upon those who wish to drive Liberalism out in order to substitute another organization. You are not going to make socialists in a hurry out of the farmers and traders and professional men in this country, but you may scare them into reaction . . . if they are threatened then they will surely sulk and harden into downright Toryism. What gain will that be for Labour?' These prophetic words are as valid today as they were in 1910; they address a reality with which every Labour leader has been obliged to contend.

It is interesting to speculate on what Mr Kinnock might do to make his party more electable. We have already compared his party's position to that of Labour's in 1959. The leader of the time, Hugh Gaitskell, aimed to modernize his party by weakening its commitment to nationalization by reforming clause four of the party constitution. He also sought to sustain his party's commitment to nuclear deterrence. On both issues he was badly beaten. Kinnock will try similarly to make his party more appealing to moderate, middle-class voters. He will certainly try to return to the issue of re-selection of MPs and will argue once again to make these decisions the subject of a vote by all constituency members and not just activists. He is also likely to attempt to reform the NEC, giving more power to representatives of the Labour heartlands. In both of these he will need the support of the major unions and, unlike Gaitskell in his battles, he is likely to get it.

This will be only the beginning of Kinnock's struggles for he must then turn his attention to Labour's policies if he is to compete successfully for the moderate, middle-class vote. The left wing of the party is not likely to be won over easily, though Kinnock, through his successful general election campaign, has acquired great personal prestige. It has to be remembered, however, that, as its own opinion polls showed, the policies which make Labour generally distinctive are unpopular.[12] Most distinctive and unpopular is Labour's support for unilateral nuclear disarmament, a policy which, as Richard Rose points out, is strongly identified with Kinnock himself,[13] though it is probably underwritten by a majority of the parliamentary party. It is worth bearing in mind, though, that if the USA and the Soviet Union manage to reach agreement on nuclear arms control, nuclear defence may not have such a high profile in the next general election campaign.

Most commentators were greatly impressed with Labour's election campaign of 1987. Rose felt that it 'has completed Neil Kinnock's substitution of his personal authority for that of the party organization . . . The strategy of selling the persona rather than the policies of the leader would have been rejected as irrational by Hugh Gaitskell, and as bad form by Clement Attlee. In the case of Michael Foot it would have been counter-productive.'[14] If Thatcher and the Conservatives took several steps towards a presidential-style campaign in 1979 and 1983, it was left to Kinnock and Labour to make the great leap forward in 1987. The Kinnock campaign was unlike any of its predecessors. For our purposes the significant feature of the campaign was the total absence of any notable left-wing figures. Meetings were entirely stage-managed, something to which, under Mandelstan's influence, party organizers had already turned their hand. At the 1986 conference, for example, the possibly damaging debate on lesbian and gay rights was timed to coincide with a break in television coverage; viewers watched *Playschool* instead.[15] The managers of the 1987 campaign, Gould, Whitty and Mandelstan, ensured quite simply that the hard left played no part. It is impossible to believe that the left will remain silent for long. For all these reasons, then, Mr Kinnock will not find it easy to make his party more acceptable to the moderate, middle-of-the-diamond voter.

Even if these major hurdles were cleared, though, it might still not be enough. If the Alliance can sustain its credibility, which will depend as much on its activists and voters as on its party leaders, it will remain the natural beneficiary of the anti-Conservative vote in the south of the country. It may well be that to secure an electoral victory Labour would have to come to an arrangement with the Alliance. This would not be easy if David Owen were Alliance leader, or even a senior figure in Alliance councils. However, if Kinnock were to be successful in reforming the Labour party there could be no reasoned objection to such an arrangement, for Labour would have become much the kind of party that the Limehouse Declaration declared to be 'Britain's best hope'. Owen is perhaps the Alliance's greatest single asset but the future is not unthinkable without him and there is little doubt that senior Liberals, disillusioned with the SDP's inability seriously to eat into the Labour vote (Greenwich being the only success in six years), will begin to consider an arrangement with Labour as the only realistic hope of power. Owen must not make himself an obstacle to such a possibility. According to some commentators the cornerstone of such an arrangement might be the promise of electoral reform.[16] If all this seems somewhat hypothetical it is worth calling to mind the pact with the Liberals which sustained the Callaghan government in power ten years earlier. On the next occasion the balance of power between the partners might be significantly different.

At any rate, if Lloyd George was correct, if Britain is to break the mould of its Conservative-dominated political system and not just, as

Curtice says, change its shape, a progressive but not socialist left of centre grouping would have to emerge, perhaps under the umbrella of a revitalized, moderate Labour party. This would result in a two-party system less damaging and divisive than the present, since Labour's moderate, left-of-centre policies would require the Conservatives to reoccupy the middle ground. Alternatively, a new progressive force might be the result of some formal arrangement between a Labour party still perhaps avowedly socialist but dominated by its moderates and an Alliance party dominated by the Liberals and like-minded Social Democrats. If one of the goals of such an arrangement were a proportional electoral system then that arrangement might become permanent. If so, its success would require three large (but not necessarily equally large) parties, each of which accepted the framework as permanent and strove to work within it. A third possibility would envisage the Labour leadership's failing to dominate the left wing, thereby giving another chance for a united Alliance, perhaps under the leadership of Owen, to capitalize on Labour's disunity. This looks the least likely but in an area where, in Brian Waldren's words, 'we are impulse buyers in a political supermarket', it should not be ruled out.

Ostrogorski, when talking about the changes in the party system after 1832, linked them explicitly to broader social changes. We have seen that an equally significant social transformation is afoot today. Tomorrow's changes will be more profound. The developed world is in the grip of a second industrial revolution. Robots and computerized machines will increasingly take the place of many traditional manual and clerical jobs. The number of workers actually involved in creating wealth has declined and looks certain to decline further, yet the wealth created could be more abundant. How is it to be shared? And how is the work which cannot be mechanized to be shared? How will the next generation be educated to make use of their increased leisure? What sort of leisure facilities will be provided and at whose expense? Who will control the wealth-producing minority and in whose interests? And how are these and other long-term strategic decisions concerning, to take only one example, energy, to be taken – and are they to be un-taken at the drop of a manifesto?

Britain's party system, locked as it is into the electoral game of bids and counter bids, limited by planning periods constrained within the life-span of individual parliaments, handicapped by adversarian procedures, hardly seems suited to tackle the problems of the twenty-first century. Those who argue that the British system, though not the most efficient, is none the less impressively stable have a point. But ultimately the two are not unconnected. A system which consistently fails to match the performance of competitors and permits the living standards of many of its people to decline will not remain stable for ever. The moral of all this (with apologies to the Water Rat) is that Britain needs a different system of government; in the fullest sense of the expression – a change of government. The two-party system as it is presently constituted can provide no such change. As H. G. Wells's Mr Britling said à propos the same system seventy years ago: 'What's the good of all this clamouring for a change of Government? We haven't a change of Government. It's like telling a tramp to get a change of linen.'

Notes

1 Richard Rose and Ian McAllister, *Voters Begin to Choose*, (London, Sage, 1986).
2 Ibid., p. 156.
3 Ibid., p. 143.
4 Ibid., p. 147.
5 Ibid., p. 149.
6 John Curtice, 'Must Labour Lose?', *New Society*, 19 June 1987, pp. 17–19.
7 Ibid.
8 Ibid.
9 Ibid.
10 Ibid.
11 See Norman Stone, 'Can the Tories govern Scotland?', *Sunday Telegraph*, 14 June 1987.
12 Richard Rose, "Labour–C'Est Moi," *Spectator*, 20 June 1987, pp. 12–13.
13 Ibid.
14 Ibid.
15 *Daily Telegraph*, 15 June 1987.
16 See "Opposition Parties", *The Economist*, 20 June 1987.

Index

Index by J. Balinski